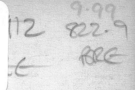

The Theatre of Bertolt Brecht

A STUDY FROM EIGHT ASPECTS

This book has become the standard guide to the work of Bertolt Brecht, the single most important figure in the theatre of this century. It is a thoroughly researched yet entirely accessible critical study by the leading British authority on Brecht, which traces the development of his style and of his ideas about the theatre and relates them to the 'modern movement' in the 1920s, to the rise and triumph of Nazism, and to Communist orthodoxy today.

It starts with a chronology of Brecht's career and a factual analysis of the forty stage and radio plays, complete with photographs of the original productions. Through a study of eight main aspects of Brecht's theatre, the book builds up a cumulative picture of a remarkable subject: the immensely live, self-contradictory world of a great artist who lived 'in a dark period,' with scepticism and hope. There is a detailed bibliography which has been completely revised for this edition.

'. . . altogether admirable and absolutely necessary. . . . This is surely one of the best books ever written on a theatrical subject. It is scholarly, lucid, economical, objective, planned with great intelligence, and superbly illustrated. . . . Anyone with the remotest interest in the theatre must read this book.' Iain Hamilton, *The Guardian*

'Seldom if ever has Brecht been looked at with such a combination of approval and commonsense, interest and detachment . . . *The Theatre of Bertolt Brecht* is brilliantly successful.' Eric Bentley, *New Statesman*

Brecht's Plays, Poetry and Prose
annotated and edited in hardback and paperback
by John Willett and Ralph Manheim

Collected Plays

The following plays are also available (in paperback) in unannotated editions:
The Caucasian Chalk Circle; The Days of the Commune; The Life of Galileo;
The Measures Taken and other Lehrstücke; The Messingkauf Dialogues; The Mother

*in preparation

THE THEATRE OF BERTOLT BRECHT

A study from eight aspects

JOHN WILLETT

METHUEN DRAMA

A METHUEN PAPERBACK

First published 5 March 1959 by Methuen & Co. Ltd.
Second edition 1960
Reprinted 1964
Third edition, revised 1967
This revised paperback edition published 1977
by Eyre Methuen Ltd.
Reprinted 1978 and 1981
Reprinted 1984, 1986 by Methuen London Ltd.
Reprinted 1991 by Methuen Drama,
an imprint of Reed Consumer Books Ltd.
Michelin House, 81 Fulham Road, London SW3 6RB
and Auckland, Melbourne, Singapore and Toronto
and distributed in the United States of America by HEB Inc.,
361 Hanover Street, Portsmouth, New Hampshire NH 03801 3959

Reprinted 1991, 1992, 1993, 1994

© 1959, 1967, 1977 John Willett

ISBN 0 413 34360 X

Printed and bound in Great Britain by
Cox & Wyman Ltd, Reading, Berkshire

Contents

List of Illustrations

9

Source of Illustrations

The Berliner Ensemble
Photos by Ruth Berlau, pages 46, 48, 51, 57, 60, 80, 152, 157, 163, 197; by Hainer
Hill, pages 154, 180, 183; by Foto Kiehl, page 175; by Carl Koch, page 171;
by Percy Paukschta, pages 48, 53, 56, 60, 158, 163, 180, 194; photographer
unspecified, pages 40, 44, 45, 84, 123, 134, 149, 156, 157, 159, 162, 188, 197,
201, 208.
Drawings by Caspar Neher, pages 31, 79, 82, 90, 92, 113, 118, 156 (of which those
on pages 92 and 156 are in the collection of the Berliner Ensemble, the present
whereabouts of the rest being unknown); page 79 (reproduced by Paukschta
from a drawing belonging to Ruth Berlau); page 82 (ditto, from the jacket of
Versuche 5).
Lithographs by George Grosz, page 190 (both from *Die Pleite*, April 1919).
Copies specially made by Percy Paukschta, from *Versuche 1*, page 34; from *Versuche
4*, page 138; from a photo lent by Ruth Berlau, page 145; from photos lent by
Otto Hopf, pages 37, 75; from a book in Brecht's possession, page 178.

Berlin
Gerda Goedhardt, page 137; Hainer Hill, page 140; Theaterwissenschaftliches
Archiv Dr Steinfeld, pages 24, 25, 29, 32, 69, 106, 115, 132, 144, 173; Ullstein,
page 23 (photo by Louise Hutchinson), 69, 106, 130, 133, 146, 147, 189, 199,
201.

London
British Museum, pages 84, 97, 103, 109 (from Moussinac, *The New Movement*);
Carl Koch, pages 30, 161; Penguin Books, page 103 (from Schweik); Society
for Cultural Relations, pages 111 (photo Huntly Carter), 182, 202, 205, 207
(Huntly Carter); Witt Library, page 204.

Paris
Cinémathèque Française, page 196.

Zurich
Doris Gattiker, page 152; B. Herbold, page 54; Teo Otto, page 122; Leonard
Steckel, page 50.

Other illustrations from books
From Brecht: *Versuche 6*, Berlin, 1932, pages 77, 91 (drawings by Grosz); from
Fuerst and Hume: *XXth Century Stage Decoration*, London, 1928, pages 27,
108; from Grosz: *Ein kleines Ja und grosses Nein*, Hamburg, 1955, pages 70, 89;
from Walter Mehring: *Europäische Nächte*, Berlin, 1924, pages 71, 87; from
Joachim Ringelnatz: *Kutteldaddeldu*, Munich, 1923, page 70.

Introduction

The original (hardbound) edition of this book appeared on 5 March 1959. It was brought up to date and slightly simplified for the third edition in 1967. For the present printing only some very minor corrections have been made to the main text, but the Bibliography has been entirely revised to take account of the great number of Brecht publications since that date. It would have been too much to amend all the detailed information in the opening Analysis of the Plays to accord with this, so I suggest that any reader needing background material or particulars of English translations for any given play should check with the Bibliography before following up what the Analysis entry says.

Three major enterprises have transformed the picture: the publication of the Brecht-Archive catalogue (or *Bestandsverzeichnis*) in four volumes, giving a wealth of information about Brecht's projects and unpublished works; the series of 'Materialien' volumes issued by Suhrkamp-Verlag, with information about individual plays; and finally the English and American editions of the Collected Plays in translation. These last have not only provided versions of several previously untranslated plays, but have likewise given much background information, some of it (e.g. for *Lucullus, Drums in the Night* and *The Good Person of Szechwan*) in advance of the 'Materialien' series. Other publications which could not be taken account of when I first wrote this book include Brecht's *Arbeitsjournal* (1938–55), the two volumes of his *Texte für Filme*, giving stories, treatments and scripts, the useful *Brecht-Chronik* by Klaus Völker, Wolfgang Gersch's pioneering study *Film bei Brecht*, and Bernhard Reich's memoirs with their eye-witness evidence as to the origins of *Verfremdung*. But however much now needs to be absorbed into our picture of Brecht, I don't think it conflicts with the framework established here.

Brecht's Dramatic Works

(As referred to in this book. Titles in italics are
not included in his collected plays)

BAVARIA

1. Baal
2. Trommeln in der Nacht
3. Im Dickicht der Städte
4. Edward II (after Marlowe)
5. Der Bettler
6. Die Hochzeit
7. Er treibt den Teufel aus
8. Lux in Tenebris

BERLIN

9. Mann ist Mann
9a. Das Elefantenkalb
10. *Mahagonny (first version)*
11. The Threepenny Opera (after Gay)
12. *Happy End (by Dorothy Lane)*
13. Mahagonny
14. *Berliner Requiem*
15. *Lindberghflug (Ozeanflug)*
16. Badener Lehrstück
17. St Joan of the Stockyards
18. Der Jasager/Der Neinsager (after Waley)
19. Die Massnahme
20. The Exception and the Rule
21. Die Mutter

SCANDINAVIA

22. Die Horatier und die Kuriatier
23. Die Rundköpfe und die Spitzköpfe
24. *Die Sieben Todsünden*
25. Furcht und Elend des Dritten Reiches
26. Senora Carrar's Rifles
27. Galileo
28. Mother Courage
29. Lucullus:
    (a) Das Verhör des Lukullus
    (b) *Die Verurteilung des Lukullus*
30. The Good Person of Szechwan
31. Puntila (with Hella Wuolijoki)
32. Arturo Ui

USA

33. Simone Machard
34. Schweik
35. The Caucasian Chalk Circle

ZURICH

36. Antigone (after Hölderlin)
37. Die Tage der Commune

BERLIN

38. Der Hofmeister (after Lenz)
39. *Herrnburger Bericht*
40. Turandot

Groundwork

Altes Theater

Richard-Wagner-Platz (Fernruf 21416)

Sonnabend, den 8. Dezember 1923
Außer Anrecht
Uraufführung

Baal

von Bertolt Brecht
In Szene gesetzt von Alwin Kronacher

Einlaß 7 Uhr   Anfang 7½ Uhr   Ende nach 9¾ Uhr

A Short Chronology
of Productions and Publications

Eugen Berthold Friedrich Brecht. Born Augsburg, 10 February 1898.

BAVARIA

1914. 17 August. First contribution to *Augsburger Neueste Nachrichten*.

1919. 21 October. First theatre criticism for *Augsburger Volkswille*.

1921. 6 September. First short story in *Der neue Merkur* (Munich).

1922. 5 September. First contribution to *Berliner Börsen-Courier*.

30 September. *Trommeln in der Nacht* première, Munich.

Publication of plays *Baal* and *Trommeln in der Nacht*.

December. *Trommeln in der Nacht* at Deutsches Theater, Berlin.

1923. 9 May. *Im Dickicht (der Städte)* première, Munich.

8 December. *Baal* première, Leipzig.

1924. 18 March. *Edward II* première, Munich. Brecht's first production.

BERLIN

1924. 29 October. *Im Dickicht* at Deutsches Theater, Berlin.

1926. 14 February. *Baal* at Deutsches Theater. Produced by Homolka and Brecht.

30 July. Interview in *Die literarische Welt* mentions the 'epic theatre'.

25 September. *Mann ist Mann* première, Darmstadt.

December. *Die Hochzeit* première, Frankfurt.

1927. First book of poems: *Die Hauspostille*.

23 March. *Mann ist Mann* broadcast, Berlin, with Helene Weigel.

17 July. *Mahagonny* ('Songspiel') première, Baden-Baden. First collaboration with Kurt Weill. Produced by Brecht.

14 October. Radio adaptation of *Macbeth* broadcast, Berlin.

December. *Im Dickicht der Städte* (revised version) at Darmstadt.

1928. 5 January. *Mann ist Mann* at the Volksbühne, Berlin.

31 August. *Threepenny Opera* première, Theater am Schiffbauerdamm, Berlin.

1929. July. *Lindberghflug* and *Badener Lehrstück* premières, at Baden-Baden. Both produced by Brecht. First 'Lehrstücke' (or didactic pieces).

31 August. *Happy End* première, Theater am Schiffbauerdamm, Berlin. Produced by Brecht.

Berliner Requiem with Weill broadcast during summer.

1930. First three issues of Brecht's *Versuche*, or miscellaneous collected writings, including first notes on the plays.

    9 March. *Aufstieg und Fall der Stadt Mahagonny* première, Leipzig Opera.

    23 June. *Der Jasager* première, Berlin.

    10 December. *Die Massnahme* première, Berlin. First collaboration with Hanns Eisler. First outspokenly Communist work.

1931. Release of *Threepenny Opera* film.

    16 January. First contribution to *Die Rote Fahne* (Berlin).

    30 January. Radio adaptation of *Hamlet* broadcast, Berlin.

    6 February. *Mann ist Mann* (revised version) at Staatstheater, Berlin. Produced by Brecht.

    21 December. *Aufstieg und Fall der Stadt Mahagonny* at Kurfürsten-damm-Theater, Berlin. Produced by Brecht and Caspar Neher.

1932. Release of *Kuhle Wampe* film. Script by Brecht and Ernst Ottwalt.

    17 January. *Die Mutter* première, Berlin.

    11 April. *St Joan of the Stockyards* broadcast, Berlin.

1933. All publications and productions in Germany interrupted.

SCANDINAVIA

1933. June. *Anna-Anna ou les Sept Péchés Capitaux* première at Théâtre des Champs-Elysées, Paris. Brecht's only ballet. His last major work with Kurt Weill (*Die Sieben Todsünden*).

1934. First (and only completed) novel: *Der Dreigroschenroman*.

Second book of poems: *Lieder Gedichte Chöre* (with Eisler).

Writing of *Die Horatier und die Kuriatier*, Brecht's last 'Lehrstück'.

1935. June. Speech to International Writers' Congress in Defence of Culture, Paris.

    19 November. *Die Mutter* in English, New York.

1936. July. First number of *Das Wort* (Moscow) edited by Brecht, Feucht-wanger and Bredel.

    4 November. *Die Rundköpfe und die Spitzköpfe* première, Copen-hagen.

Winter issue of *Life and Letters* (London) prints Brecht's essay 'The Fourth Wall of China', with first mention of 'Verfremdung', or alienation.

1937. 16 October. *Senora Carrar's Rifles* première, Paris.

1938. First (and only) two volumes of *Malik* edition of Collected Plays.

    21 May. *Furcht und Elend des Dritten Reiches* première, Paris. Produced by Brecht.

August. *The Exception and the Rule* première, Palestine.

1939. March. Final number of *Das Wort*.

Third book of poems: *Svendborger Gedichte*.

1940. 12 May. *Das Verhör des Lukullus* broadcast, Beromünster.

1941. 19 April. *Mother Courage* première, Zurich Schauspielhaus.

U.S.A.

1942. Release of film *Hangmen also Die*. Story by Brecht and Fritz Lang.

1943. 4 February. *The Good Person of Szechwan* première, Zurich Schauspielhaus.

9 September. *Galileo* première, Zurich Schauspielhaus.

1945. June. *Private Life of the Master Race* (adaptation of *Furcht und Elend*)
in English, San Francisco and New York.

1947. August. *Galileo* (second version; translated by Brecht and Laughton)
in Hollywood.

ZURICH

1948. First (and only) volume of short stories: *Kalendergeschichten*.

15 February. *Antigone* première, Chur (Switzerland). Produced by
Brecht and Neher. Helene Weigel's first professional appearance
since 1933.

4 May. Student production of *The Caucasian Chalk Circle* in English,
Northfield (Minnesota).

5 June. *Herr Puntila und sein Knecht* première, Zurich Schauspielhaus.

BERLIN

1949. 11 January. *Mother Courage* at Deutsches Theater, East Berlin. Produced by Brecht and Engel, with Helene Weigel.

12 November. *Herr Puntila und sein Knecht* at Deutsches Theater.
Produced by Brecht and Engel. First production of the Berliner
Ensemble.

Publication of the *Versuche* resumed. 'Kleines Organon für das Theater', Brecht's chief theoretical work, appears in a special number of
Sinn und Form (Potsdam).

1950. 15 April. Lenz's *Der Hofmeister* in Brecht's adaptation, at Deutsches
Theater. Produced by Brecht, with Berliner Ensemble.

8 October. *Mother Courage* in Munich Kammerspiele. Produced by
Brecht.

1951. First selected poems: *Hundert Gedichte*.

10 January. *Die Mutter* at Deutsches Theater. Produced by Brecht,
with Berliner Ensemble.

17 March. *Das Verhör des Lukullus*, opera version by Paul Dessau, given trial performance in East Berlin State Opera.

August. *Herrnburger Bericht* première at World Youth Festival in East Berlin.

12 October. *Die Verurteilung des Lukullus* put into State Opera's repertoire after changes to title, score and text.

1952. 16 November. *Senora Carrar's Rifles* at Deutsches Theater, with Berliner Ensemble.

1953. First two volumes of *Stücke*, or Complete Dramatic Works.

17 May. Erwin Strittmatter's *Katzgraben* at Deutsches Theater. Produced by Brecht, with Berliner Ensemble.

1954. March. First performance by Berliner Ensemble in Theater am Schiffbauerdamm as an independent State Theatre.

March. *The Threepenny Opera* (English adaptation by Marc Blitzstein) begins a five-year run in New York.

15 June. *Caucasian Chalk Circle* German première at Theater am Schiffbauerdamm. Produced by Brecht, with Berliner Ensemble.

July. International Theatre Festival, Paris. Berliner Ensemble production of *Mother Courage*.

1955. Illustrated war verses: *Kriegsfibel*.

12 January. J. R. Becher's *Winterschlacht* produced by Brecht and Wekwerth, with Berliner Ensemble.

June. Second International Theatre Festival, Paris. Berliner Ensemble production of *Caucasian Chalk Circle*.

1956. 14 August. Brecht dies at his home in East Berlin.

Analysis of the Plays

The following deals in chronological order with Brecht's completed dramatic works, under the numbers used in the list at the beginning of the book. The majority of the illustrations show the original production; about a third are of later productions under Brecht's own direction. At the end there is a short reference to his unfinished works and projects, and to some of his collaborations on other writers' works. The collaborations and adaptations where Brecht played a major creative part have been included with the main body of his work. So many of his plays began life as one or the other that it would be pedantic to count them separately.

The classification is an admittedly inconsistent one, designed only for the purposes of this book, and it may well be disputed. *Happy End*, which Brecht himself always disowned, is included because it seems no less his than the *Threepenny Opera*. *Der Hofmeister*, alone of the Berliner Ensemble's adaptations, is included because it has appeared elsewhere under Brecht's name and the reader might be puzzled if it were not. Again, Weill's *Berliner Requiem* is counted as a radio work because it has no other existence; but *Die Erziehung der Hirse*, which Dessau turned into a cantata, is omitted because it exists as a long poem on its own. The object of these rather arbitrary decisions is not to define the corpus of Brecht's work, but to help explain subsequent references in the text.

Some of the terms used need explaining:

Modellbuch: a collection of photographs illustrating a complete production of a given play by the Berliner Ensemble, and kept there for loan to would-be producers. (See page 162.)

Theaterarbeit: an illustrated volume describing the Ensemble's first six productions. (See bibliography, section 5.)

Versuche. Malik. Stücke. The three main editions of the plays. (See bibliography for details.)

Plays. Two volumes of selected plays published by Methuen, London.

SzT: Schriften zum Theater. Collected theoretical writings in seven volumes.

For English translations see Bibliography as well as entries on individual plays.

1. BAAL

Baal, a play.

Early twentieth-century German setting, against a background chiefly of darkness, wind and rain.

Baal, a poet and singer, drunk, lazy, selfish and ruthless, seduces (among others) a disciple's 17-year-old mistress, who drowns herself. He mixes with tramps and drivers, and sings in a cheap night-club. With his friend the composer Ekart he wanders through the country, drinking and fighting. Sophie, pregnant by him, follows them and likewise drowns herself. Baal seduces Ekart's mistress, then kills him. Hunted by the police and deserted by the woodcutters, he dies alone in a forest hut.

1926

Twenty-two scenes of heightened prose. Four songs, plus fragments of songs and an introductory Choral.

Written 1918. First produced Altes Theater, Leipzig, 8 December 1923, by Alwin Kronacher, scenery Paul Thiersch, with Lothar Körner (Baal).

Revised and produced Deutsches Theater, Berlin, 14 February 1926, by Brecht and Oskar Homolka, scenery Caspar Neher, with Homolka (Baal). Vienna, Theatre in der Josefstadt, 21 March 1926, by Herbert Waniek, with Homolka. London, Phoenix Theatre, 17 February 1963, by William Gaskill, with Peter O'Toole.

Published: Kiepenheuer, Potsdam, 1922; *Stücke I* (substitutes earlier version of first and last scenes). The songs, with Brecht's own melodies, are to be found in his *Hauspostille*, Propyläen-Verlag, Berlin, 1927. *Baal. Drei Fassungen*, Suhrkamp,

1966, gives three further versions, dated 1918, 1919 and 1926, together with details of alternative readings and notes by the editor, Dieter Schmidt. The first two of these contain several scenes and characters not in the published texts; the third (under the title *Lebenslauf des Mannes Baal. Dramatische Biografie*) is a shortened version of the 1922 text, with a more urban setting—Baal is a garage mechanic—and with 'epic'-style titles to the scenes.

Three short notes in *SzT 2*. See also introduction (1955) to *Stücke I* ('I admit – and advise you: this play is lacking in wisdom'). Fictitious note on the origin of the play in *Die Szene* (Berlin), 1926, I, p. 26. Hofmannsthal wrote a prologue for the Vienna performance.

English translation by Eric Bentley and Martin Esslin in *Baal, A Man's a Man and the Elephant Calf*, Grove Press, New York 1964.

2. TROMMELN IN DER NACHT

Drums in the Night, drama. (Later called 'Comedy'.)

Set in Berlin, November 1918. (Changed in revised version to January 1919.)

The soldier Andreas Kragler returns from a prison camp in Morocco to find his fiancée Anna just engaged to the prosperous Friedrich Murk. She is already expecting a child. In the Piccadilly Bar, against sounds and reports of the Spartacists storming the newspaper offices, he quarrels with her parents and the now drunken Murk. Lost in the streets, he follows the rioting; Anna follows him. He drinks in a small schnapps-bar, and in desperation leads the (partly drunken) company to the newspaper offices. In the early morning he and Anna meet in the streets. Contemptuously he refuses to go back to the fighting; then Anna and he go home together.

Five Acts prose. One song: the 'Legende vom toten Soldaten'.

Written *c*. 1918–20. Kleist Prize 1922. First produced in Munich Kammersieple, 29 September 1922, by Otto Falckenberg. Cast included Erwin Faber, Hans Leibelt, Kurt Horwitz, Maria Koppenhöfer.

Also produced in Deutsches Theater, Berlin, 20 December 1922, by same producer, with Alexander Granach (Kragler); in English at Arena Theatre, Albany, 2 August 1961.

Published: Dreimasken-Verlag, Munich, 1922; Propyläen-Verlag, Berlin n.d.; Kiepenheuer, Berlin, 1927; *Stücke I* (with considerable changes to Acts 3, 4, 5, cutting down the alcoholic haze). The 'Legende vom toten Soldaten', with Brecht's own melody, is in his *Hauspostille*, Propyläen-Verlag, Berlin, 1927.

Preface, notes and discussion in *SzT 2*. See also introduction to *Stücke I*.

According to Feuchtwanger (*Weltbühne*, No. 36, 1928) the play was at first called *Spartakus*.

English translation by Frank Jones in *Jungle of Cities and other plays*, Grove Press, New York, 1966.

3. IM DICKICHT DER STÄDTE

In the Cities' Jungle. A contest between two men in the giant city of Chicago.

Set in Chicago, August 1912–November 1915.

1923

Shlink, a Chinese timber dealer of 51, quarrels deliberately with an assistant in a bookshop, George Garga. Shlink and underworld friends (names like The Worm, The Baboon) turn his lover Jane and his sister Marie into prostitutes; the former marries George, the latter falls vainly in love with Shlink. So as to fight on level terms, Shlink hands his business over to Garga, who demolishes the business at the cost of himself going to gaol. There he denounces Shlink for enticement of the two girls, and arranges that he should be lynched at the time of his own release. They escape the lynchers together. Shlink says he loves George, and fought for fighting's sake. But George fought only to survive. Shlink dies as the mob arrives; George sets fire to the timber business and leaves for New York.

Eleven scenes prose (largely heightened).

Written 1921-4. First produced under title *Im Dickicht* in Munich Residenz-theater, 9 May 1923, by Erich Engel, scenery Neher, with Otto Wernicke (Shlink), Faber (George), Koppenhöfer (Marie).

Also produced in Deutsches Theater, Berlin, 29 October 1924, by Engel, scenery Neher, with Fritz Kortner (Shlink), Walter Frank (George). Franziska Kinz, Paul Bildt, Gerda Müller, under title *Dickicht* (Untergang einer Familie). Revised version produced in Hessisches Landestheater Darmstadt, December 1927, by Carl Ebert. New York, Living Theatre, 16 December 1960, by Judith Malina. London, Theatre Royal, Stratford, 14 June 1962, by Michael White.

Published: Propyläen-Verlag, Berlin, 1927 (revised version); *Stücke I*.

Note in all editions: ('You are about to observe an incomprehensible wrestling-match between two humans. . . . Do not worry unduly as to the motives of this struggle . . .'). Notes of 1924 (on relation of language to that of Rimbaud and Verlaine) and 1928 in *SzT* 2. Note of 1955 in introduction to *Stücke I*. Style discussed in essay 'Über reimlose Lyrik' in *Versuche 12*.

English translation by Eric Bentley in *Seven Plays by Bertolt Brecht*, Grove Press, New York 1961. By Gerhard Nellhaus in *Theatre Arts*, New York, August 1961. By Anselm Hollo in *Jungle of Cities and other plays*, Grove Press, 1966.

4. EDWARD THE SECOND

Leben Eduards des Zweiten von England (after Marlowe). History.

Set in England 1307-26.

1924

The broad outline is Marlowe's. Edward on his coronation sends for his favourite Gaveston; the peers and the church turn against him, and so does his wife; Gaveston is murdered; Edward, after a short-lived victory, is captured by Mortimer and eventually killed; his young son then has Mortimer hanged and the Queen sent to the Tower. But not more than a twentieth of the play is direct translation. Brecht has simplified Marlowe's plot and rewritten it, cutting out Gaveston's banishment and second return, and the

Queen's trip to France. A number of characters are cut or elided. Motives are altered: for Gaveston's release, for Mortimer's escape from execution by Edward. When captured, Edward here refuses to abdicate, and imprisonment is designed to break his spirit; he refuses again in a final scene with Mortimer, and so is murdered. Mortimer is made to require the support of parliament and peers; Edward that of the common soldiers. Neither has the independence allowed by Marlowe. (There are also unexplained changes of detail: Queen Isabella is 'Anna', the Archbishop 'Archbishop of Winchester', Gaveston an Irishman, and his Christian name 'Danny', not Piers.)

Twenty-one scenes irregular free verse, apart from a few lines of prose. Scene 7 (Battle of Killingworth) is subdivided in time into eleven episodes. Two songs, of which one is Marlowe's.

Written with Feuchtwanger. Produced in Munich Kammerspiele, 19 March 1924, by Brecht, scenery Neher, with Faber (Edward), Homolka, Koppenhöfer, Hans Schweikart.

Published: Kiepenheuer, Berlin, 1924 (with cover and four drawings by Neher) *Stücke II*. Translation by Eric Bentley, Grove Press, 1966

Mentioned by Brecht in introduction to *Stücke I*. Style discussed in essay 'Über reimlose Lyrik' in *Versuche 12*. First production described by Marieluise Fleisser in article in *50 Jahre Schauspielhaus*, Munich, 1951, and by Bernhard Reich in *Studien*, supplement to *Theater der Zeit*, E. Berlin, 1966 no.14.

5. DER BETTLER ODER DER TOTE HUND

The Beggar or the Dead Dog.

A victorious king, on his way to the official celebrations, falls into conversation with a beggar. Paying no attention to his rank, the beggar upsets all the king's ideas. At the end he proves to be blind.

One-act play in heightened prose.
Probably written in 1919. Published in *Stücke XIII*.

6. DIE HOCHZEIT

The Wedding.

A contemporary German wedding party where everything goes wrong. Guests quarrel or make love, the bridegroom's home-made furniture falls to pieces, the bride is revealed to be pregnant.

One-act farce in realistic prose.
Probably written in 1919. Produced in Frankfurt Schauspielhaus, 11 December 1926, by Melchior Vischer.
Published: *Stücke XIII* under the title *Die Kleinbürgerhochzeit*.

7. ER TREIBT DEN TEUFEL AUS

Driving Out the Devil.

Outside her peasant home, a Bavarian girl and her lover flirt heavily while her parents try to call her in. He visits her at night, but her father takes his ladder away, and drives them on to the roof.

One-act farce in prose.
Probably written in 1919. Published in *Stücke XIII*.

8. LUX IN TENEBRIS

Set in a street in a contemporary South German town.

Paduk, organizer of an exhibition to discourage venereal diseases (much visited by the godly), is shown to be a former client of the brothel opposite. The proprietress convinces him that her business has the better prospects. He is shown round and ends up as a partner.

One-act farce in prose.
Probably written in 1919. Published in *Stücke XIII*.

9. MANN IST MANN

A Man's a Man. The transformation of the docker Galy Gay in Kilkoa barracks during the year nineteen hundred and twenty-five. Comedy. (Termed 'Parable' in 1931.)

Vaguely set in British India, but both time and geography are largely non-sensical. (It is 1925, but Queen Victoria is on the throne. The 'temple' is a Tibetan Pagoda, and its worshippers are Chinese.)

1926

Four private soldiers loot an Indian temple, but one is left behind.

27

Terrified of their fierce Sergeant, they get Galy Gay, an Irish docker, to pose as the fourth man. By threats and blackmail he is forced to take this new identity; at the same time the missing soldier is presented as a miracle-working statue in the temple and the Sergeant, finishing up in civilian clothes, is seen as a harmless drunk. Galy Gay witnesses his own supposed execution and funeral, and delivers the funeral speech. In the last two scenes he takes part in a war against Tibet and single-handed reduces a fortress: he has become the perfect soldier. The missing man tries to rejoin his comrades, but is turned away with Galy Gay's old identity papers.

Eleven scenes, of which the ninth (transformation) scene is subdivided into five or six separate episodes. Prose, with a verse prologue to Scene 9 and one free verse speech; two songs. (Revised version changes one song and adds a third, also further free verse passages.)

Collaborators: Burri, Dudow, Hauptmann, Neher, Reich.

Music (1931) by Weill (lost); (1956–60) by Dessau.

Written 1924–6. First produced in Landestheater, Darmstadt, 25 September 1926, by Jacob Geis, scenery by Neher, with Ernst Legal as Galy Gay.

Also produced in Volksbühne, Berlin, 5 January 1928, by Engel, scenery Neher, music Edmund Meisel, with Heinrich George (Galy Gay) and Helene Weigel (Begbick, the canteen woman). In Staatstheater, Berlin, 6 February 1931, by Brecht (revised version), with Peter Lorre (Galy Gay), Weigel (Begbick), Theo Lingen, Wolfgang Heinz and Alexander Granach as the three soldiers. New York, The Living Theatre, by Julian Beck, 6 September 1962, and Masque Theatre, 19 September 1962. Radio version given by Radio Berlin, 27 March 1927, with Weigel as Begbick.

Published: Propyläen-Verlag, Berlin, 1927. (Scenes mis-numbered. Brecht's tune to the 'Mann-ist-Mann song' is given in this version only.) *Malik I* (revised version, cutting Scenes 10 and 11). *Stücke II* (same version, but with these two scenes restored. The 1931 version shortened the play, and cut out Begbick's three daughters). Four songs in Dessau's *Lieder und Gesänge*, Berlin, 1957. *Gedichte 2* includes a poem from an early version under title *Der grüne Garraga*.

Notes of 1931 and 1936 in *Malik* and *Stücke* editions. Earlier prologues and discussion in *SzT 2*. Discussed in introduction to *Stücke I*, where Brecht says the play's subject is 'the false, bad collectivity (the "gang")' as opposed to the 'historic-ally timely, genuine social collectivity of the workers'.

Translation by Eric Bentley in *Seven Plays by Bertolt Brecht*, Grove Press, New York 1961. Adaptation by Eric Bentley in *Baal, A Man's a Man and The Elephant Calf*, Grove Press 1964.

9a. DAS ELEFANTENKALB

The Baby Elephant.

One-act surrealistic prose farce for the three soldiers and Galy Gay, printed as Annex to the above in Propyläen and *Stücke* editions. In the latter it is called 'an interlude to be played in the foyer'. The former subtitles it 'or You Can Prove Anything'.

Includes one song.

English version by Nellhaus in *Wake*, Cambridge, Mass., No. 8. Autumn 1949.
By Eric Bentley in *Baal, A Man's a Man and The Elephant Calf*, Grove Press, 1964.

10. MAHAGONNY

Mahagonny. 'Songspiel'. (Sometimes known as *The Little Mahagonny*.)

1927

Basis of the subsequent opera (13). Six songs with orchestral interludes, lasting about forty-five minutes in all. Five of these are the Mahagonny Songs included, with their melodies, in Brecht's first collection of poems. The sixth—'Aber dieses ganze Mahagonny'—recurs in the opera. Slonimsky in *Music Since 1900* describes the work as a very short chamber opera: a 'skit pretending to idealize degeneration of life in some country very like New York, set to music of a jazzy accent similarly pretending to be ideal'.

Music by Kurt Weill.

Produced at Deutsche Kammermusik, Baden-Baden, 17 July 1927, with Lotte Lenja. At Theater am Schiffbauerdamm, E. Berlin, 10 February 1963, by Matthias Langhoff and Manfred Karge with Berliner Ensemble (much adapted).

Song texts published by Universal-Edition, Vienna, 1927. Less finale, but with Brecht's original tunes, in *Hauspostille*, Propyläen-Verlag, Berlin, 1927. Music unpublished. Programme note for first performance says: 'Weill's recent works show him to be moving in the same direction as those artists in every field who foresee the collapse of the social arts. *Mahagonny* is a short epic play which simply draws conclusions from the irresistible decline of our existing social classes. It is already turning towards a public which goes to the theatre naïvely and for fun.' See also David Drew: 'The History of Mahagonny' in *The Musical Times* (London). January 1963.

11. THE THREEPENNY OPERA

Die Dreigroschenoper. After John Gay: *Beggar's Opera.*

Set in London about 1900.

The outline is Gay's: Macheath secretly marries Polly, daughter of his fellow-crook Peachum. Peachum plans his arrest; he flees, but is caught through the treachery of Jenny and her co-whores. In gaol he finds another old love, Lucy, who helps him to escape. He is recaptured with yet another woman, taken to be executed, and reprieved in a deliberately artificial happy ending. But about nine-tenths of the dialogue has been rewritten. Innovations include the second scene (the stable wedding), the character of Tiger Brown (*vice* Gay's Lockit), and Peachum's whole business of organizing and fitting out beggars; in Gay he is a simple receiver. None of Gay's songs have been retained, and the whole angle of the satire is altered. In Gay the target was an aristocracy whose affairs were much like those of the underworld; here it is a bourgeois society which allows there to be an underworld at all.

1928

Prelude and three acts, each of three scenes. Prose dialogue, with nineteen songs. (After 1945 Brecht made new topical versions of two songs and additions to two others.)

Collaborators: Hauptmann, Weill.

Written 1928. First produced in Theater am Schiffbauerdamm, Berlin, 31 August 1928, by Engel, scenery Neher, conductor Theo Mackeben, with Harald Paulsen (Mac), Roma Bahn (Polly), Lotte Lenja (Jenny), Erich Ponto (Peachum), Kurt Gerron (Brown), Ernst Busch (Smith) and the Lewis Ruth Band.

Second cast included Hermann Thimig, Carola Neher, Rosa Valetti, Leonard Steckel.

Produced New York Empire Theatre, 13 April 1933 (Krimsky translation); Illinois University, 15 November 1946 (Vesey translation); New York De Lys Theatre, 10 March 1954 (Blitzstein translation), with Lenja as Jenny; London Royal Court Theatre, 9 February 1956 (Blitzstein translation), by Sam Wanamaker, conductor Berthold Goldschmidt. Broadcast BBC, 8 February 1935, adapted and produced by C. Denis Freeman, conductor Edward Clark.

Published: Universal-Edition, 1929, *Versuche 3*; *Malik I*; *Stücke III*; and separately by Malik-Verlag, London, 1938, and Suhrkamp, Frankfurt, 1958. *Songs aus der Dreigroschenoper* (including two new ones and amendments to others),

Gebrüder Weiss, Berlin, 1949. Piano score Universal-Edition, 1928, omitting scene 8 and the 'Ballade der sexuellen Hörigkeit'.

Notes in all editions. Film treatment (*Die Beule*) and account of film and lawsuit in *Versuche 3*. Essay on *The Beggar's Opera* in *Das Stichwort*, Berlin, September 1928. Weill's 'Briefwechsel über die Dreigroschenoper' in *Die Szene* (Berlin), 1929, p. 64. *Brechts Dreigroschenbuch*, Suhrkamp 1960, contains reprints of various critiques, texts of the play, the *Dreigroschenroman* and the 'Dreigroschenprozess', plus some new material including Brecht's discussion with Giorgio Strehler, 1955. Selections recorded (1930) on Telefunken LGX 66053. Fuller version (post-1950) on Philips S 06715 R. For film see p. 65.

English translation by Vesey and Bentley in *Modern Theatre I*, Doubleday, 1955, and *From the Modern Repertoire I*, University of Denver Press, 1949; revised version, with notes, in *Plays I*. Songs translated by Christopher Isherwood in *A Penny for the Poor*, Hale, London, 1937.

12. HAPPY END

'By Dorothy Lane, arranged for the theatre by Elisabeth Hauptmann. Songs by Bert Brecht.' Music Weill.

Set in contemporary Chicago.

1929

Bill Cracker, gangster and proprietor of 'Bill's Ballhaus', falls in love with Lieutenant Lilian Holiday of the Salvation Army, who has come to his establishment with Lieutenant Hannibal Jackson to make converts. Lilian is thrown out of the Salvation Army; Bill, who fails his part in a safe robbery, out of the gang. Bill goes to an Army meeting to find Lilian, but the gang follow in order to murder him. The gang's mysterious leader, the Lady in Grey, recognizes Hannibal as her long-lost husband, and so the Army and the crooks join forces. Bill gets an Army uniform, and all unite to found a bank.

Verse prologue and three acts. Prose dialogue; six songs.

First produced in Theater am Schiffbauerdamm, Berlin, September 1929, by

31

Brecht and Engel, scenery Neher, with Carola Neher, Weigel, Homolka, Lorre, Lingen, Gerron. At Pollock Hall, Edinburgh, August 1964, by Michael Geliot with Bettina Ionic, and at Royal Court Theatre, London, 11 March 1965.

Disowned by Brecht. See No. 17 below. Not published. Stage script by Felix Bloch Erben, Berlin. Piano score Universal-Edition 1959. Four songs in *Gedichte 2*. E. J. Aufricht's memoirs *Erzähle, damit du dein Recht beweist*, Ullstein, Berlin, 1966, gives a vivid account of the first production.

No notes.

13. AUFSTIEG UND FALL DER STADT MAHAGONNY

Rise and Fall of the Town of Mahagonny. Opera. ('An attempt at an Epic Opera: an account of mores.') Based on No. 10.

1930

Fleeing the police, the Widow Begbick and two fellow-crooks found the boom town of Mahagonny. It is to be a 'net-city' to catch all comers. Yet the customers leave disappointed, because it is too uneventful and too hedged-in with injunctions and prohibitions. In the crisis of an approaching hurricane a lumberman from Alaska called Paul Ackermann (or Johann, or Jimmy Mahoney, the name varying in different editions) finds the answer: everything must be allowed. Within a year this has become the one rule: they eat, make love, fight and drink, sometimes to death. But Paul runs out of money; Jenny, the tart whom he loves, refuses to help; and for that he is tried, condemned and electrocuted. In chaotic demonstrations, as the city burns behind them, the inhabitants show that their pleasures, their morality, their whole civilization depend only on money: that there is nothing else to help them, and nothing to help a dead man at all.

Twenty scenes. Eight soloists, chorus of six girls, male chorus. Text almost entirely rhymed or free verse. Scarcely any break in the score; songs, choruses, arias, recitatives and occasional speaking through or to the music.

Collaborators: Hauptmann, Neher, Weill.

Written 1927–9. First produced at Leipzig, 9 March 1930, by Walther Brugmann, conductor Gustav Brecher, scenery and projections by Neher, with Paul Beinert (Ackermann), Mali Trümmer (Jenny).

Also produced in Kurfürstendamm-Theater, Berlin, 21 December 1931, by Brecht and Neher, conductor Zemlinsky, with Lenja (Jenny), Paulsen (Ackermann), Hesterberg (Begbick). At Sadler's Wells, London, 16 January 1963, by Michael Geliot, with Adele Leigh (Jenny).

Published: *Versuche 2*; *Malik I*; *Stücke II*; and Universal-Edition, 1929. Piano score: Universal-Edition, 1929. Full score and parts taken by Gestapo in 1938 and lost till mid-1950s.

Full recording (1956–7) on Philips L 09418–20 L. Selections (1931) Electrola EH 736.

Notes by Brecht and Suhrkamp in first three editions, dated 1930. Notes by Weill in *Die Musik*, Stuttgart, XXII/6, March 1930. Weill's 'Vorwort zum Regiebuch' in *Anbruch* (Vienna) 1930, pp. 5–7. See also David Drew: 'The History of Mahagonny' in *The Musical Times* (London), January 1963.

Translation with U.S. Columbia KL 5271–3 (the Philips recording).

14. DAS BERLINER REQUIEM

Berlin Requiem

A work by Kurt Weill to poems by Brecht. These are: 'Ballade vom Tod der Männer im Hatourywald'; 'Können einen toten Mann nicht helfen' (used for finale of No. 13); 'Lobet di eNacht'; 'Ballade vom ertrunkenen Mädchen'; 'Marterl'; 'Wir kamen von den Gebirgen'; 'Tod des Unbekannten Soldaten'; 'Zu Potsdam unter den Eichen'.

Broadcast, summer 1929, in Südwestfunk, Baden-Baden. Commissioned by Frankfurt Radio.

Only other performance known was 18 November 1966 in Staatsoper, E. Berlin.

Listed by Universal-Edition, Vienna. Most of the poems can be found in *Hauspostille* or *Lieder Gedichte Chöre* (details in Bibliography). Two songs in Weill: *Song-Album*, Universal-Edition, 1929.

15. DER OZEANFLUG (originally LINDBERGHFLUG)

The Flight over the Ocean (Lindbergh's Flight). A didactic radio feature for boys and girls. ('One of a series of attempts which use poetry for purposes of self-instruction.')

Radio, but can be performed on concert platform.

A flier (Lindbergh) describes his preparations for his solo flight of 1927 across the Atlantic. His enemies—Fog, Snowstorm, Sleep—express their determination to beat him; ships at sea and both continents make reports: all through the mouth of the chorus. Against this he repeats his aim (to overcome the Primitive) and also his fears. He lands, and the work ends in praise of man's achievement in flying.

1929

Seventeen sections of irregular unrhymed verse (of which three are additional to the score) for tenor (Lindbergh), bass and baritone solos, and chorus. According to Brecht the whole of Lindbergh's part is to be sung by the listener or, in a concert performance, by the choir. (The score gives no indication.)

Collaborators: Hauptmann, Weill. Hindemith also composed four numbers for the first performance.

Written 1928–9. First produced at Deutsche Kammermusik, Baden-Baden, July 1929: radio production by Hardt, followed by platform production by Brecht. Performed Berlin, 5 December 1929, under Klemperer. At Philadelphia Academy of Music, 4 April 1931, under Stokowski.

Published: *Versuche* 1. 1959 reprint gives amended version. (Not included in *Stücke*.) Also in *Uhu*, Berlin, V, 7, April 1929. Piano score (shorter text): Universal-Edition, 1930. (Hindemith's music has never been published.)

Notes by Brecht and Suhrkamp (1930) in *Versuche 1*. The work was originally called *Lindberghflug* or *Flug der Lindberghs*, but a letter of Brecht's of 3 January 1950 to Stuttgart Radio directs that in view of Lindbergh's political history the title must be changed, a new prologue added and the name Lindbergh struck out. 'The changes may cause some slight damage to the poem, but the striking out of the name will prove instructive.' Letter and prologue are in the 1959 reprint.

English translation by George Antheil, Universal-Edition, Vienna. (In full score only.)

16. BADENER LEHRSTÜCK VOM EINVERSTÄNDNIS

Baden-Baden Cantata of Acquiescence. 'A further attempt at a didactic piece.'

Concert platform, with possibly the wreckage of a crashed aeroplane.

1929

Four airmen have crashed and are in danger of death. Are we, the chorus, to help them? No. Power, not help, is what matters until our world is altered: the airmen must reconcile themselves to dying. When the first pilot, Nungesser, tries to stand out against this he is sent off the platform as worthless; his claim to be heard ceased with his (social) function. The chorus then tells the others to help us change the world, while renouncing both it and themselves.

Eleven short sections for four soloists, speaker and chorus. Interpolated knockabout scene with three clowns and short section of film.

Collaborators: Dudow, Hauptmann, Hindemith.

First produced at Baden-Baden music festival, 28 July 1929, producer Brecht, conductors Ernst Wolff and Alfons Dressel with soloists including Joseph Witt, Oskar Kalman, Gerda Müller-Scherchen (speaker), Theo Lingen, Karl Paulsen and Benno Carle (the three clowns).

Also produced in various German towns and Vienna, and on Brussels Radio in 1934. Disagreement between Brecht and Hindemith blocked further performances till that of 14 May 1958 in German and English at 316, East 63rd Street, New York, conducted by Margaret Hillis and sponsored by the B. de Rothschild Foundation.

Published: *Versuche 2*; *Stücke III*. Piano score (shorter text): Schott, 1928.

Notes by Hindemith in latter, disputed by Brecht in a note following the other two editions.

English translation by Gerhard Nellhaus in *Harvard Advocate*, CXXXIV, 4, February 1951. By Lee Baxandall in *TDR* 4, 4 (1960).

17. ST JOAN OF THE STOCKYARDS

Die Heilige Johanna der Schlachthöfe. ('. . . is meant to show the present evolutionary stage of Faustian Man. The play is derived from Elisabeth Hauptmann's play "Happy End" . . . .')

Set in the stockyards and commercial exchanges of modern Chicago.

1959

In a falling market the meat-packer king Pierpont Mauler contracts to buy his competitors' total production for the next two months, then corners the livestock and cuts off their supplies. The Salvation Army girl Johanna Dark imagines that this is in answer to her pleas that he should save the market and prevent unemployment. But the canning factories remain closed, and Mauler overreaches himself so that the whole market crashes. Always genuinely moved by Johanna, he presents himself as a ruined penitent; she helps the workers to organize a general strike. Mauler's competitors then persuade him, with the help of his Wall Street friends, to lead the meat ring out of its troubles, and the troops clear the strikers from the stockyards. Johanna herself collapses. Taken desperately ill to Salvation Army HQ, she is canonized by Mauler and his friends for her work among the poor and vainly denounces the class system as she dies.

Eleven scenes. Classical blank verse, prose, irregular unrhymed verse, Salvation Army hymns. Final apotheosis in parody of Goethe and Schiller. Considerable use of choruses—of workers, cattle dealers, Salvationists, etc.

Collaborators: Borchardt, Burri, Hauptmann. Songs (1936) by Dessau.

Written about 1929–31, and first produced Deutsches Schauspielhaus, Hamburg, 30 April, 1959, by Gründgens, scenery Neher, music Siegfried Franz, with Hanna Hiob as Johanna. Gaiety Theatre, Dublin, 18 September 1961, by Hilton Edwards, with Siobhan McKenna. Queens Theatre, London, 11 June 1964. Broadcast by Berlin Radio, 11 April 1932, producer Alfred Braun, with Carola Neher (Johanna), Kortner (Mauler), Weigel, Busch, Lorre, Bildt, Friedrich Gnass.
Published: *Versuche 5*; *Malik I*; *Stücke IV*.
Notes in *SzT. 2*.
English translation by Frank Jones in *Plays II*. Also in *From the Modern Repertoire III*, Indiana University Press, 1956 and in *Seven Plays by Bertolt Brecht*, Grove Press, New York, 1961.

18. DER JASAGER/DER NEINSAGER

He who said Yes/He who said No. After the Japanese play *Taniko*, in the English version by Arthur Waley. ('School operas . . . intended for schools. The two little plays should, if possible, always be performed together.')

No indication of time or place. Stage or platform divided into two, with chorus either side.

1930

Der Jasager: A teacher leads an expedition to the mountains, taking with him a boy whose mother is ill. On the journey the boy falls ill too; the custom is that the other members of the party should hurl him into the valley, and this they regretfully do, with the boy's own acquiescence. (The version set by Weill is largely identical with Elisabeth Hauptmann's translation of Waley, but with a new opening chorus, and the trip is not a religious pilgrimage but a quest for medicine for the sick woman; the custom when the boy falls ill is not that he be immediately hurled into the valley, but that he should first be asked whether they are to leave him behind, and should answer Yes. In other words, it is the boy himself who insists on being killed.) *Der Neinsager* is simply the same play, with a different ending; the boy refuses to be killed and demands that a new custom be instituted: 'the custom that one must think afresh in every new situation'.

Two parts (ten musical sections). Six soloists, chorus and orchestra. Prose and unrhymed irregular verse. All sung.

Collaborators: Hauptmann, Weill.

Written 1929–30. *Der Jasager*. First produced 23 June 1930 at Zentralinstitut für Erziehung und Unterricht, Berlin, by Brecht and Weill, with Otto Hopf (Teacher) and schoolboys, and amateur orchestra under Kurt Drabek. (It is not clear when the *Neinsager* version was used. The first known production of both plays was by the Comenius-Gymnasium, Düsseldorf, on 18 July 1958.)

Produced New York Grand Street Playhouse, 25 April 1933.

Published: *Versuche 4*; *Malik II*; *Stücke IV*; all with amendments softening the play's severity, and separately by Kiepenheuer, Berlin, 1930. Piano score (*Jasager* only): Universal-Edition, 1930, with first version of text. Elisabeth Hauptmann's original translation from Waley appeared in *Der Scheinwerfer*, Essen, during 1929–30. It is included in *Der Jasager und der Neinsager. Vorlagen, Fassungen und Materialien*, Suhrkamp, 1966, edited by Peter Szondi, which also prints Waley's *Taniko*, the first version of *Der Jasager* and various contemporary criticisms. Complete recording on MGM 3270.

Notes of a school discussion on the play in first three editions above. It is on the basis of this that the new ending was evolved.

(Retranslation into English by Gerhard Nellhaus in *Accent*, Urbana, VII, 2, autumn 1946. *Taniko* is in Arthur Waley: *The Nō Plays of Japan*, Allen and Unwin, 1921.)

19. DIE MASSNAHME

The Decision. Didactic piece.

Concert platform.

Four political agitators from Moscow report to a controlling and commenting Chorus how they had to kill a young communist who accompanied them into China. In a succession of short scenes they act out his mistakes. Out of sympathy he spoke too openly to the coolies; during a strike he interfered to prevent police injustice; sent to win bourgeois support, he quarrelled with the bourgeois; when the city became restless he disclosed himself too soon and tried to lead a hopeless revolution. In all these ways he made their work impossible. They cannot smuggle him out, so they decide to kill him, and he acquiesces in their decision. They shoot him and return to their work, and the chorus agrees that they were right.

1930

Eight sections. Prose and unrhymed irregular verse. Six major songs. All parts performed by the four soloists.

Collaborators: Dudow, Eisler.

First produced in Grosses Schauspielhaus, Berlin, 10 December 1930; conductor Rankl, with Weigel, Busch, Granach, Topitz and Arbeiterchor Gross-Berlin. Also produced in 1931 in Philharmonie, Berlin, by the Arbeitersängerbund. (According to Schumacher, p. 368, changes were made at the suggestion of the Communist Party after the first performance.) By students at Amherst, Mass., 20 May 1960, with music by Philip Gossett.

Published: *Versuche 4*; *Malik II*; *Stücke IV*. Piano score: Universal-Edition, 1931. Also published as a 'Vordruck' from the *Versuche*, with differences.

Joint note by the collaborators in all three editions: 'The attempt to use a didactic piece to make familiar an attitude of positive intervention. . . .' According to Mrs Hauptmann there is an unpublished letter of Brecht's, written since 1949, which gives reasons why the work should no longer be performed. A note at the end of *Stücke V* says that 'The writer has always turned down proposed productions of Die Massnahme, as only the Young Comrade can learn anything from it, and even he can only do so if he has also played one of the Agitators and sung in the control-chorus.' Further short note in *SzT 2*.

English translation by Eric Bentley in *The Colorado Review* (Fort Collins), Vol. I, No. 1, winter 1956–7, under title *The Measures Taken*. Rough translation (*The Punitive Measure*) in Ruth Fischer: *Stalin and German Communism*, Oxford University Press, 1948.

20. THE EXCEPTION AND THE RULE

Die Ausnahme und die Regel. A short play for schools.

Set in Mongolia, some time between 1900–30.

A merchant is hastening to gain a concession. He mistrusts his guide because he is too friendly with the coolie who carries the baggage; so sends him back. The coolie loses the way in the desert; they run short of water; and when the coolie approaches him with a waterbottle the merchant thinks he is going to attack him, and shoots. A court judges the case and decides that it was self-defence. The rule is that the underdog must want to attack his employer, and the merchant could not be expected to know that here was an exception.

Nine sections. Prose, with verse prologue and epilogue and six songs.
Collaborators: Hauptmann, Burri. Musical score (1948) by Dessau.
Written 1930. First produced in August 1938 at Givath Chajim, Palestine.
Produced at Unity Theatre, London, 12 October 1956 (Bentley's translation), by Bill Norton.
Published in *Internationale Literatur* (Moscow), 1937, No. 9; *Malik II*; *Versuche 10*; *Stücke V*.
English translation by Bentley in *Chrysalis* (Boston), 1954, Nos. 11–12, and *New Directions*, 15 (1955).

21. DIE MUTTER

Mother. After Gorki. Partly based on a dramatization by G. Stark and G. Weisenborn.

Set in Russia between 1905 and 1917.

1932

Pelagea Vlassova, mother of the metal-worker Pavel, is drawn by her son into the revolutionary movement. Though hostile to it at first, she refuses to let him distribute leaflets, preferring to run the risk herself. She takes part in a peaceful demonstration, where Pavel is arrested; she learns to read, helps striking peasants, works an illegal press. Pavel escapes from Siberia, but is caught and shot. Pelagea is beaten up for protesting against the 1914 war.

She argues effectively with women who support it, and finishes by carrying the red flag in a huge anti-war demonstration in the winter of 1916.

Fifteen short scenes. Prose dialogue with unrhymed irregular verse. Originally ten songs; three others added later. Chorus.

Collaborators: Eisler, Weisenborn, Dudow.

Written 1930–1. First produced in Komödienhaus (Theater am Schiffbauerdamm), Berlin, 17 January 1932, by Burri, scenery Neher, with Weigel (Vlassova), Busch (Pavel), Lingen, Gerhard Bienert.

Also produced in Deutsches Theater, Berlin, 10 January 1951, by Brecht, scenery Neher, with Weigel (Vlassova), Kahler (Pavel), Busch (Lapkin) and Berliner Ensemble; at Theater am Schiffbauerdamm, 10 December 1957, same production revised by Manfred Wekwerth, with cast changes.

The 1957 production has been filmed by DEFA and the Berliner Ensemble.

Produced in English at Civic Repertory Theatre, New York, 19 November 1935, by Victor Wolfson for Theatre Union; scenery Mordecai Gorelik.

Published: *Versuche* 7; *Malik II* (with slight change in order of scenes); *Stücke V*; Mundus-Verlag, Basel, 1946. Piano score: Lied der Zeit (Berlin).

Songs recorded on Eterna 110006–10.

Notes in all editions, though *Versuche* does not include references to New York production which are in others. 'Written in the style of the didactic pieces, but requiring actors, *Die Mutter* is a piece of anti-metaphysical, materialistic, non-aristotelian drama.' Account of 1951 production in *Theaterarbeit*. Further notes in *SzT 2* and *SzT 4*.

English translation by Lee Baxandall, Grove Press, New York, 1965.

22. DIE HORATIER UND DIE KURIATIER

The Horatii and the Curiatii. School Play. '. . . a didactic play for children about dialectics.'

Platform.

The Curiatii decide to attack the city of the Horatii; both sides organize their armies. Thanks to better weapons the Curiatii win the bowmen's and pikemen's engagements, and in the engagement between the swordsmen the Horatii run away. But the pursuit splits up the Curiatii, so that the Horatian swordsmen can engage them singly and beat them.

Introduction and three episodes, almost entirely in unrhymed irregular verse. Three soloists on each side, carrying pennants to indicate their exact military strength, represent the bowmen, pikemen and swordsmen of the two armies: a convention of the Chinese stage. Each side has also a chorus, sometimes split into men and women.

Collaborator: Steffin.

Written 1933–4. First produced at Halle, Theater der Jungen Garde, 26 April 1958, to music by Kurt Schwaen (1956).

Published: *Malik II*; *Versuche 14*; *Stücke V*.

English translation by H. R. Hays in *Accent* (Urbana), VIII, 1, autumn 1947.

23. DIE RUNDKÖPFE UND DIE SPITZKÖPFE

Round Heads and Pointed Heads. Or 'Reich und Reich gesellt sich gern' (untranslatable pun). An atrocity story.

Set in the imaginary contemporary country of Yahoo and its capital Lima or Luma. The characters have Spanish names.

1936

This play, which was begun in 1931 as an adaptation of *Measure for Measure* for the Berlin Volksbühne, deals with the attempt to substitute racial doctrines for the realities of the class struggle. The attacks on the Pointed-Head minority by Angelo Iberin, a strong-man politician, at first lead men like the tenant farmer Callas to forsake the class movement known as 'the Sickle' in the hope that Iberin will reduce the power of the landlords. After Iberin has defeated 'the Sickle' Callas's Pointed-Head landlord is condemned to death for seducing a Round-Head girl (Callas's daughter), but his possessions remain intact. Callas gets his rent reduced in return for taking the landlord's place in gaol, while his daughter poses as the landlord's sister Isabella, a nun whom the gaol commandant wishes to ravish. Both these moves are fruitless, for the Viceroy returns and Iberin is forced to release the landlord, with the result that the play ends with Domed Heads and Pointed Heads mingling, but the rich and the poor once again separate: the landlords feasting on one side, the condemned members of 'the Sickle' waiting to be hanged on the other.

Eleven scenes prose and blank verse. Thirteen songs (not in pre-1933 version). Collaborators: Eisler, Burri, Hauptmann, Steffin.

Written 1931-4. First produced in Danish (but with Brecht's collaboration), in Riddersalen Theatre, Copenhagen, 4 November 1936, by Per Knutzon, with Asbjorn Andersen (Iberin), Niels Bing (Landlord), Lulu Ziegler (Nanna Callas), Astrid Schmahl (Isabella).

Published: *Malik II*; *Stücke VI*; in *Neue Deutsche Literatur* (Berlin), October 1956. Pre-1933 version called *Die Spitzköpfe und die Rundköpfe* in *Versuche 8* (1959), signed Brecht, Burri, Hauptmann. Two songs in Hanns Eisler's *Lieder und Kantaten I*, Berlin and Leipzig. Eight more in vols II and IV.

Notes in *Malik* and *Stücke*: 'This play, the parable type of non-aristotelian drama. . . .' Mentioned in essay 'Über die Verwendung von Musik' in *Schriften zum Theater*, pp. 248-9, as a play 'which unlike *Die Mutter* is addressed to a "wide" public and takes more account of purely entertainment considerations . . .'.

English translation by N. Goold-Verschoyle in *International Literature* (Moscow), 1937, No. 5. Also in *Jungle of Cities and other plays*, Grove Press, New York, 1966.

24. DIE SIEBEN TODSUENDEN DER KLEINBUERGER

Les Sept Péchés Capitaux. *The Seven Deadly Sins* (sometimes called *Anna-Anna*). A spectacle based on poems by Bertolt Brecht.

Set in modern America.

Two sisters, Anna 1 and Anna 2, are sent out by their family in Louisiana to earn their fortune. 'One of the two Annas is the Manager, the other the artist; one (A 1) is the saleswoman, the other (A 2) the article sold.' In seven years they traverse seven cities, in each of which A 2 is tempted by one of the seven deadly sins, which would have ruined her. These sins are in fact virtues: Pride (in one's own best self), Sloth (in performing an injustice), Anger (at a mean action), etc. She avoids the lot; she succeeds as blackmailer, cabaret star, film extra; and so the two Annas are able to return home with enough money for their family to build a house. In a final episode, other Annas are foolish enough to commit these sins, and are ruined.

Ballet libretto in seven sections. Ten songs.
Music: Weill. Choreography: Balanchine and Kochno.
First produced in Théâtre des Champs Elysées, Paris, by Edward James's Ballets 1933, 7 June 1933, scenery Neher, with Tilly Losch, Lenja, Roman Jasinsky, etc., and the Orchestre Symphonique de Paris under Maurice D'Abravanel.
Produced in Savoy Theatre, London, 30 June 1933, by Ballets 1933, conductors Constant Lambert and Maurice D'Abravanel. At New York City Centre by Balanchine, 2 December 1958.
Published Suhrkamp-Verlag, Frankfurt, 1959. Also in *Gedichte 3*. Omitted from *Stücke*. English translation by Edward James in full score (since apparently lost); by W. H. Auden and Chester Kallman in *TDR* 6, 1 (1961); anonymous translation with American Columbia recording KL 5175.

25. FURCHT UND ELEND DES DRITTEN REICHES

Terror and Misery of the Third Reich. (Original title: *Deutschland – ein Greuelmärchen: Germany – an Atrocity Story.*)

Set in Nazi Germany.

1938

A sequence of realistic sketches, often very short, designed to be played separately or together. They deal with the brutality and jocular ingenuity of the individual Nazi; the fear of betrayal; the divisions and mutual mistrust within the family; the cowardice of the liberal professions; the lack of cohesion among the opposition; the realities underlying such institutions as Labour Service, Winter Help, the Hitler Youth and the concentration camps; the imminence of war. Each sketch concerns a different group of characters.

Twenty-four scenes introduced and linked by a long poem. Eight extra scenes. Collaborator: Steffin. Music by Dessau (1938); Eisler (1945).

Written about 1935-8. Produced Paris, 21 May 1938, by Brecht under title 99%, with Helene Weigel. Also produced in New York (in German), 28 May 1942, by Berthold Viertel; at Los Angeles, 7 June 1945, by Henry Schnitzler for University of California (Bentley's translation); in Pauline Edwards Theatre, New York, 12 June 1945, by Viertel (Bentley's translation).

Published: Malik-Verlag, London, 1938 (twenty-seven scenes); Meshdunarodnaya Kniga, Moscow, 1941 (thirteen scenes); Aurora Verlag, New York, 1945 (twenty-four scenes); Aufbau, Berlin, 1948 (twenty-four scenes); Volk und Wissen, Berlin-Leipzig, 1949 (ten scenes); *Stücke VI* (twenty-four scenes).

Notes in Aurora, Aufbau and *Stücke* versions. The play 'is based on eye-witness accounts and newspaper reports'. Alternative version played in US is given: seventeen scenes linked by new choruses, to be sung by German soldiers in an armoured troop carrier. In *SzT 4* there is an essay on Nazi Germany which bears the title of the play. Filmed by Pudovkin, 1942, but not released.

44

English translation published by Meshdunarodnaya Kniga, Moscow, 1942, under title *Fear and Misery in the Third Reich* (twelve scenes only); by Eric Bentley under title *The Private Life of the Master Race* (translation of the alternative seventeen-scene version above), published by New Directions, New York, 1944; Gollancz, London, 1948).

26. SENORA CARRAR'S RIFLES

Die Gewehre der Frau Carrar. Partly based on an idea by J. M. Synge.

Andalusian fisherman's cottage in April 1937.

1937

The widow Carrar refuses to let her two sons join the Spanish Republican Army, or to let her worker brother have the rifles which were concealed by her fisherman husband before his death. As they wait at night for the elder son to bring his boat in, neighbours come to argue with her: she feels it her duty to be neutral, and thinks that this neutrality will be respected by the rebel generals. But her brother claims that 'who is not with us is against us': he sees neutrality as a form of hostility to the republic. Then the elder son is carried in dead; he has been machine-gunned at sea by the rebels. As the distant gunfire increases, mother and son decide to take the hidden rifles and leave with her brother for the front. (The play is a modern version of Synge's *Riders to the Sea*.)

One act prose.
Collaborator: Steffin.
Written 1937. First produced in Salle Adyar, Paris, 16 October 1937, by Dudow with Weigel (Carrar), Steffi Spira, H. Altman, W. Florian.
Produced in English at Unity Theatre, London, 13 September 1938, by John Fernald, scenery S. John Woods, with Lilian Hinton and Peggy Cochrane (Carrar), John Slater (Pablo). This production toured in other English towns. Produced at San Francisco Green Street Theatre, 3 February 1939 (Wallis translation), by George Altman.

Published: *Malik II*; also separately by Malik-Verlag, London, 1937; as *Versuche Sonderheft* (Aufbau only) 1953; and in *Stücke VII*. Also by VEB Verlag der Kunst, Dresden, 1952, with photographs of Paris, Copenhagen and Greifswald productions.

Note by Brecht at end of *Malik II* and *Stücke VII*. Notes by Ruth Berlau in Verlag der Kunst edition. Modellbuch. Further note in *SzT 4*. Prologue and Epilogue, written by Brecht for the Swedish 'Freie deutsche Bühne', in Werner Mittenzwei: *Bertolt Brecht*, Aufbau, E. Berlin. 1962, pp. 390-2.

English translation by Keene Wallis in *Theatre Workshop* (New York), April–June 1938.

27. GALILEO

Leben des Galilei. Play.

Set in Italy, 1609–37.

1947

Galileo, an easy-going, not too scrupulous hedonist, uses the telescope to establish Copernicus's theories. The philosophers at the Medici court refuse to accept his evidence; so do the monks at the Collegium Romanum, but the papal astronomer Clavius has to admit its truth. Yet the Holy Office denounces the idea of a solar system as heretical, for the ultimate reason that an attitude of mind which queries the existing cosmic order is likely to query the religious, economic and social orders too. So for eight years Galileo keeps off astronomy, till he can no longer resist the current researches into sunspots. His subversive ideas begin to spread. In 1633 the Medici deliver him to the Inquisition; Urban VIII (the former Cardinal Barberini), himself a mathematician, refuses to protect him; he is scared into publicly abjuring his theories. For the rest of his life he lives privately with his daughter Virginia, writing the *Discorsi* under the eye of the Church, which impounds the MS. as written. But he keeps back a copy, and this his former pupil Andrea is able to smuggle out of the country.

Fifteen scenes prose. One song. In the 1947 English version a rhyming verse introduced each scene, and Scenes 5 and 14 were cut. Brecht translated the verses for the 1957 Berlin production, when the same cuts were made.

Collaborator: Steffin. Music by Eisler.

Written 1937–9. Second (American) version written 1945–7. First produced in Zurich Schauspielhaus, 9 September 1943, by Leonard Steckel, scenery Teo Otto, with Steckel (Galileo), Karl Paryla, Wolfgang Langhoff.

Produced in Theater am Schiffbauerdamm, January 1957, by Engel, scenery Neher, with Busch (Galileo) and Berliner Ensemble.

Produced in Los Angeles Coronet Theatre, 30 July 1947 (Brecht's and Laughton's translation) by Joseph Losey and Brecht, with Laughton (Galileo), Hugo Haas (Barberini), Frances Heflin (Virginia), scenery Robert Davison; same production given in New York, Maxine Elliott's Theatre, 7 December 1947. Mermaid Theatre, London, 16 June 1960, by Bernard Miles, with himself as Galileo.

Published: *Versuche 14; Stücke VIII*; separately by Suhrkamp-Verlag, 1959; Reclam (Leipzig), 1959. *Aufbau einer Rolle – Galilei*, Henschel, Berlin, 1958, contains text, photographs, and Brecht's account of the collaboration with Laughton.

Notes on *Stücke*, also in supplement to *Theater der Zeit*, Berlin, 1956, No. 11. More notes in *SzT 4* and in *Materialien zu Brechts Leben des Galilei*, Suhrkamp, 1963. Rejected version of Scene 14 in *Versuche 15*, with some of Eisler's settings of the verses. Full score in Eisler's *Lieder und Kantaten IV*. See also para. 63 of the *Kleines Organon* with reference to this play, and detailed account by Käthe Rülucke of Brecht's rehearsing of the last scene in *Sinn und Form* (Potsdam), Zweite Sondernummer Bertolt Brecht, 1957.

Abridged English translation by (Brecht and) Laughton in *Seven Plays by Bertolt Brecht*, Grove Press, 1961. Also separately by Grove Press, 1966. Full version by Desmond Vesey in *Plays I*.

28. MOTHER COURAGE AND HER CHILDREN

Mutter Courage und ihre Kinder. A chronicle play of the Thirty Years' War.

Set in Sweden, Poland and Germany between 1624 and 1636.

Mother Courage, who owns a travelling canteen wagon and makes her living from the troops, loses her two sons to the Protestant army. The Catholics overrun her, and she changes sides, but they catch and kill one son. The other is shot by the Protestants for looting during a temporary armistice. Her dumb daughter Kattrin loses her life giving warning of a surprise Catholic attack. Throughout all these tragedies (which she feels deeply) Courage's main concern is to keep her business going: against the background of great historical events she expounds her materialist, matter-of-fact view of war. At the end she is left alone with her wagon, old and wretched but still determined to get her cut.

Twelve scenes prose (with strong dialect and period flavour). Nine songs. Music by Dessau.

1951

Written 1938–9. First produced in Zurich Schauspielhaus, 19 April 1941, by Leopold Lindtberg, scenery Teo Otto, music Paul Burkhard, with Therese Giehse (Courage), Langhoff (Eilif), Bienert (Sergeant), Gerda Müller (Old Woman), Paryla (Schweizerköbi). Also produced in Deutsches Theater, Berlin, 11 January 1949, by Brecht and Engel, scenery Otto, with Weigel (Courage), Hurwicz (Kattrin), Bildt (cook), Hinz (chaplain), Kahler (Eilif). New production, 11 September 1951, with Busch as cook, Geschonneck or Kaiser (since 1955) as chaplain, and Berliner Ensemble.

Produced at Barnstaple, June 1955, by Theatre Workshop, producer Joan Littlewood (who also played Courage). Produced at Marines Memorial Theatre, San Francisco, 17 January 1956, by Herbert Blau; at Ambassador Theatre, New York, October 1962, by Jerome Robbins, with Anna Magnani; at National Theatre, London, by William Gaskill, 12 May 1965, with Madge Ryan.

Published: *Versuche 9* (1949). Later impressions (e.g. Aufbau printing of 1953) include a few modifications, notably the insertion of 'I must get back into business' at the end. In *Stücke VII*. Separately by Suhrkamp, 1958; Reclam (Leipzig), 1959. Nine songs Thüringer Volksverlag Weimar, 1949. Scene 6 in *Internationale Literatur*, 1940, No. 12 (text differs).

Note by Brecht in both editions, giving changes from Zurich text. *Materialien zu Brechts 'Mutter Courage und ihre Kinder'*, Suhrkamp, 1964. Modellbuch *Courage-modell 1949* Henschel, Berlin, 1958. A film version has been made by DEFA and the Berliner Ensemble, using their stage cast under direction of Wekwerth and Peter Palitzsch (première 1961). Songs recorded by the Ensemble on Eterna I 10 002–5 or Eterna 5 10 005.

English translation by H. R. Hays in *New Directions* (Norfolk), 1941; by Eric Bentley in *Plays II*, in *Modern Theatre*, II (Doubleday, 1955) and *Seven Plays by Bertolt Brecht*, Grove Press, 1961.

29. LUCULLUS

(a) DAS VERHÖR DES LUKULLUS

The Trial of Lucullus. A radio play.

Set in classical Rome.

After all the pomp of his funeral procession and burial, the great Roman general Lucullus is judged in the underworld by a peasant, a slave, a fish-wife, a baker and a courtesan; all representatives of the living future. The figures from his triumphal frieze are called as witnesses to his victories, his booty, his sacking of cities, his haul of slaves, his cuisine, his introduction of the cherry tree into Europe. Only the latter speaks for him. Thus his bloody hands are not entirely empty: but 80,000 dead is a high price to pay. The court withdraws to consider its verdict.

Fourteen short sections: one in rhyme, remainder unrhymed irregular verse. Collaborator: Steffin.

Written 1938–9. Broadcast by Studio Bern (Beromünster), 12 May 1940, producer Ernst Bringolf.

Produced in English at Los Angeles, 18 April 1947, by Henry Schnitzler for University of California, in Hays's translation, with music by Roger Sessions. Also at Princeton, 29 April 1955, and in BBC Third Programme, 26 October 1958 by H. B. Fortuin, music Humphrey Searle.

Published: *Internationale Literatur*, Moscow, 1940, No. 3; *Versuche* 11 (expanded version, with final scene of Lucullus's condemnation, as in opera – below, and notes giving differences between the radio play and the opera). *Stücke VII* (ditto, with extra footnotes by Elisabeth Hauptmann).

Translation by H. R. Hays, New Directions, NY, 1943. Revised for *Plays I*.

(b) DIE VERURTEILUNG DES LUKULLUS

The Condemnation of Lucullus. Opera.

1951

Text largely identical with the above. There are minor changes in allotment of lines and order of sections (e.g. Section 2 is absorbed in Section 1, Section 3 is put after Section 5, Section 12 is cut). Section 8 is changed so that the frieze is not actually brought in; instead, the shades of the persons represented on it are summoned. In Section 9 the king from the frieze is preferred to Lucullus because he was fighting a defensive war, not one of conquest. In the final scene the court does not withdraw, but condemns Lucullus to be hurled into nothingness.

Music by Dessau.

First produced in Berlin Staatsoper, 17 March 1951, under original title (29(*a*)), conductor Scherchen, producer Wolfgang Völker, scenery Neher, with Alfred Hülgert (Lucullus), Willi Heyer-Krömer (Judge), Otto Hopf (King). Then withdrawn for revision and put into repertoire under new title, 12 October 1951 (see page 203).

Broadcast in English in BBC Third Programme, 20 March 1953, conductor Scherchen.

Published under original title by Aufbau, Berlin, 1951 (all copies withdrawn); also by Ars Viva Verlag Hermann Scherchen, Zurich, 1951. Published under new title by Aufbau, Berlin, 1951. All subsequent publications under original title, q.v. Piano score, Henschel, E. Berlin., 1951 and 1961. Ten songs in Dessau: *Lieder und Gesänge*, Henschel, 1957.

Note by Dessau in *Leipziger Theater* (Leipzig), No. 19, 1956–7. His essay 'Wie es zum Lukullus kam' is in *Erinnerungen an Brecht* (edited by Herbert Witt), Reclam, Leipzig, 1964.

30. THE GOOD PERSON OF SZECHWAN

Der Gute Mensch von Sezuan. A parable play.

Set in pre-war China, in the capital of Szechwan province.

1943

To justify their existence, the gods have to produce a good person. They choose Shen Teh, a penniless prostitute, set her up in a tobacconist's shop and watch her progress. She finds that she cannot remain good and survive. She disguises herself as a man (her supposed cousin) who has the necessary ruthlessness to put order in her affairs. These prosper, at the cost of her going wholly over into his identity. The gods disentangle the position in a court scene, but return to heaven leaving Shen Teh's problem unsettled.

Ten scenes, with prologue, short interludes and verse epilogue. Prose with heightened passages, sections of free verse and six songs.

Collaborators: Berlau, Steffin. Music by Dessau. (Brecht also planned incidental music with Weill.)

Written 1938–42. First produced in Zurich Schauspielhaus, 4 February 1943, by Steckel, scenery Otto, music by H. G. Früh, with Maria Becker (Shen Teh), Paryla (Sun), Giehse (Mrs Mi Tzü).

Produced in English (Bentley's translation) at Hamline University Theatre, St Paul, 16 March 1948, by James R. Carlson, music by John G. Flittie; in Royal Court Theatre, London, 31 October 1956, by George Devine, scenery Otto, music Dessau, with Peggy Ashcroft; in Phoenix Theatre, New York, 18 December 1956, by Eric Bentley, scenery Otto, music Dessau, with Uta Hagen.

Published: *Versuche 12*; *Stücke VIII*; and separately by Suhrkamp, 1959. Five songs in Dessau: *Lieder aus Der Gute Mensch von Sezuan*, E. Berlin, 1952.

No notes. Alternative epilogue given in *Stücke*. Summarised story in *SzT 4*. Brecht's diary indicates that the play was first conceived before 1933, under the title *Die Ware Liebe*.

English translation by John Willett in *Plays II*. Also under title 'The Good Woman of Setzuan' by Eric and Maya Bentley in *Parables for the Theatre*, University of Minnesota Press, 1948. Revised version by Eric Bentley in 1966 reprint (Penguin Books) and in *Seven Plays by Bertolt Brecht*, Grove Press, 1961.

31. HERR PUNTILA UND SEIN KNECHT MATTI

Herr Puntila and his Man Matti. '. . . is a Volksstück (popular play) . . . after some stories and a scheme for a play by Hella Wuolijoki.'

Set in pre-war Finland.

1949

Puntila is a big farmer and a bigger drinker. When drunk he is friendly and human; when sober, surly and selfish. Oscillating unsteadily between these two poles, he hires new farmhands, invites the village women to his daughter's engagement party, wrecks her engagement to a Foreign Office official and insists that she marry Matti, his sardonic chauffeur. Or he dismisses the farmhands, throws out the village women, propitiates the fiancé and threatens Matti with gaol. At the apex of a drunken spell Matti leaves him; he cannot stand so false and uncertain a relationship.

Twelve scenes prose with verse prologue and epilogue and two songs. A 'Puntila-song' of eight verses links the various scenes.

Music by Dessau (who has also made an opera of this work).

Written August and September 1940 for a Finnish competition. First produced in Zurich Schauspielhaus, 5 June 1948, by Kurt Hirschfeld (and Brecht), scenery Otto, with Steckel (Puntila), Gustav Knuth (Matti), Giehse (Emma), Regine Lutz (Dairy Girl).

Also produced in Deutsches Theater, Berlin, 12 November 1949, by Brecht and Engel, scenery Neher, with Steckel (Puntila) and Geschonneck (Matti).

Produced in English at Wilbur Theatre, Boston, 4 May 1959; at Aldwych Theatre, London, 15 July 1965, by Michel Saint-Denis with Roy Dotrice (Puntila) and Royal Shakespeare company.

Published: *Versuche 10*; *Stücke X*; and separately by Suhrkamp-Verlag, 1959. Finnish version by Brecht and Wuolijoki published as *The Master of Iso-Heikallä and His Man Kalle*, Helsinki, 1946.

Notes by Brecht on the Zurich production, and suggestion for telescoping Scenes 4 and 5, in both editions. 'Notes on the Volksstück' and eight songs by Dessau in *Versuche* only. Account of Berliner Ensemble production in *Theaterarbeit*. Modellbücher. For the play's relationship to the Finnish version and to Hella Wuolijoki's film script, see Margaret Mare's introduction to the school edition of the play (Methuen, 1962). A potted recording of the songs and other extracts is on Eterna 7 10 006.

32. DER AUFHALTSAME AUFSTIEG DES ARTURO UI

The Resistible Ascent of Arturo Ui. '. . . a parable play, written with the aim of destroying the usual disastrous respect which we feel for great murderers.'

Set in Chicago 1938–9.

The five men who control the wholesale greengrocery trade in Chicago face an economic crisis. They bribe Dogsborough, their respected Mayor, to grant a loan. The Press get wind of this, but Ui the gang leader, who wants to 'protect' the wholesalers and is blackmailing Dogsborough, murders the one witness. With his lieutenants Giri, Givola and Roma, Ui then establishes a system of 'protection', and sets fire to one of the wholesalers' warehouses. For this crime a half-wit picked up by Giri is tried and, with the judges' connivance, found guilty. The gangsters fall out over Dogsborough's testament, which names Ui as his successor, and when Roma opposes Ui's plan for extending operations to the suburb of Cicero, Ui has him treacherously shot down by the others. Then Dullfeet of Cicero, whose newspaper has criticized the lawlessness in Chicago, is likewise murdered after every appearance of friendship. So the wholesalers of Cicero, too, are scared into asking (unanimously) for Ui's protection, and Ui concludes by sketching sweeping plans for the future.

1959

Sixteen scenes with (new) rhymed prologue. Mainly blank verse, but with patches of prose. Shakespearean scene endings; one song. One scene includes the whole of 'Friends, Romans and countrymen'; another is a parody of the garden scene from *Faust I*. Each scene finishes with the stage direction 'AN INSCRIPTION APPEARS WHICH RECALLS CERTAIN EPISODES IN THE IMMEDIATE PAST'.

Collaborator: Steffin.

Written March–April 1941. First produced Stuttgart 10 November 1958 by Peter Palitzsch; by Palitzsch and Wekwerth, scenery Von Appen, music Hosalla, with Ekkehard Schall as Ui and Berliner Ensemble, 23 March 1959; at Lunt-Fontanne Theatre, New York, 11 November 1963, by Tony Richardson, with Christopher Plummer as Ui.

Published in *Sinn und Form* (Potsdam), Zweites Sonderheft Bertolt Brecht, 1957, and *Stücke IX*.

Notes in the latter. 'In order that the play may retain all its (regrettable) significance, it must be produced on the Grand Scale, and preferably with obvious harkbacks to the Elizabethan theatre . . . pure parody however must be avoided, and the comic element must be to some extent revolting. The actual presentation has got to go at top speed. . . .' Notes 'Aus dem Arbeitsbuch' in *Sinn und Form* edition. Texts of 'inscriptions' to go between the scenes, in *Stücke*.

33. DIE GESICHTE DER SIMONE MACHARD

The Visions of Simone Machard.

Set in a small town in Touraine in June 1940.

Simone is an adolescent girl employed at the Hostellerie du Relais during the German breakthrough of 1940. Her brother is serving in the army and she herself is reading the story of Jeanne d'Arc. In four dream interludes the real personages in her life become the historical figures in the story: her brother appears to her as an angel, and she herself is Jeanne. This identification enables her to stop her employer from taking all the food and transport in his flight; to distribute food to hungry refugees; and to deny the town's petrol resources to the enemy by setting them on fire. All this against the opposition of her employers, of the French Pétainistes, and of the Germans when they arrive. She is caught and handed over to a mental institution run by nuns. But already others have begun to follow her example.

1957

Four acts prose, including four dream interludes.
Collaborator: Feuchtwanger. Incidental music by Eisler.
Outlined December 1941; mainly written November 1942-spring 1943. First produced for Frankfurt Städtische Bühnen, 8 March 1957, by Harry Buckwitz, scenery Otto, with Dorothea Jecht as Simone. In English at Unity Theatre, London, 2 June 1961, by Heinz Bernard; Glasgow Citizens' Theatre, 28 February 1967.
Published in *Sinn und Form*, Potsdam, 1956, Nos. 5-6; in *Stücke X*.
Notes in *SzT 4*. Notes from Brecht's diary and account by Feuchtwanger ('Zur Entstehungsgeschichte des Stückes "Simone"') in *Schauspiel*, Frankfurt, 1956-7, No. 9. Typescript of the play says it is based on a work by Jacques Malorne. Feuchtwanger wrote a novel on the same story: *Simone*, Neuer Verlag Stockholm, n.d.; English translation by G. A. Herrmann, Hamish Hamilton, London, 1944.
Translation by Carl Richard Mueller, Grove Press, 1965.

34. SCHWEYK IM ZWEITEN WELTKRIEG

Schweik in the Second World War.

Set in Prague and on the Russian front.

Schweik the dog-fancier wanders innocently and deliberately through the

Second World War. He passes through Gestapo HQ, the Voluntary Labour Service and a military prison full of malingerers, without ever betraying whether his idiocy is real or sham; and is finally sent off to Russia to join a unit fighting near Stalingrad. His adventures with Bullinger the SS man, Brettschneider the Gestapo spy, the gargantuan photographer Baloun and the 'Flagon's' landlady Mrs Kopecka, and his final anabasis in the wastes of Russia are all much in the spirit of Hašek's novel. They are set against the short pantomimic ('in the style of an atrocity story') Interludes in the Higher Regions, where Hitler expresses his recurrent concern about the attitude of the Common Man. At the end of the play Hitler and Schweik meet, both utterly lost. But Schweik has lost himself accidentally-on-purpose.

1959

Eight scenes in prose, with a prelude, postlude and two interludes in rhymed couplets. Eight songs and verse epilogue.

Music by Eisler. (Originally planned as opera with Weill.)

Written 1941–3 and not finally revised. First produced Warsaw, Teatr Dramatyczny, 15 January 1957, by Ludvik René; at Erfurt, 1 May 1958, by Eugen Schaub; at Frankfurt Municipal Theatre by Buckwitz, 22 May 1959. In English at Mermaid Theatre, London, 21 August 1963, by Frank Dunlop, with Bernard Miles (Schweik).

Published in *Stücke X*. Also separately by Suhrkamp-Verlag, 1959.

Short note in latter. Résumé of the story in *SzT 4*.

35. THE CAUCASIAN CHALK CIRCLE

Der Kaukasische Kreidekreis.

Set in feudal Georgia, before the invention of firearms.

A prelude shows two Soviet collective farms meeting in 1945 to decide which should have a certain valley. They are told the following story, which constitutes the play proper: The Governor of a Georgian city is overthrown and killed by a nobles' revolt. His wife flees, leaving her baby son. Grusha, a servant girl, takes it and looks after it; she escapes to her brother's in the mountains, where she has to marry a supposedly dying peasant in order to give it a name and a status. When the revolt ends the Governor's wife sends troops to fetch Grusha and the child back to the city, and sues for the child's return. With the beginning of the fourth Act the story flashes back to the day of the revolt to trace the disreputable career of Azdak, a tramp-like village rogue whom the rebellious soldiers appoint judge. In the last Act he tries the case, and settles it by reversing the old test of the Chalk Circle: the child is given to Grusha because she cannot bear the traditional tug-of-war which is supposed to end in the child's being drawn out of the circle by maternal attraction. At the same time he gives Grusha a divorce so that she can return to her soldier fiancé. The final moral is that both child and valley should go to whoever serves them best.

1954

Prelude and five acts, mainly prose. Narrative chorus of three or four singers in unrhymed irregular verse. Twelve songs, of which four sung by the singers.

Collaborator: Berlau. Music: Dessau.

Written 1943–5. First produced in English (see below). Produced in Theater am Schiffbauerdamm, Berlin, 15 June 1954, by Brecht, scenery von Appen, with Hurwicz (Grusha), Weigel (Governor's Wife), Busch (Azdak) and Berliner Ensemble.

Produced (in English) at Nourse Little Theatre, Northfield (Minn), 4 May 1948, by Henry Goodman, music Katherine Griffith; at Aldwych Theatre, London, 29 March 1962, by William Gaskill, with Royal Shakespeare Company; at Actor's Workshop, San Francisco, 13 December 1963, by Carl Weber; at Lincoln Center Repertory Theatre, New York, 28 March 1966, by Julius Irving, music Morton Subotnick.

Published: *Sonderheft Sinn und Form*, Potsdam, 1949; *Versuche 13*; *Stücke X*. Also separately by Suhrkamp, 1959; Reclam, Leipzig, 1959.

Modellbücher. Résumé of the story by Brecht in Kulisiewicz's *Zeichnungen zur Inszenierung des Berliner Ensembles*, Henschel, Berlin, 1956. Reprinted with other notes in *SzT 6*.

English translation by James Stern and W. H. Auden in *Plays I*; by Eric and Maja Bentley, less prologue, in *Two Parables for the Theatre*, University of Minnesota Press, 1948; also published separately by Oxford University Press, London, 1956; with prologue, in *Seven Plays by Bertolt Brecht*, Grove Press, 1961; same, revised by Eric Bentley, in reprint of *Two Parables*, Minnesota and Penguin, 1966.

36. ANTIGONE

Die Antigone des Sophokles. Adapted for the stage by Bertolt Brecht from Hölderlin's translation.

Set in Thebes, outside Creon's palace.

1948

Perhaps two-thirds of the play follows the Hölderlin version, but even here Brecht has largely reshaped the verse so that although much of the sense, many of the images, and even the words themselves are the same as Hölderlin's the cadence is different. Almost indistinguishable in style, his new passages are woven into this. Considerable changes result. A prologue set in Berlin of 1945 shows two sisters whose brother has deserted from the German army and is found hanged: should they risk being seen by the SS cutting his body down? In the play itself Creon becomes a brutal aggressor, who has attacked Argos for the sake of its iron ore; Polyneikes deserts in protest against this war which has killed his brother; and Antigone is partly moved by a like disapproval of her uncle's policy. There is only minimum reference to the supernatural: Tiresias, instead of prophesying the future, becomes a pessimistic analyst of the present; while the chorus of elders, always reserved in its attitude, eventually turns against Creon too. Not only Antigone and Hamon die; at the end a wounded messenger announces disaster in Argos and the death of Megareus, the one son on whom Creon still relies. The fall of Thebes itself is impending.

Prologue of 93 lines and play 1,300 lines, of unrhymed irregular verse.

57

Collaborator: Neher.

Written 30 March–12 December 1947. First produced in Chur Stadttheater (Switzerland), February 1948, by Brecht, scenery Neher, with Weigel (Antigone), Hans Gaugler (Creon).

Published as a Modellbuch *Antigonemodell 1948* by Gebrüder Weiss, Berlin, 1949; republished by Henschel-Verlag, Berlin, 1955, with new (alternative) prologue. In *Stücke XI*.

Antigonemodell 1948 contains marginal notes by Brecht, and a résumé of the play in hexameters. The foreword to it, together with the prologue and notes for the Greiz production, are published in *Stücke XI*: 'According to the picture of the ancients man is delivered over more or less blindly to Fate; he has no power over it. In Bertolt Brecht's adaptation this picture has given way to the view that man's fate is man himself.' Further notes and material are printed in *Die Antigone des Sophokles. Materialien zur Antigone*, Suhrkamp, 1965.

37. DIE TAGE DER COMMUNE

The Days of the Commune. '. . . written after reading Nordahl Grieg's *Die Niederlage*. A few characters and features were adapted from this, but on the whole *Die Tage der Commune* is intended as a kind of counter to it.'

Set in Paris between January–April 1871.

1956

The story of the Paris Commune is told through fictional Men in the Street – a seamstress and a schoolmistress, a worker and his mother, a student priest and his baker brother, all grouped round a Montmartre café – and a number of historical personages including Thiers and Bismarck and some of the delegates to the Commune itself. The Men in the Street resist Thiers's attempt to disarm the National Guard, watch its Central Committee seize power at the Hôtel de Ville, dance and discuss in the streets. The Commune

58

holds its meetings; the Governor of the Bank of France preserves his independence; Bismarck presses for Paris to be 'pacified'; the Men in the Street put up a barricade, on which they fight and die. Watching from a safe distance, the bougeois and the aristocrats congratulate Thiers.

Fourteen scenes prose, some of which are subdivided.
Three songs.
Music by Eisler.
Written 1948-9, but not finally revised. First produced Municipal Theatre, Karl Marx-Stadt (ex-Chemnitz), 17 November 1956, by Besson and Wekwerth, setting Neher. Also at Theater am Schiffbauerdamm, E. Berlin, 7 October 1962, by Wekwerth and Joachim Tenschert, with Berliner Ensemble.
Published: *Versuche 15; Stücke X.*
English translation by Leonard Lehrman, *Dunster Drama Review*, 10/2, 1971.

38. DER HOFMEISTER

The Tutor. By J. M. R. Lenz. (An adaptation) . . . 'designed for the Berliner Ensemble.'

Set in Insterburg (Prussia) and Halle (Saxony) after the Seven Years' War.

1950

Lenz's story is that Läuffer, engaged as tutor for a retired major's two children, seduces (or is seduced by) the daughter in the absence of her real lover. Pursued by the major and his friends, he takes refuge with a village schoolmaster, who exploits him as a cheap assistant. In the presence of the teacher's young ward he feels the same disaster about to recur. He castrates himself; and finds that he is then universally acceptable. To this piece of tragic satire Brecht has added the discussions about love and philosophy between the students in Halle; the dialogue has been almost entirely rewritten; and he has sharpened the moral. This self-castration now comes to represent the collapse of the German intellectuals before their country's problems, and also the dismal pedagogic tradition to which it led. At the end Läuffer is hailed as the perfect teacher who shall mould the youth of Germany in his own image.

Five acts (seventeen scenes) prose, with rhymed prologue and epilogue.
Collaborators: Berlau, Besson, Monk, Neher.
First produced 15 April 1950 for Berliner Ensemble by Brecht and Neher, scenery Neher, with Hans Gaugler (Läuffer).
Published: *Versuche 11*; *Stücke XI*.
Notes by Brecht in former, with analysis 'Über das Poetische und Artistische'. Account of the production in *Theaterarbeit*.

39. HERRNBURGER BERICHT

Report from Herrnburg. 'This piece needs no dynamics. It is a report.'

Concert platform, with uniforms and a frontier barrier.

The story is based on an actual incident, and can be told in the titles of the songs: 'Encounter near Herrnburg – the Youth refuse to give the West German police their names – the Policeman asks the Youth how they got on in the German Democratic Republic – Dance Song – the Children's request – Refreshing Song – Invitation – the Police caution the Free German Youth that they must not sing when marching through Lübeck – Mocking Song.'

1951

Ten songs, for youth chorus, each introduced by a very short commentary. Two fragments of film.
Music by Dessau.
Produced in Deutsches Theater, Berlin, August 1951, by Egon Monk, with the Free German Youth, for the World Festival of Democratic Youth. Awarded National Prize, First Class.

Published by Central Committee of Free German Youth (FDJ), Berlin, 1951.
Omitted from *Stücke*.

No notes known.

40. TURANDOT ODER DER KONGRESS DER WEISSWÄSCHER

Turandot, or the Whitewashers' Congress.

Set in China at some indeterminate past time.

There is no cotton to be bought in China; the Emperor and his brother have a monopoly, but are waiting for a rise in price. Clothes-makers and clothesless unite in protest, and a revolutionary opposition is led by Kai Ho, an ex-Tui. The Tuis (or 'Tellect-Ual-Ins'), a group of futile thinkers who live by hawking opinions and arguments, are called in to invent excuses for the shortage: the most successful whitewasher to marry the Emperor's daughter Turandot. The competitors all fail and are beheaded. Gogher Gogh, the gangster (a would-be Tui), then burns half the imperial cotton stock under the nose of the remaining Tuis, so that the rest can be sold on a rising market. The Tuis flee; one of them goes to join Kai Ho. Gogher Gogh makes a putsch, but Turandot does not care to marry him, and before he can force her Kai Ho's supporters break in. (The idea of the competition comes from Gozzi or from Schiller's adaptation, but the rest of the story is new.)

Ten scenes prose. Scene 5 (one-third of the whole play) is subdivided.
Music by Eisler.
Written about 1953–4 and not finally revised.
First produced at Zurich Schauspielhaus, 14 February 1969, by Benno Besson and Horst Sagert.

UNFINISHED WORKS

Absalom und Bathseba
Brecht's Augsburg friend, H. O. Münsterer, says this play, originally called *David*, was virtually finished by December 1919. See his *Bert Brecht. Erinnerungen aus der Jahren 1917–22*, Verlag der Arche, Zurich, 1963. It has not survived.

Sommersinfonie
As for the above. Münsterer says it anticipated *Mahagonny* and included the song 'Gegen Verführung' later taken into that work.

Der reiche Mann und der arme Mann
One song is in *Gedichte 2*.

Joe P. Fleischhacker aus Chicago
Unfinished play about a wheat king; billed as *Weizen* on programme of Piscator's company for the 1927–8 season. See *Sinn und Form*, Sonderheft, 1957, p. 243. One song in *Gedichte 2*. Verses in *Gedichte 9*.

Der Fischzug

One-act play of uncertain date included in *Stücke XIII*, 1966. It is suggested there that it may date from as early as 1919.

Untergang des Egoisten Johann Fatzer

Fragment of ten pages published in *Versuche I*. Set in Weimar Germany, and written in uneven blank verse. Mentioned in Piscator's *Das Politische Theater* (1929) as under consideration by his company. Three verse passages and poem 'Fatzer, komm' in *Gedichte 2* and *9*.

Aus Nichts wird Nichts

Referred to by Schumacher, p. 441; also by Piscator (*op. cit.*) as 'pedagogical-philosophical' play, likewise under consideration by him. Collaborators: Burri, Hauptmann. 'Der Aus-nichts-wird-nichts Song' is in *Gedichte 2*. Other verses in *Gedichte 9*.

Der Brotladen

Seemingly the most important of the unfinished plays: being written about 1929–30. Two scenes and note in *Sinn und Form* (Potsdam) 1958, No. 1. Four items in *Gedichte 9*. Collaborators: Burri, Hauptmann. Here is part of an unpublished note by Brecht:

'Our re-working of what is, classically speaking, tragic, must always refer back to the Bread Shop. Depriving a mother of her children – near the Bread Shop, a terrible blow. Idem, away from it – liberation. Freedom: a permanent necessity when one has bread in one's pocket, but no use when one is hungry. Even wisdom (even its lowest form = cunning) at some distance from the Bread Shop becomes quite irrelevant.'

Der Moabiter Pferdehandel

One-act work planned in collaboration with Weill. Might be identical with

Der Stalljunge

'School opera'. Microfilm of MS. is in New York Public Library.

Was kostet das Eisen or *Kleine Geschäfte mit Eisen*

Short play in four episodes with verse prologue. Dated 1939.

Dansen

Another short contemporary play of the same time. Included with the previous item in *Stücke XIII*, 1966.

Die Reisen des Glücksgotts

Opera planned with Dessau in the 1940s. Prologue and first scene were written, and the whole work sketched out; the introduction to *Stücke I* describes its theme and relates it to that of *Baal*. Four preliminary 'Lieder des Glücksgotts' and one aria from the opera are in Brecht/Dessau: *Lieder und Gesänge*, Henschel-Verlag, Berlin, 1957, which also gives a note on the work. Nine songs are included in *Gedichte 6* and *9*.

Salzburger Totentanz

An open-air play like Hofmannsthal's *Jedermann*, to be performed outside Salzburg cathedral. Fragments and relevant correspondence quoted by Siegfried

Melchinger in 'Bertolt Brecht's Salzburger Totentanz', *Stuttgarter Zeitung*, 5 January 1963.

PROJECTS

These include *Der dicke Mann auf der Schiffschaukel* (1918), *Quintus Fabius Maximus, Condel*, a Büchner-like tragedy, and *Herr Makrot* (all 1919), *Klamauk* (1922), *Karl der Kühne* (c. 1926), *Dan Drew* (Die Erie Bahn) to *Joe P. Fleischhacker*), *Inflation* (*Mentscher*) (1926), *Simon von Mühlheim, Revue für die Ruhr* (c. 1930, with Weill, for Essen), *Goliath* (opera; two items in *Gedichte 5*), *Das wahre Leben des Jakob Gehherda* (two items ditto), *Die Freuden und Leiden der kleineren Seeräuber* (with Ruth Berlau and Eisler, presumably the operetta which Brecht told the *Berlingske Tidende* of 14 January 1935 he hoped Mae West would act in,) *Julius Cäsar* (three songs in *Gedichte 9*, where it is said to have been dropped for the novel on the same theme,) *Die Strasse der Ministerien* and *Pluto-Revue* (a song from each in *Gedichte 9*), *Leben des Konfuzius* (1940 and 1944), *Dunant* (1942), *Life and Death of Rosa Luxemburg* (1944), *Ulenspiegel* (1948), *Clownspiel* (with Dessau), *Büsching*, about the East German Stakhanovite building worker Hans Garbe, and a play about Einstein.

A scene from *Leben des Konfuzius* is in *Neue Deutsche Literatur*, 1958, No. 2; translation by H. E. Rank in *The Kenyon Review*, Summer, 1958. Quotations from *Büsching* are in *Bertolt Brecht, Leben und Werk*, Volk und Wissen, E. Berlin, 1963. pp. 172–3; a translation by Eric Bentley of the *Salzburger Totentanz* fragment in *The Jewish Wife and Other Short Plays by Bertolt Brecht*, Grove Press, New York, 1965.

No doubt there were many others. These titles are only given in case they are of use, and because they help show the development of Brecht's interests.

ADAPTATIONS, COLLABORATIONS, ETC., NOT COUNTED ABOVE

For the Berliner Ensemble:

Coriolanus by Shakespeare

Brecht's unfinished translation and adaptation (made about 1951–3) is printed in *Stücke XI*, together with a 'Study of the first scene' in the form of a dialogue between him and his collaborators. The study is also published in *Versuche 15* and *Schriften zum Theater*. First produced Frankfurt Schauspielhaus, 22 September 1962, by Heinrich Koch. By Berliner Ensemble, September 1964.

Der Prozess des Jeanne d'Arc zu Rouen 1431 by Anna Seghers

Documentary radio play, adapted in sixteen scenes for the stage, 1952, and produced by Besson, with Käthe Reichel. In *Stücke XII*.

Don Juan by Molière

Made in 1952 and published in *Stücke XII*, with short notes on the play and on Besson's production. Four acts. Collaborators: Besson, Hauptmann.

Pauken und Trompeten after Farquhar's The Recruiting Officer

Twelve scenes (1955), produced by Besson with Kaiser and Regine Lutz, and published in *Stücke XII*. Collaborators: Besson, Hauptmann. Music by Rudolf Wagner-Regeny. Potted recording on Eterna 710001.

Others:

Hannibal

First scene from an unfinished adaptation of Grabbe, published in *Berliner Börsen-Courier*, 13 November 1922. See two early letters in *Sinn und Form* (Potsdam), 1958 No. 1.

Gösta Berling by Selma Lagerlöf, dramatized by E. Karin.

Prologue to an adaptation by Brecht in *Das Kunstblatt* (Potsdam) January 1924. See also Arnolt Bronnen: *Tage mit Bertolt Brecht*, Munich, 1960, pp. 146–9 for account of negotiations.

Pastor Ephraim Magnus by Hans Henny Jahnn

See Arnolt Bronnen's *Gibt zu Protokoll* (Rowohlt, Hamburg, 1954) for reference to his and Brecht's adaptation and production of this work about 1923.

La Dame aux Camélias by Alexander Dumas, translated by Ferdinand Bruckner

Revised by Brecht for Deutsches Theater production by Bernhard Reich.

Kalkutta 4 Mai by Lion Feuchtwanger

Published in *Drei Angelsächsische Stücke* (Propyläen, Berlin, 1927) and *Stücke in Prosa* (Querido, Amsterdam, 1936) and in translation by Willa and Edwin Muir in *Two Anglo-Saxon Plays* (Viking, New York, 1928). Revision by Brecht and Feuchtwanger during 1925 of a play published in 1916 under title *Warren Hastings*.

Macbeth by Shakespeare

Brecht's radio adaptation was broadcast from Berlin on 14 October 1927. Foreword in *SzT 1*.

Rasputin by Alexei Tolstoy and P. Shchegolev
Die Abenteuer des braven Soldaten Schweiks by Hašek, adapted by Brod and Reimann.
Konjunktur by Leo Lania

Brecht helped on the adaptation of these three works for Erwin Piscator's 1927–8 season in Berlin. His diary for 24 June 1943 suggests that he was wholly responsible for the second, and calls it 'a pure piece of montage from the novel'.

Ich will ein Kind haben ('Die Pioniere') by Sergei Tretiakoff

Translated by Ernst Hube, adapted by Bert Brecht. Duplicated MS. published by Max Reichard-Verlag, Freiburg im Breisgau n.d.

Hamlet by Shakespeare

Brecht's radio adaptation was produced by Alfred Braun for Berlin Radio on 30 January 1931 with Fritz Kortner and Oskar Homolka.

Alle wissen Alles by Ruth Berlau

'. . . represents an adaptation of a forgotten English farce of the 'nineties with a certain amount of advice from me.' Written about 1938 for Robert Storm Petersen ('Storm P.'). Introduction by Brecht in *SzT 4*. Not produced.

Nothing but the Best with Mordecai Gorelik

American setting, written in California in 1940s. According to Mr Gorelik it never got beyond a first draft. He did most of the writing.

The Duchess of Malfi by Webster

Adapted *c.* 1943 with H. R. Hays and W. H. Auden for Elisabeth Bergner. Text in English only. Produced at Boston, September 1946, by George Rylands, with Elisabeth Bergner and Canada Lee; on 15 October 1946 at Ethel Barrymore Theatre, New York.

Plays for which Brecht wrote songs include Paul Schurek's *Kamrad Kasper* (1932: three songs in *Gedichte 2*) and Rudolf Wagner-Regeny's and Caspar Neher's opera *Persische Legende* (one song in *Gedichte 7*). He helped adapt *Volpone* for a production in Vienna in 1952 (two songs in *Gedichte 7*), and had a hand in virtually all the plays staged by the Berliner Ensemble.

FILMS

Die Dreigroschenoper

Director: G. W. Pabst. Script by Ernst Vadja, Leo Lania and Bela Balazs; sets by Andreiev; music by Kurt Weill. Version 1 (in German) with Carola Neher, Lotte Lenja, Rudolf Forster, Ernst Busch. Version 2 (in French) with Albert Préjean. Nero-Film, 1931.

Première 19 February 1931.

(Brecht began working on the script with Lania and Balazs. His own treatment was rejected, so he disowned the film and sued for an injunction to stop it from being made. The treatment, under the title *Die Beule*, is published in *Versuche 3*, together with Brecht's account of his suit. Some of its ideas were later absorbed in the *Dreigroschenroman*.)

A new version directed by Wolfgang Staudte on a script by himself and Günther Weisenborn starred Curt Jürgens and Hildegard Knef. Première March 1963.

Kuhle Wampe

Director: Slatan Dudow. Producer: Georg Hoellering. Script by Brecht and Ernst Ottwalt; music by Hanns Eisler. With Herta Thiele, Ernst Busch and the voice of Helene Weigel. Praesens-Film, 1932.

Première 30 May 1932.

(Semi-documentary middle-length film of Berlin working-class life, culminating in a Communist sports day. Banned on political grounds soon after release.)

Ubitzi vykhodyat na dorogu ('Murderers are on their way')

Directors: Vsevolod Pudovkin and Yuri Tarich. Scenario by Pudovkin and E. Bolshintsov. Music by Nikolai Kryukov. Combined Studio, 1942.

Never released.

(Scenes from *Furcht und Elend des Dritten Reiches*. Also titled, at earlier stages, *The Face of Fascism* and *School for Villainy*.)

Hangmen also Die

Director: Fritz Lang. Producer: Arnold Pressburger. Story by Brecht and Lang; script by John Wexley; music by Hanns Eisler. With Brian Donlevy, Walter Brennan, Anna Lee. United Artists, 1942.

(Story of the assassination of Heydrich, in fictionalized form. Brecht thought that his contribution had been distorted, and brought a case to ensure that the credits distinguished it from the actual script.)

Herr Puntila und sein Knecht

Director: Alberto Cavalcanti. Play adapted by Vladimir Pozner and Ruth Weiden; script by Cavalcanti; music by Hanns Eisler. With Curt Bois. Wien-Film, 1955.

Première 29 May 1955.

(Colour film of the play, made in Austria. Brecht originally wished Joris Ivens to be the director.)

Film Treatments by Brecht:

These include *Lady Macbeth of the Yards*, *Caesar's Last Days*, *Wie der Brotkönig lernte Brot zu backen* and *Simone* (with Vladimir Pozner, from his own play). Brecht is also supposed to have helped revise the script adapted from Remarque's *Arc de Triomphe* in 1947 and to have worked on Richard Tauber's *Bajazzo*. About 1953 he wrote the songs for *Song of the Rivers* (Director: Joris Ivens. Script: Vladimir Pozner. Music: Shostakovitch. Producers: DEFA for the World Federation of Trade Unions.) These are published in Ivens and Pozner: *Lied der Ströme*, Verlag Tribüne, Berlin, 1957.

Films by the Berliner Ensemble:

Under Manfred Wekwerth's direction the Ensemble has made a documentary record of Brecht's production of *Die Mutter* (1958). A Cinemascope version of *Mother Courage* was completed in 1961, produced by DEFA and under the joint direction of Wekwerth and Peter Palitzsch.

Eight Aspects

ONE

The Subject Matter

The violent poetry of Brecht's first works emerges from even the shortest account. Crime, drink, rape, murder, prostitution, mob violence: nothing is spared. The moon hangs over the stage as figures with names like Glubb and Gloomb, Shlink and Bulltrotter, Bolleboll and Gougou stalk about in aimless desperation. Indoors it is a bar or a cheap hotel; outside it is waste land at night; in the stage directions the wind is continually howling. 'Voici le temps des ASSASSINS', Rimbaud had foretold:

> Oh! tous les vices, colère, luxure –
> Magnifique, la luxure
> Surtout mensonge et paresse.

An exaggerated lawlessness grips the theatre; an embittered and anarchic re-action against the shortcomings of orthodox morality. The outcast, the dis-illusioned tough becomes the hero; he may be criminal, he may be semi-human, but in plays like *Baal* he can be romanticized into an inverted idealist, blindly striking out at the society in which he lives.

> Consumed by tempests and sun, eroded and maddened,
> A looted wreath crowning his tangled head,
> He had forgotten his whole childhood except for the dreams which he had then,
> Quickly the roof, but never the sky overhead.

Such creatures savage one another against a tattered and shabby jungle back-ground, far below the semi-naturalistic level of Hemingway and Traven; haunted by beggars, tramps, ballad singers, whores: figures drawn from a tradition of squalor which stretches from the nineteenth-century realists to the dustbins of Mr Bratby and Mr Samuel Beckett today.

In the Germany of the 1920s the vivid experiences of war, revolution and economic collapse gave a sharp topical relevance to this vogue, so that a number of the liveliest artists and writers were using similar terms of refer-ence to Brecht's. George Grosz drew his murderers and adventurers, and tried to make the bourgeois' hair stand on end; Joachim Ringelnatz wrote his poems of tough sailors shouting, boozing, fighting, drowning; Walter Mehring wrote a 'Ballad of an Adventurer' –

> I'd slide beneath a pile of corpses
> Contented as a tired-out child.

68

The early plays. *Left*: *Im Dickicht* (1924): Walter Franck knifing Fritz Kortner. *Right*: *Baal* (1926): Oskar Homolka throttling Paul Bildt

– who was like a caricatured version of Baal himself. A whole school of synthetic debauchery sprang up, which set out in its own way to match the gangster and Western story, and took much of its inspiration from overseas. It was at once aggressive and frivolous, like the Berlin Dadaist movement to which Mehring and Grosz and the Herzfelde brothers (two later associates of Brecht's) all belonged: and it showed a consciously anti-patriotic concern with foreign manners and even with foreign words:

> I want to be down home in Dixi
> Und cowboys rings
> Bei echten drinks
> My darling girl schenk ein and mix sie!

Thus Mehring; or, less jazzily but more phonetically, Ringelnatz:

> Swiethart! Manilahaariges Kitty-Anny-Pipi –
> Oder wie du heisst –
> Bulldog aheu!
> Bei Jesus Chreist
> Ich war – seit Konstantinopel – dir immer treu
> Scheek hands! Ehrlich und offen
> Ich bin gar nicht besoffen.
> Gif öss a Whisky, du, ach du! Jesus Chreist!

Here was a combination of the new language of the dance-band with Rimbaud's notions of exotic adventure: a pungent flavour that recalled the great international sea-ports and the newly translated stories of Kipling, and even the traditional cowboy-and-Indian world of Fenimore Cooper and Karl May.

The exotic background. Drawings by Karl Arnold (*left*: 1923)
and George Grosz ('*New Yorker Vision*', 1915)

A spurious Anglo-Saxon mythology grew up, and Brecht embraced it in
his plays and even in his life. Bertolt was Bert, Georg (Grosz) became George,
Walter Mehring passed as Walt Merin; Hellmut Herzfelde had earlier taken
the name of John Heartfield as a deliberate gesture against the war. Sport was
the culture of this mythical world, jazz its music, the Salvation Army the
most intriguing religion.[1] It was the same rowdy, popular combination as
fascinated other poets of the 'twenties: Cocteau, Lorca, Mayakovsky.[2] 'Ah,
those women's voices . . .' wrote Brecht,

> That's how they sang (take care of those records!) in the golden age.
> Soft sound of evening breakers at Miami!
> Irresistible humour of the people speeding on unending highways!
> Shattering sorrow of melodious girls, trustfully
> Lamenting their broadshouldered man, yet ever surrounded
> By broadshouldered men!
>
> What men they were! Their boxers the strongest!
> Their inventors most adept! Their trains the swiftest!
> And the most crowded!
> And it all looked like lasting a thousand years.

[1] E.g., Rudolf Arnheim's article 'Die Heilsarmee' in *Die Weltbühne*, Berlin, 6 July 1926.
Wedekind had also taken a certain interest in this organization and its hymns.
[2] Typical products of Mayakovsky's American visit of 1925 were the poems 'Cross-
section of a Skyscraper' and 'A Decent Citizen'. The Salvation Army figures in the latter.

Boxing, wrestling, racing became the symbolic forms of struggle, whisky and ale the drinks, 'Virginia' the correct brand of cigar. Lion Feuchtwanger (himself one of Brecht's earliest friends and collaborators) compiled *Pep: J. L. Wetcheek's Amerikanisches Liederbuch*; the Expressionist playwright Georg Kaiser included a hectic bicycle race and a Salvation Army scene in his play *Von Morgens bis Mitternachts*; Ringelnatz put a boxing match, a wrestling match and another bicycle race in his *Turngedichte* of 1923. In 1925 Brecht's friend Arnolt Bronnen summed up his view of literature in these fashionable terms: 'I look at it in the broadest sense, ranging from the boxing match to the jazz band.'

Viertes Bild:
(Der Manager durchs Megaphon:)

6 Tage Rennen

Hart
Am Start
Die Muskeln auf der Lauer
Zweimalhunderttausend
Augen:

The cult of sport. Cabaret sketch by Walter Mehring (1924)

Brecht himself presented *Im Dickicht der Städte* as a wrestling match and advised the reader in a foreword to 'Judge the competitors' form impartially and concentrate on the finish' (auf das Finish); 'Alle ab zum Boxkampf' 'all off to the prizefight' is the closing stage direction of the *Elefantenkalb*. In such ways sport became an interest, and to some extent an affectation, which left its stamp all over Brecht's work. Motoring apart, he never actually practised a sport of any kind. But in his early days in Berlin he made friends with the then German middleweight champion Paul Samson-Körner,[1] and they spent

[1] Brecht also wrote a short story 'Der Kinnhaken' ('Hook to the Chin') in *Scherls Magazin*, Berlin, January 1926, and an essay 'Die Krise des Sports' in Willy Meisl: *Der Sport am Scheidewege*, Heidelberg 1928. A boxing play *Harte Bandagen* by his friend Ferdinand Reyher was produced in Berlin in 1930. Samson-Körner lost his title to Hans Breitensträter, and is now dead. Breitensträter in turn had appeared in 1921 as one of the contributors to Alfred Flechtheim's *Der Querschnitt*, 'Zeitschrift für Kunst und Boxsport', together with Apollinaire, Sternheim, Vlaminck and others. For sport and the theatre see pp. 146-7. Note also the boxing-ring effect in the illustrations on pp. 29, 132, 138.

Left: 'The Human Fighting-Machine'
Right: The Salvationist from *Happy End*

part of 1926 collaborating on an unfinished work called *Die Menschliche Kampfmaschine*, the Human Fighting-Machine. Very characteristically that same year, when he was asked to judge a poetry competition by the *Literarische Welt*, he put aside all the entries in favour of a poem written by his friend Hannes Küpper and published in some bicycling paper. This told of the feats of the Australian cyclist MacNamara, ending each verse (in English) with the refrain 'Hé, hé! The Iron Man!'[1]

This half-romantic, half-satirical Anglo-Saxon world forms the background of nearly all Brecht's plays between 1921 and 1928: from *Im Dickicht der Städte* to *Mahagonny*. And so they are full of inaccuracies and inconsistencies that present a certain obstacle to the Anglo-Saxon audience: they make us giggle. Sergeant Blody Five tells how the Army captured Shiks at Lake-Tchad-River;[2] twentieth-century British soldiers drink cocktails, eighteenth- drink whisky, fourteenth- play whist. Characters are called Caruther or Dockdaisy or I. N. Smith; London becomes the seamy pseudo-Dickensian town of the *Threepenny Novel*. Such fantasies recall that passage in Isherwood's *Prater Violet* where 'Bergmann' (based on Brecht's old friend Berthold Viertel) sees London through just these spectacles, or an uninten-

---

[1] Küpper, a friend of Brecht's, was a 'Dramaturg' at the Essen Municipal Theatre around 1930. He figures in the picture on p. 146.

[2] See *Mann ist Mann* (1926 edition), p. 92. In later editions 'Blody Five' was amended to 'Blutiger Fünfer', 'Dschadseefluss' to 'Tschadsefluss' and 'Shiks' to 'Hindus'.

tionally comic report by Egon Erwin Kisch (also a friend of Brecht's) where 'dark London' is described in terms of Whitechapel and Jack the Ripper and the Salvation Army:

> The publican places the empty glass behind the counter . . . pulls on a black handle that stands on its surface above the glass, and the glass fills with brandy from a tap. About thirty such handles are screwed to the surface: one for each drink. Beer is also served. . . .[1]

We have to note the absurdities, because with time the myth may come to be accepted. Already there are Communist critics who present Brecht's picture as an accurate account of Western bourgeois life, fit to be compared with Engels's inquiry of 1844.[2]

In his own view such aberrations simply did not matter. 'If his attention is drawn to some internal distortion,' wrote Feuchtwanger in 1928,

> he will not hesitate ruthlessly to scrap a year's work; but he won't waste a single minute over setting right a gross error in external probability. . . . For he minds more about the inner curve of his characters than about the outer curve of the plot. And so the plots of his plays are full of the crassest improbabilities.

Twenty years later he still felt the same, writing in the 'Short Organum' that

> Incorrectness, or considerable improbability even, was hardly or not at all disturbing, so long as the incorrectness had a certain consistency and the im-

[1] See Isherwood: *Prater Violet*, Methuen, London, 1946, p. 41; and Egon Erwin Kisch: *Der Rasende Reporter*, Sieben-Stäbe, Verlag, Berlin, 1930 (originally published 1924), p. 242.

Jack the Ripper seems to have been a favourite English figure for German writers ever since he appeared in Wedekind's *Büchse der Pandora* (the basis of Berg's opera *Lulu*). Wedekind took the part himself.

[2] For instance, Ernst Schumacher's *Die Dramatischen Versuche Bertolt Brechts 1918–1933*, Rütten and Loening, E. Berlin, 1955, pp. 112–13, on *Mann ist Mann* ('A piece of grisly colonial reality . . .'), or pp. 103–4 on Galy Gay as a 'proletarian' illustrating certain ideas of Lenin's, or pp. 236–7 on *The Threepenny Opera* as a 'vague reflection' of Engels's *Condition of the Working Classes in 1844*. See also N. Poliakova's unpublished thesis on Brecht, which quotes *Im Dickicht der Städte*, *Mahagonny* and *The Threepenny Opera* as giving a true picture of the contemporary bourgeoisie. 'He saw the US as a land of merciless exploitation,' says Galina Znamenskaya in an article on Brecht in *Soviet Literature* (Moscow), 1955, No. 6, 'a stronghold of reaction and a major centre of imperialism. He exposed the so-called American democracy in *Mahagonny*.' Again, of the mythical London of the *Dreigroschenroman*: 'Brecht depicts imperialist vultures . . . exposes the imperialist bourgeoisie and in doing so discloses the essence of the class forces that produced Fascism. . . . He leads the reader to the idea that imperialism and Fascist tendencies are inseparable.'

The other, supposedly 'positive', side of this kind of criticism may be seen in the same lady's verdicts on *Mother Courage* ('the most important of all Brecht's anti-war writings') and *The Caucasian Chalk Circle* ('tells of the struggle of Soviet collective farmers to transform nature'). Fortunately, later Soviet criticisms of Brecht have been on a much higher level (see pages 208–9 below).

probability remained of a constant kind. All that mattered was the illusion of compelling momentum in the story being told. . . .

And so in *Baal* what matters is the outcast's struggle for life and pleasure; in *Im Dickicht der Städte* the pointless competitive fight; in *Edward II* the feudal contest for power; in *Mann ist Mann* the farce of the military Team Spirit; in *The Threepenny Opera* and *Mahagonny* the violence of the satirical attack. The crooks and beggars, the soldiers, the tarts and the Anglo-Saxon trappings are none of them anything but incidentals; the liveliness of the narrative and the force of the writing are all that counts.

It is true that Brecht could achieve this crazy logic; and in *Trommeln in der Nacht* there was something more: a passionate despair, both personal and political, that was set out in largely natural terms. But the phoney world became far too solidly, even lovingly established to be taken as a mere setting, and it undoubtedly appealed to Brecht for its own sake. Thus when about 1928 he began to take a different attitude to the theatre and to his own part in it the old myths were too closely woven into his work to be discarded. In later works like *Die Rundköpfe und die Spitzköpfe* or *Turandot* or *Arturo Ui* they are plainly visible; they seem to underlie a number of his theatrical conventions; they probably explain his interest in Beckett's *Waiting for Godot*; and again and again their half-hidden presence can be felt in what are ostensibly quite different plays. Not only that, but the public too has always felt their nostalgic charm, so that Brecht came to have many admirers who would look eagerly for traces of the familiar freakish background in any new production, and grumble bitterly if none could be found.

* * *

Lindberghflug and the *Badener Lehrstück*, both produced for the first time in 1929, mark a new stage in Brecht's work: the starting-point of his unmistakable didactic style. The wild, mad world drops away, or is at least subordinated to other considerations. Where its conflicts recur, as in *St Joan of the Stockyards*, it is as an illustration of a serious anti-capitalist or anti-Nazi thesis; they no longer run their own independent course. Instead, we find the beginnings of a new, inquiring, critical theatre which substitutes for the old Anglo-Saxon exoticism an impassivity and detachment of a more Oriental kind. Wisdom itself now begins to seem a Chinese speciality; self-subordination and self-discipline, a gift of the Japanese. The physical setting of the plays changes to match. If six out of Brecht's eight major plays up to 1929 have the Anglo-Saxon background, three of the next seven are more or less Oriental; while from 1933 on the proportions are fairly evenly mixed, with two West (*die Sieben Todsünden*, *Arturo Ui*) and three East (*The Good Person of Szechwan*, *The Caucasian Chalk Circle* and *Turandot*), as well as two

Before and after the 1929 crisis. *Above*: *Im Dickicht* (1924). A fantastic play set in Chicago, staged by Erich Engel in Max Reinhardt's Deutsches Theater with Fritz Kortner (*left*) and other leading actors. Setting by Caspar Neher. *Below*: *Der Jasager* (1930). A didactic play from the Japanese, staged by Brecht on a lecture platform. Music by Kurt Weill

classical works and some others that come rather nearer home. With this shift of setting the plays themselves become less like a story, more and more like a court of investigation: a development already foreshadowed in the mock-trials of *Mahagonny* and *Mann ist Mann*. Deprived of a sustaining 'plot', we are thrown back on the bare words and the bare ideas, and these lead us to an (ostensibly) firm judgment and an (apparently) clear-cut conclusion.

The social interests which determined this change are not new: they are incidentally present in much of Brecht's previous writing. Even in early poems like 'Jakob Apfelböck' or 'Marie Farrar', with their stories of squalid and pathetic crime, there is more than mere *nostalgie de la boue* (or vicarious self-degradation); they express genuine sympathy with the down-and-out. This concern is at its plainest and most despondent in *Trommeln in der Nacht*, which is a strong and moving play, even though Brecht later found that it had 'become alien' to him, and came to deplore the 'shabbiness' of the solution reached. But it also steadily increases in the other works till it breaks out in the biting and highly explicit verses of *The Threepenny Opera*, verses that redeem any triviality in the setting:

> How does man keep alive? Because his fellows
> Are persecuted, tortured, plundered, strangled and die.
> Man only keeps alive because he well knows
> How to suppress his own humanity.
> For once you must try not to shirk the facts:
> Man only keeps alive by bestial acts.

Here again is the idea of a social system whose cruelty freezes all human feeling:

> Don't punish our misdeeds too harshly; never
> Will they withstand the frost, for they are cold.
> Think of the darkness and the bitter weather,
> The fear and pain that echo round this world.

Later Brecht saw this compassion as too all-embracing, and characteristically added a new verse to exempt those major criminals from whom, in his view, the fear and the pain arose.

But what is new in Brecht's work from 1929 on is that such criticism and sympathy should get a dominating grip on his technique and force it into a simple, direct form. And here outside factors played a part. He had become convinced by the Marxist system of dialectical analysis and the conception of the class war to which this led. Mounting tensions within Germany gave him a new sense of urgency; his own successes perhaps allowed him a certain independence of the commercial stage; and at the end of 1929 the world crisis showed the old Anglo-Saxon mythology in a new light:

They still sell gramophone records, not many however,
But what have these cows really got to tell us, that
Never learnt singing? What
Is the sense of such songs?
What have they really
Been singing to us during all these years?
Why do we now feel distaste for these once famous voices?
Why
Do the photographs of their cities now leave us cold?
Because the rumour has got around
That these people are bankrupt!

What a bankruptcy! How great a glory
Here has vanished! What a discovery:
That their system of communal life has the same
Wretched weak points as that of
Less pretentious people.

The world economic crisis. Drawing
by Grosz to a poem by Brecht (1931)

A good few other writers and producers, moreover, were now throwing their weight into what seemed an increasingly clear political struggle. The Dadaists, for instance, had become outspokenly pro-Communist as early as 1921-2; Erwin Piscator (of whom more later) had organized a monster pageant under Ruth Fischer's chairmanship for the Communist Party's 1925 congress; poets like Erich Weinert, Kurt Tucholsky and Erich Arendt were writing political poems and songs;[1] and Hanns Eisler, with works like the Comintern Song of 1928, was setting them to rousing music. To this whole movement, which continued in Germany or in exile right into the 1939-45 war, Brecht began to make his very individual contribution.

[1] A selection of such poems, all taken from the *Arbeiter-Illustrierte-Zeitung*, appeared under the title *Rote Signale*, Berlin, 1931. Weinert and Tucholsky were chief contributors. It included nothing of Brecht's, though he sent a message for the paper's tenth birthday number: No. 41 of 1931. There are in fact no known contributions by him to the Berlin Communist press before that year.

He wrote little that can be seen as specifically Communist, though *Die Mutter*, the outstanding instance, is in some ways his most perfect work. *Die Massnahme*, with similar revolutionary songs and illegal party agitation as its subject, deals with that subject in a strictly personal way; *St Joan of the Stockyards* is at bottom more concerned with the fascination of American Big Business than with the class war that rages in the background. *Furcht und Elend* is primarily an anti-Nazi document; and only the Spanish War one-acter *Senora Carrar* seems truly to suit the Party line. What his change of direction meant to Brecht was something at once deeper and broader: a self-identification with the workers which went beyond the earlier bohemian sympathy, a new concern with working-class players and an unsophisticated audience, and a general conception of the theatre as a means of teaching and transforming his society. 'That is to say,' concludes the 'Short Organum',

> our representations must take second place to what is represented, human social life, and the pleasure felt in their perfection must be converted into the higher pleasure felt when the rules emerging from this social life are treated as imperfect and provisional. With this the theatre will leave its spectators fruitfully disposed, even after the spectacle is over.

The object was not so much to preach the political slogans of the moment as to query the rules under which men lived. It was no longer to shock, but to make men think.

The same methods of thought that led to scientific progress must be applied to society. Thus the *Badener Lehrstück*:

SOLOIST: Many of us have thought carefully
About the earth's movement round the sun, about
The human body, the laws
Of universality, the composition of the air
And the fishes of the ocean.
And they have
Made great discoveries.

CHORUS: That did not bring down the price of bread.
In fact
Poverty has increased in our cities. . . .

'So, too,' says Brecht's Lindbergh – who is the obvious symbol both of technical advance and of the transatlantic myth with which it had so far been associated –

there still remains
In our improved cities confusion
Which arises from lack of knowledge and resembles God.

But the machines and the workers
Will attack it, and you too
Take part in
The attack on what is backward.[1]

For Brecht scientific thought in the social field was henceforward to be identified with Marxism, but that did not lead him to talk Party jargon, or simply to present stock conclusions. It meant rather that he felt the scientific attitude to be developing 'among the new class of workers whose element is large-scale production'. 'Propaganda in favour of thinking,' he believed, 'whatever form it may take, helps the cause of the oppressed.'

The essence of all science, for Brecht, was scepticism: a refusal to take anything for granted: an active, burrowing doubt. It was this that must be applied to our social surroundings, if we were ever to learn to control them. *The Exception and the Rule*, for instance, opens with a prologue addressed direct to the audience:

'The Doubter'. Drawing by
Neher on a scroll

Closely observe the behaviour of these people:
Consider it strange, although familiar,
Hard to explain, although the custom.
Hard to accept, though no exception.
Even the slightest action, apparently simple
Observe with mistrust. Check whether it is needed
Especially if usual. . . .

For nothing must be taken for granted, in order that nothing may seem unalterable. Here is the theme of all Brecht's later writing, and the key to his dramatic theories. 'The same attitude as men once showed in face of unpredictable natural catastrophes,' he wrote in the 'Short Organum' nearly twenty years later, 'they now adopt towards their own undertakings.' Or again: 'One can describe the world today to the people of today only if one

[1] *Der Flug des Lindberghs*, Section 8: Ideologie. Sub-section 4. (This, the nub of the whole work, is not included in Weill's piano score.)

describes it as capable of alteration.' And in a note to *Antigone* in 1951 he again warned against passive acceptance: 'Man's fate is man himself.'

The sceptic. Galileo after his recantation

'Scepticism,' he said, 'moves mountains.' Repeatedly we find this concern with the nosy, sardonic, dissatisfied human intellect. 'Dizzy with shouted commands,' says a poem characteristically called 'In Praise of Doubt',

>   examined
> For physical fitness by bearded doctors, inspected
> By shining beings with golden badges, cautioned
> By ceremonious priests who hurl at him a book written by God in person
> Taught
> By irritable schoolmasters, the poor man stands and hears
> That this world is the best of all worlds and that the leak
> In his attic roof was put there by God himself.
> Really, it is difficult for him
> To query this world.

Similarly the neatly-managed letter X from an alphabet:

> Xantippe said to Socrates
> You're drunk: just look at you.
> He said: One must doubt what one sees –
> Nothing is wholly true.
> He ranks as a philosopher
> She as the classic shrew.

– or speech after speech from *Galileo* with its deep faith in scientific scepticism and its dispassionate account of the obstacles. The whole restless conception is at once fundamental to Brecht's character and congenial to his theatrical ideas. It allows him to attack, to judge, to startle, to demolish; thus showing the world itself as changeable, and the familiar as very odd.

* * *

It is hard for a man to become aware of problems of such urgency and scope, without his interest becoming to some extent diverted from the individuals concerned. This is the snag for writers, just as it is for politicians and philosophers, and Brecht only began to overcome it in the late 1930s, when the political and intellectual tension of his work seems to slacken, and a new warmth comes into his characters and his plays. His natural sympathy with the underdog then combines with his deliberate allegiance to 'the workers' to give him a special interest in creating unpretentious plebeian figures, often with a sardonic or even slightly disreputable twist. 'I grew up as son', he wrote around this time,

> Of well-to-do people. My parents tied
> A collar round my neck and brought me up
> To be accustomed to service
> And practised in the art of command. But
> When I was grown up and looked about me
> I did not care for the people of my own class
> Not for commanding, not for being served.
> And I left my own class and associated
> With unimportant persons.

So the leading characters of many of his later works (*Die Mutter*, for instance; *Mother Courage*, *The Caucasian Chalk Circle*), and many of the minor figures too, are shabby and down-to-earth, and even those who come from a slightly higher social grade (like Puntila or Galileo) have a healthy vulgarity which leads them again and again to adopt the unheroic pose.

There is bound to be a certain degree of unreality in any work when the original impact on the playwright was a generalized one, bigger than the individual examples whence it derives. Even in Brecht's later and less schematized plays this is often so, and as a result not only are the settings themselves kept remote, but the broader moral problems with which he begins to deal are occasionally simplified out of all recognition. He will present, for instance, the good poor man or the bad rich, without going into detailed explanations of what makes them good or bad: a habit that M. Ionesco has called 'bien-pensant' and 'boy-scout': 'the condescension of a Left-wing petty bourgeois'. There is a strong flavour of such stylized and class-conditioned virtue in *The Caucasian Chalk Circle* and the *Good Person of Szechwan*; and many critics have remarked the leading role played by dedicated working-class women in Brecht's plays, from *St Joan of the Stockyards* on. The

DIE HEILIGE
JOHANNA DER
SCHLACHTHOFE

Brecht's first heroine.
Joan Dark (1930).
Jacket design by Neher

humble and selfless St Joan seems indeed to have had a particular fascination for him, for she recurred not only in *Simone Machard* (as a quite young girl) but also in the Berliner Ensemble's production of Anna Seghers's documentary account of the Rouen trial. Children, too, made an increasing appearance in his later productions, whether as innocent participants in the story or as a choir to sing the incidental songs.

But in spite of this slightly forced *naïveté* Brecht often managed, as he intended, to shed an unfamiliar light on our moral and social behaviour, illuminating, in his very personal way, that interesting and largely neglected area where ethics, politics and economics meet. Such concern with conduct is most evident in the plays written under the shadow of the 1939 war, when the didactic impulse had become softened and the immediate need to expose the Nazis had gone: in *Galileo* and *Puntila* and *Mother Courage*. But it had long been an important element in Brecht's work. 'Food is the first thing, morals follow on', says a famous phrase in *The Threepenny Opera*, and this is not the pure cynicism that it is often taken to be. It means, not that only animal needs matter, but that it is hard for any man to behave decently if they have not been seen to. What seems at first sight like amorality is really a nagging concern with the circumstances under which moral conduct is (*a*) possible and (*b*) worth while.

Sacrifice and denial were specially fascinating to him, especially when conducted at the cost of what seems superficially right and dear. And in this there is a strong element of self-denial and self-abasement, sometimes in favour of the community but sometimes for its own sake. Thus, where in the early ballad of Marie Farrar the refrain was a straight appeal for sympathy:

For every creature needs help from all.

the didactic plays came to overrule the individual's claims. In the *Badener Lehrstück*, for instance, there is a double sacrifice: the crashed airmen agree that they must be left to die, and the chorus agree that they cannot interfere, on the (very questionable) grounds that

So long as force rules, help can be denied
When force rules no longer, help is no longer needed.[1]

In *Der Jasager* the student agrees to be killed so that the expedition may go on; in *Die Massnahme* the young Communist agrees to be shot for the sake of the Party, and the chorus agree that this is right. It is the same attitude of rejection of whatever is closest to one as we find in the St Peter-like episodes of denial in *Edward II*, *Mann ist Mann*, the *Fatzer* fragment ('Decline of the Egoist . . .') and *Mother Courage*, or in the strange plunge into the mud of the poem 'Fatzer, komm':

> He who is beaten cannot escape
> From wisdom
> Keep hold of yourself and sink! Be afraid! But sink! At the bottom
> The lesson awaits you.

Even the individual's own highest standards may have to be discarded, as the poem 'An die Nachgeborenen' sadly points out:

> Oh we
> Who wanted to prepare the ground for friendliness
> Could not ourselves be friendly.

It is a badly distorted society which makes us sacrifice not only ourselves and our friends, but sometimes our principles too.

The harshness of such a view comes at times near to Oriental fatalism, or to the ruthless asceticism of Rimbaud's 'Sur toute joie pour l'étrangler j'ai fait le bond sourd de la bête féroce'. The audiences for whom these lessons were meant found them often hard to stomach: schoolchildren (in the case of *Der Jasager*) and Communists alike were unconvinced that this spirit of 'acquiescence' was so very necessary. As a result of their criticisms Brecht rewrote *Der Jasager* as *Der Neinsager*, with a 'happy' but unheroic ending; and from then on self-sacrifice had to be queried just like 'help' or charity or friendliness, or any other ethical principle. All had to be tested in the light of the ruling conditions. Thus Brecht put the case of Galileo's moral cowardice:

ANDREA: . . . In Ethics too you were several centuries ahead of us.
GALILEO: Elaborate that, will you, Andrea?
ANDREA: We thought with the man in the street: He will die, but he will never recant. You came back: I have recanted, but I am going to live. Your hands are dirty, we said. You said: Better dirty than void.

[1] *Badener Lehrstück*, Section IV: Die Hilfeverweigerung. (Not in Hindemith's piano score.)

This is no excuse for Galileo's recantation, in Brecht's own opinion,[1] but it is none the less true. And so we arrive at a shifting system of social ethics, where nothing can be taken as fixed outside its context or its time.

The temptation of goodness; the strain of being evil. *Left:* Drawing by Kulisiewicz from *The Caucasian Chalk Circle*. *Right:* Woodcut by Hokusai from a Nō play

Goodness and friendliness remain deep instincts, but that does not mean that they are always right. 'Frightful is the temptation to goodness,' says the singer in *The Caucasian Chalk Circle*, as Grusha risks her life and her love for a baby's sake. 'What a strain it is to be evil,' is the converse conclusion of the short poem 'Die Maske des Bösen'; and this fits Brecht's early Greene-like sympathy with the wicked: a sympathy which hovers between the purely human and the perverse. 'Why are you so unpleasant?' asks Shen Teh in the *Good Person of Szechwan*:

> To trample on one's fellows
> Is surely exhausting? Veins in your temples
> Stick out with the strenuousness of greed.
> Loosely held forth
> A hand gives and receives with the same suppleness. Yet
> Greedily snatching it has got to strain. Oh
> How tempting it is to be generous. How welcome
> Friendliness can somehow feel. A kindly word
> Escapes like a sigh of contentment.

Beyond this natural, almost aesthetic moral appeal it is a question of practicability. It is no good, says Mother Courage in her 'Song of the Great

[1] A note of Brecht's refers to Galileo's insistence that his scientific achievements make no difference to his guilt, adding: 'In case anyone is interested, that is also the playwright's verdict.'

Surrender', adopting positions which one cannot hold. And here again arises the whole question of the social conditions: the question posed in *The Three-penny Opera* and *St Joan of the Stockyards*, and most persistently in the *Good Person of Szechwan*, with its moral that in a competitive society good-ness is often suicidal.

Such relative ethics, with their ever-changing social basis, fit Brecht's in-terest in the double character: an interest that first appeared in *Mann ist Mann*, with its changes of identity, then in *St Joan of the Stockyards* and *Die Sieben Todsünden*. Neither principles nor people are what they appear. The theatrical possibilities of this continual fluidity of our world occurred to Pirandello too, but in Brecht's case the social and moral aspects are much more clearly picked out. The ethical confusion of a confused society means that evil actions may be undertaken from good intentions, or that good actions may have evil consequences, or that evil intentions may be thrust on men who carry them out laboriously and with reluctance: that the individual himself is often a peculiar mixture of extreme good and extreme bad. Anyone may be shown, as are Shen Teh and Puntila and, less schematically, Mother Courage, as having two conflicting sides. This suits both Brecht's conception of the Dialectic and his own instinct for sharp oppositions.

'Man!' shouts a chorus in parody of Goethe to Pierpont Mauler the financier at the end of *St Joan of the Stockyards* as he laments the opposing tugs of business and altruism,

> you have two rival spirits
> Lodged in you!
> Do not try to weigh their merits,
> You have got to have the two.
> Stay disputed, undecided!
> Stay a unit, stay divided!
> Hold to the good one, hold the obscener one!
> Hold to the crude one, hold to the cleaner one!
> Hold them united!

One of Brecht's Marxist acquisitions which will be discussed in more detail later was an idea of Dialectics which matched his sense of the incompatible and the comic as well as his political views.[1] This led him to take particular delight in such unresolved confusion, whether in the individual or in society itself. And this is what gives his theatre its peculiar richness, allowing one play to sprawl over time and space and seventy or eighty characters, another to restrict itself to the simplest, driest means, so that his work is full of clashes and surprises and apparent inconsistency. It means that sometimes

---

[1] 'I have never found anybody without a sense of humour who could understand dia-lectics,' says a character in the *Flüchtlingsgespräche*.

his characters are caricatures or deliberately bloodless dummies, and that he always disclaimed any interest in psychology as such; yet that in the later plays he could build up such complicated living figures as Galileo, Courage, Puntila, Schweik, each of whom finishes by dwarfing not only the background but often the actual ideas which he represents. Above all, it allowed him to take over unblushingly the fantastic, confused, corrupt world of his early plays into the wiser and more purposeful theatre of his middle age. 'My contradictory spirit,' he called it in an essay written two years before his death. 'I suppress the instinct to slip in the word "youthful", as I hope I still dispose of it in undiminished strength.'

So there are the three main elements of Brecht's theatre, and indeed of his whole work: the highly flavoured, half-nostalgic artificial world of the early plays; the very clear didacticism of his thirties; and, arising out of this, the more complicated, less schematized moral-social arguments of the plays from about 1938 on. They overlap, so that his songs for the adaptation *Trumpets and Drums* (for instance) spring from the first, while later works like *Lucullus* and *Antigone* continue the second. They intermingle in almost every work, so that a play like *The Caucasian Chalk Circle* combines the old romantic attitude towards blood and sweat, rags and tatters, with almost undiluted argument and a rambling ethical parable. Much of the interest of Brecht's theatre lies in this combination of barely reconcilable features: lesson and entertainment, individualism and collective; scepticism and myth, the fake world and the real. They all tug us in different directions, and in every work the proportions of the mixture vary. There is a continual feeling of movement and life.

Somehow they are held together. This is partly due to the consistently beautiful language in which they are written, partly to Brecht's elaboration over the years of suitable theatrical methods which he was able to shuffle into an apparently coherent theory. But ultimately their force is due to a profound obstinacy, which allowed Brecht to weather all changes in political climate or artistic fashion and develop steadily along his own lines. This made him a much more elastic and indiarubbery writer than those who have to iron out all conflicts and present a consistent, unwrinkled face. He freely revised his plays, only perhaps to return to the original text; he sometimes discouraged performances of his early works, but only where he felt that they pointed to false (social) conclusions; he reprinted them in 1954 because he felt 'that my present opinions and capabilities would be of less value without some knowledge of my previous ones—that is, presuming there to have been a certain improvement'. Life itself was inconsistent, and that meant that it was a great deal funnier and more complicated than either poets or politicians will normally admit. It had to be viewed with humanity and humour; and so does his work. 'God,' he said, 'spends all day long laughing at himself.'

TWO

The Language

Aside from the surging mainstream of German poetry there is a disregarded tradition of neat, light, often satirical writing. Heine, for instance, Georg Herwegh, Hoffmann von Fallersleben were highly explicit poets whose verses sometimes recall Byron's *Don Juan* or the slighter poems of Peacock and Thackeray; and following them there were Wilhelm Busch, with the simple, pungent couplets of *Max und Moritz*, and at the turn of the century Christian Morgenstern, whose delicate and imaginative wit seems to look forward to the paintings of Klee. It was then that the tradition of the Paris *chansonnier* was first imported into Germany. Bierbaum's *Deutsche Chansons* were published in 1900, and the next year the cabaret called Die Elf Scharfrichter was launched in Munich, with Frank Wedekind as its principal star. Wedekind was then a 'Dramaturg' (or play-reader and adapter) at the Munich Schauspielhaus, fresh from a nine-months' sentence for lèse-majesté which had been imposed for his satirical poems in the early numbers of *Simplizissimus*. Through him this class of German writing came to establish itself, quite unpretentiously, in the theatre; and a whole new group of satirists later arose around the cabarets and such papers as Siegfried Jacobsohn's *Weltbühne*, which became the liveliest and most intelligent weekly in post-war Berlin. Kurt Tucholsky (writing under four pseudonyms), Walter Mehring,

Das Internationale Kabarett auf der Reeperbahn.

(Der Plüschvorhang teilt sich; Musik: Rule Britannia.)

1. Englisch: Miß Ellinor mit ihren 25 Niggerboys; starkes Flitterdécolleté, aus dem sie über die erste Jugend hinausgewachsen; etwas kreischende Stimme:

's war ein schicker niggerboy boy boy
Und er handelte mit sunlight
In der moonlightbay bay bay.

A cabaret sketch
by Walter Mehring
(1924)

Joachim Ringelnatz and Erich Kästner were all bitter social critics who used direct, stinging satire as the best means of attack and wrote a large part of their always intelligible light verse to be declaimed or sung. The newspaper *feuilleton*, the cabaret *chanson* or *song* became their medium (perhaps significantly there were no German words for these things); their poetry sold in editions of five and ten thousand; and their songs were performed by Trude Hesterberg, Rosa Valetti, Blandine Ebinger, Paul Graetz: actors also in Brecht's early plays.

87

This, not the apocalyptic confusion of the expressionists or the wordy bombast of the socialist utopians, was the background into which Brecht fitted. It is neglected in many respectable anthologies, and it is something for which we in England have no real equivalent. One has to imagine a combination of Sagittarius, Mr Auden and Mr Paul Dehn writing for the kind of highbrow (also clean) cabaret that we belatedly hoped to establish during the 1960s satire boom but somehow could not quite assimilate. The German poet of the 'twenties could communicate with a large public; and he had to have an ear for music. Nobody thought it profound or clever if he was impossible to understand.

*   *   *

Like Wedekind, Brecht set many of his early poems to his own tunes, and sang them himself. 'Then he planted himself in the middle of the room', says Feuchtwanger of 'Kaspar Pröckl' (a fictionalized version of Brecht) in Bavaria about 1922,

> and with open effrontery in a horribly loud shrill voice began to deliver his ballads to the twanging of the banjo, pronouncing his words with an unmistakably broad accent. But the ballads dealt with everyday happenings in the life of the ordinary man from the point of view of the large town, and as they had never been seen before; the verses were light and malicious, spiced with impudence, carelessly full of character. . . .[1]

There was a strongly local, popular flavour about many of these early songs, for Brecht found his models in the old ballads sung at Bavarian fairs – German equivalents of 'Frankie and Johnnie' or 'She was poor, but she was honest' – and in the street-singer's *Moritat*, such as gives *The Threepenny Opera* its haunting theme. At the same time there was also a ritual, protestant undertone which was sometimes authentic, sometimes flippant. *Die Hauspostille*, he called his first book of poems: 'A Few Sermons for the Home'; the Lutheran (Bach-like) chorale recurs time and again in his verse; and behind much of his prose or free verse can be heard the thunder of the Lutheran bible. 'What work has influenced you most?' a women's magazine once asked him. 'The Bible. Don't laugh. . . .'

It seemed laughable, because he concealed this firm and very German foundation with a number of foreign influences that were thought unpatriotic, disreputable and even diabolic. 'I occupied myself,' he wrote of his third play, *Im Dickicht der Städte* 'with the heightened prose of Arthur Rimbaud's

---

[1] Lion Feuchtwanger: *Success*, London, 1930, p. 223. A similar picture has been given by Tristan Tzara in an obituary tribute (in *Les Lettres Françaises*) and by Sergei Tretiakoff (in *International Literature*, Moscow, May 1937). The tradition, supported by Brecht's own accounts to friends, is that he used to sing his songs in bars in Augsburg and/or Munich. So did his character Baal.

"Saison en Enfer" '; and Rimbaud's vagrant, anarchic spirit infects much of *Baal* and the *Hauspostille* poems. Brecht read very little French – so little that he did not, for instance, know Musset's plays – but Rimbaud was translated both by Theodor Däubler (an older friend of the Dadaist group) and by Alfred Wolfenstein, who worked as 'Dramaturg' for Piscator; and his poems had a strong impact on a number of Brecht's contemporaries, including Paul Zech, whose Rimbaud play *Das trunkene Schiff* was produced by Piscator in about 1926 against settings by Grosz. The actual opening of 'Le Bateau ivre' –

> Comme je descendais des Fleuves impassibles,
> Je ne me sentis plus guidé par les haleurs;
> Des Peaux-Rouges criards les avaient pris pour cibles,
> Les ayant cloués nus aux poteaux de couleurs.

– fits perfectly the Fenimore Cooper mythology of those days and Brecht's own big-city nostalgia for a life of violence, whether in the great open spaces –

> The men of Fort Donald – hohe!

– with pale skies and light winds and sudden death; or scouring the infinite oceans like raucous pirates; or simply lying waterlogged like 'Das Schiff' and 'The Drowned Girl', in sea, lake or river:

> Once she had drowned and started her slow descent
> Through streams into the rivers' broader eddies,
> The opal sky seemed most magnificent,
> As if it must be gentle to her body.

Men curse and grimace; the air is stormy and scorching or deceptively *mild* and *violett*; all flesh is as seaweed; amorality and exoticism and hairy swagger lead finally to deliquescence and decomposition.

But Brecht's rotting, sodden 'Ship'

> Through the clear waters of many oceans drifting

is not only first cousin to the Bateau Ivre; she is also a sister of Kipling's 'The Derelict' in *The Seven Seas* (1894)

Grosz: illustration to Daudet' *Tartarin*, 1921

> Wrenched as the lips of thirst,
> Wried, dried and split and burst,
> Bone-bleached my decks, wind-scoured to the graining . . .

who in turn seems to descend from Melville's 'Aeolian Harp':

> It has drifted, waterlogged,
> Till by trailing weeds beclogged:
> Drifted, drifted, day by day
> Pilotless on pathless way . . .

Neher: illustration to
Mann ist Mann

And Kipling provided the poetic setting for Brecht's Anglo-Saxon mythology of the 'twenties, from the troops' song in Scene 4 of *Mann ist Mann*

> Mit Toddy, Gum und hai, hai, hai
> Am Himmel vorbei, an der Höll entlang
> Mach das Maul zu, Tommy, halt den Hut fest, Tommy
> Auf der Fahrt vom Sodabergchen bis zum Whiskyhang.[1]

– with its recollections of 'O, it's Tommy this, an' Tommy that . . .' to the 'Kanonen-Song' of *The Threepenny Opera*

> John war darunter und Jim war dabei
> Und George ist Sergeant geworden . . .[2]

[1] With toddy, gum and hi, hi, hi
By-passing heaven and skirting hell
Shut your big mouth, Tommy; keep your hair on, Tommy,
On the trip from Soda Mountain down to Whiskey Dell.

[2] John was all present and Jim was all there
And George had got his promotion . . .

Compare the 'soldiers three' of *Mann ist Mann* and *Die Drei Soldaten*. Brecht also translated some Kipling poems, including 'Banjo' and 'The Ladies' (in *Die Dame*, LIV, 8, 1927, p. 4), and is said to have used Kipling as a model for 'Denn wie man sich bettet' in *Mahagonny* and for 'Surabaya-Jonny'. The temple episode in *Mann ist Mann* is strongly reminiscent of Kipling's story 'Krishna Mulvaney' in *Life's Handicap* (1891), even if it

then all the Bilbao-Benares-Surabaya-Mandalay[1] *songs* of *Mahagonny* and *Happy End*. Far more than Rimbaud's, this influence lasted into Brecht's later

work; for even in his most serious plays he never quite shed the Anglo-Saxon convention, which reappears in the 'Ballad of the Woman and the Soldier' in *Mother Courage*,[1] and (more obviously) the 'Song of the Eighth Elephant' in the *Good Person of Szechwan*, as well as in such relative frivolities as the 'Song of the Women of Gaa' in *Trumpets and Drums*. Kipling is the real ancestor of all Brecht's bloated and caricatured soldiers, and he remained till the last among those few twentieth-century writers for whose work Brecht had any deep regard.

Grosz: drawing for
Die Drei Soldaten

Whitman is sometimes suggested as another influence, but the relationship is much less direct. Admittedly Gustav Landauer, who was shot for his part in the Munich Soviet of 1919, had introduced and translated some of his work in Herzfelde's *Neue Jugend*, which was where Däubler's Rimbaud versions had also appeared. But nothing could be more foreign to Brecht

---

also relates, as Dr Schumacher suggests, to Döblin's novel *Die Drei Sprünge des Wang-lun* (1921) – which this writer has not read.

In view of Jaroslav Hašek's influence on Brecht it is worth pointing out a certain relationship between Kipling's soldiers and the Good Soldier Schweik. Left-wing commentators often see nothing but evidence of Kipling's imperialism in these stories, and forget his pioneering interest in the characters, exploits and language of the Other Ranks.

[1] 'Bills Ballhaus in Bilbao', 'Surabaya-Jonny' and 'Der Song von Mandalay', all from *Happy End* (MS. only). 'Stimmt ihn an, den Song von Mandalay', in Scene 14 of *Mahagonny*; reference to 'Die Bar von Mandelay' in Scene 8; 'Benares-Song' in 'Songspiel' version of 1927 and in *Hauspostille*, p. 112. The last-named in English: thus –

There is no whisky in this town
There is no bar to sit us down
Oh!
Where is the telephone?
Is here no telephone?
Oh, Sir, God damn me:
No!
etc. etc.

[1] *Mutter Courage*, Scene 2. Previously appeared as 'Die Ballade von dem Soldaten' in *Hauspostille*, p. 98; *100 Gedichte*, p. 71; *Selected Poems*, p. 36. 'After Kipling', according to note in *100 Gedichte*: presumably meaning the verse at the end of 'Love-o-Women' in *Many Inventions* (1893), though 'Soldier, Soldier' in *Barrack Room Ballads* also relates.

than Whitman's egotism and rather hollow rhetoric, and what looks like a parallel is more often parody, as in the poem on 'The Vanished Glories of the City of New York' quoted earlier. All that the two writers really have in common is the biblical foundation which they also share with Claudel. The similarity of parts of Whitman's 'Europe'

> But the sweetness of mercy brewed bitter destruction, and the frightened
>   rulers come back;
> Each comes in state with his train – hangman, priest, tax-gatherer,
> Soldier, lawyer, lord, jailer and sycophant.

– with passages in *The Caucasian Chalk Circle* like the 'Song of Chaos' -

> The son of him we looked up to is no longer recognizable; the mistress's child
>   becomes
> The son of her servant.
> Councillors are seeking shelter in barns; he who could barely lodge
> On the city walls now sprawls in bed.

– might seem at first sight to relate to the Whitman readings which Brecht helped Charles Laughton to prepare in California during the mid-1940s. But these particular lines of Brecht's were already written by 1934, and Whitman's influence in the 1920s was much more evident in the work of such writers as Johannes R. Becher and Ernst Toller: poets, certainly, of the Bavarian Left wing, but in almost every other way profoundly unlike Brecht.

His other main model was Villon. Here was somebody far more congenial:

Neher:
The Easy Life
(after Villon's
'Il n'est trésor que
de vivre à son
aise')

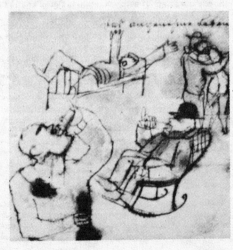

the most vivid and indestructible of outsiders, whom Brecht could present in the early poem 'Of François Villon' almost as if he were a precursor of the monstrous Baal. There was a very good German translation of his Ballads by K. L. Ammer (later there appeared also a version by Paul Zech, who had written the Rimbaud play): and Brecht took it as the basis for several of *The Threepenny Opera* songs. In 1930, after a controversy with the critic Alfred Kerr as to whether or no this constituted plagiarism,[1] he prefaced a reprint of Ammer's translations with the sonnet:

ON A TRANSLATION OF VILLON

Once more the fading letters become clear
In this new version of his Testament
Where he doles out his lumps of excrement –
Will those who qualify please answer 'Here!'?

Where is the snot you spat as he walked past?
Where is the man you told to stuff himself?
Only his verses figure on the shelf
But how much longer do you think they'll last?

Here, for the price of fifty cigarettes,
You buy another chance to look them through
(A chance to find out what he thought of you . . .)

It's sour but cheap; you pay three marks for it
And what a lucky dip the buyer gets!
In my own case it yielded quite a bit . . .

It yielded, in fact, major portions of five of the songs, and the rest – apart from the famous *Moritat*: the great hit tune – are strongly impregnated with Villon's spirit. This was natural so long as Brecht was concerned with the attack on the bourgeois from a beggar's-eye point of view: with individual acts of aggression. In his later work there is little of this flavour left.

Such are the most obvious influences on the *Hauspostille* and on most of the early plays and the operas with Weill. There is nothing about them that

[1] Villon: *Balladen*. Übersetzung von K. L. Ammer. Berlin, 1930; Weimar, 1949. Brecht's sonnet is quoted by Schumacher (p. 242), who goes closely into the relationships between Ammer's and Brecht's versions, and into the accusations of plagiarism made by Alfred Kerr. (Kerr in *Berliner Tageblatt*, 3 May 1929; Brecht's reply in *Die Schöne Literatur*, Leipzig, July 1929, p. 332.)

Kurt Fassmann's picture biography of Brecht (Kindler, Munich, 1958), reproduces the programme for the first night of *The Threepenny Opera*, which reads 'From the English of John Gay (additional ballads by François Villon and Rudyard Kipling). Translation, Elisabeth Hauptmann. Adaptation, Brecht. Music, Kurt Weill . . .' Ammer (pseudonym of a retired army officer named Klammer) was in fact paid a royalty by Brecht.

is flabby or esoteric; they put unexpected guts in the cabaret-cum-dance-tune style which Brecht sometimes aped –

> O Moon of Alabama
> We now must say goodbye . . .

and they distinguish him clearly from the smoother, slighter verse of his fellow-satirists. It was easy for the latter to see something ridiculous in his mannerisms: Tucholsky, for instance, called him 'Rudyard Brecht', and *The Threepenny Opera* 'stylized Bavaria': parodying him thus:

> It's literature which can't do harm
> Or cause the capitalists alarm
> > *Remington to larboard!*
> Sometimes we're lyrical, sometimes the Strong Man
> We curse on the altar and pray on the pan. . . .[1]

But the songs and poems which Brecht wrote in his twenties do seem to be standing the test of time, and already the great Austrian satirist Karl Kraus saw them as something quite distinctive.[2]

> The wet medium in which the whole lot work is nothing compared with the single figure of Bert Brecht, even though he does act as his own private vampire and suck his blood away with theorizing. He still has enough individuality to generate the poem of the cranes and the clouds, and the Trial scene in *Mahagonny*, and it cannot be stamped out by any Press campaign (launched by Kerr or anybody else).

The poem Kraus refers to is the famous duet in *Mahagonny*, and after many further Press campaigns against Brecht what he says remains true. The exotic touch of which Tucholsky complained in his work combines with much that is straightforward or epigrammatic or purely lyrical, to make a varied and often moving whole. It has resilience, which is what less easily criticized writers so often prove to lack.

*   *   *

About four years before the *Hauspostille* and the first version of *Mahagonny*, Brecht worked with Feuchtwanger on the adaptation of Marlowe's

---

[1] There is also a dialogue of Tucholsky's which goes:
> Who's the play by?
> The play's by Brecht.
> Then who's the play by?

[2] It is perhaps relevant that Wedekind was a contributor to Kraus's one-man review *Die Fackel*, and that Kraus helped to organize the world première of his play *Büchse der Pandora* in Vienna in 1905. Brecht himself contributed to *Stimmen über Karl Kraus* (Lanyi, Vienna, 1934), a volume celebrating Kraus's sixtieth birthday.

Neher: stage design for *Edward II*, after Marlowe (1924)

Edward II. He was struck, so he later said in his essay 'Über reimlose Lyrik', by the superiority of the Schlegel-Tieck translation of Shakespeare to the much smoother version of Reinhardt's translator Hans Rothe; and saw its relative roughness and irregularity as the right means 'to show human dealings as contradictory, fiercely fought over, full of violence'. To express Marlowe's savage conflicts, he wrote,

> I needed elevated language, but was brought up against the oily smoothness of the usual five-foot iambic metre. I needed rhythm, but not the usual jingle.

According to Marieluise Fleisser, another Munich playwright, it was Feuchtwanger who insisted that the lines must 'stumble', and Brecht's first drafts were often too smooth. Between them they produced a translation which almost entirely rewrote Marlowe in a broken free verse, with what Brecht called 'free but irregular rhythms'. This style could express not only the liquid, half-putrid world of *Baal* and 'The Drowned Girl' – thus Mortimer:

> Dragging a slight burden out
> Of a long-stagnant pond I still,
> My flesh more dulled, see hanging from it
> Human matter. More and more
> Drawing myself up I feel ever greater
> Weight.

– but also a new, drier, more critical class of idea, which became very typical of his later work. Here is Mortimer again, a long way from Marlowe:

Plutarch tells of Caius Julius Caesar
That all in one he read and wrote and made his clerk
Take letters and beat the Gauls. It seems
That people of his stature owe their fame
To what is really just a shortage
Of insight into the triviality of human
Acts and concerns, linked with an
Amazing lack of seriousness: in short to their
Superficiality.

And the same style can be seen in a poem of Feuchtwanger's on 'Adaptations' (an evident by-product of the collaboration) or in Brecht's moving Christmas poem of 1924, which the Prussian Ministry of Justice was asked to prosecute for blasphemy.

It then seemed to drop out of Brecht's repertoire, and perhaps he might never have used it again if he had not turned to a new and didactic conception of the theatre. But in 1928–9 when he made this change here was the right language lying, so to speak, ready to hand. Then it was farewell to the drowned girls and the great violet skies; farewell to Villon; farewell even to the home-made English of

O show us the way to the next whisky-bar . . .

For *Lindberghflug* and the *Badener Lehrstück* were expressed in the bare, austere phrases whose point is defined in the 'Lesebuch für Städtebewohner' poems published in 1930:

When I address you
Cold and broadly
In the driest terms
Without looking at you
(I apparently fail to recognize you
Your particular manner and difficulties.)

I address you merely
Like reality itself
(Sober, incorruptible thanks to your manner
Tired of your difficulties)
Which you seem to me to be disregarding.

And from then on this was his characteristic voice.

Just about this time, Brecht's collaborator Elisabeth Hauptmann discovered Arthur Waley's translation of the *Nō Plays of Japan*, and turned four of them into German. Waley's poetry had many of the qualities at which Brecht was aiming; 'an experiment in English unrhymed verse', he had called his earlier Chinese translations; and the Japanese conception of

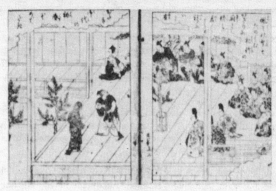

A Japanese Nō stage

a high-flown prose which 'often heightens into verse' also suited the new didactic kind of play. In the fragment *Kagekiyo*, for instance (which is one of those that Frau Hauptmann translated), the language seems to anticipate Brecht's:

> He that of old gave welcome
> To casual strangers and would raise an angry voice
> If any passed his door,
> Now from his own child gladly
> Would hide his wretchedness.

And when in 1930 Brecht turned *Taniko* into the school opera *Der Jasager*, he bodily took over nearly all Waley's text. Most plainly in its ending:

> Foot to foot
> They stood together
> Heaving blindly,
> None guiltier than his neighbour.
> And clods of earth after
> And flat stones they flung.

we see both the stuff and the style of Brecht's first didactic works. Later, his interest in the Far East again led him to Waley, so that seven of the nine 'Chinesische Gedichte' (1939) were retranslated from Waley's versions, and one of them was subsequently included in the second scene of the *Good Person of Szechwan*.

With the didactic works began also Brecht's theorizing; and this further explained the sense of the new style. For such irregular unrhymed verse fitted his notion of the *Gestus*: of the essential attitude which underlies any phrase or speech. The dry, chopped-off style of the new poems and plays, the political songs which he was starting to write, even the political slogans to which he had opened his ears all helped him to put his finger on the fundamental sense: they purified his language and showed him the practical and aesthetic value of saying just what one really means and no more. Here was an attitude to language something like that which Claudel had shown thirty years earlier in his play *La Ville*:

> I worked out this verse which had no rhyme or metre
> And in the privacy of my heart I allotted it that double reciprocal function
> By which a man absorbs life and gives back, in the supreme act of exhalation
> An intelligible word . . .

Every sentence now had to be examined with the care of an advertising man weighing a slogan: 'the language must exactly follow the attitude of the person speaking'. At the same time it had to sound right to the ear. 'It must be remembered that my main work was in the field of the theatre: I was always thinking of actual delivery.'[1]

The lines as spoken had to convey the direction in which the speaker was aiming: to imply the basic purpose of the speech, not just to give elegant expression to the ideas and images through which this might be attained. It became a technique of writing pointedly, and from the essay which Brecht wrote to describe his work with Charles Laughton on *Galileo* we can see how it applied also to his prose. Here were an actor who knew no German and a playwright who spoke little English collaborating not just to produce, but also to translate, a vast play:

> . . . we had to decide the gist of each piece of dialogue by my acting it all in bad English or even in German, and his then acting it back in a variety of ways until I could say: that is it. . . . Our first care throughout was for the smallest fragments, for sentences, even for exclamations, each treated separately, each demanding to be given the simplest, freshly produced form. . . . We were compelled to do what better equipped translators should do too: translate the underlying attitudes. For language is theatrical in so far as it conveys the mutual attitude of the speakers.

---

[1] It is interesting that Erich Kästner, another exceptionally intelligible poet, should have worked in advertising, and that among the first highbrow writers to do so was Wedekind, who worked with Maggi the soup firm in Switzerland in 1886.

This notion that language itself is a form of gesture is not new. See the *Ideen zu einer Mimik* of J. J. Engel, director of the Prussian royal theatre at the end of the eighteenth century. (*Schriften*, VIII, Berlin, 1804; edited by Henry Siddons as *On Gesture and Action*, London, 1822.) Letter 32 (No. 29 in Siddons) opens by referring to the 'resemblance which exists between the fundamental ideas of the art of gesture and that of declamation'. Engel incidentally disliked verse plays, and praised English acting for its freedom from exaggeration.

As a result, the translation was exceptionally faithful. For these were the same principles as Brecht followed to give his own German such bite.

He did not forsake more traditional styles, as his sonnets and many of his songs will show. But this irregular unrhymed verse makes the backbone of all his writing during the 1930s; and less than a fifth of the collected *Svendborger Gedichte* of 1939 are written in any other form. 'Rhyme seemed to me unsuitable', he said of his anti-Nazi poems,

> as it easily makes a poem seem self-contained, lets it glide past the ear.

Exile led him gradually to turn from the immediate political struggle to the great figures of the past: Buddha, Lao–Tse, Empedocles, Lucullus, Antigone. Here, too, he used the same free yet firm and dignified style:

> A victory on every page.
> Who cooked the banquet that followed?
> A great man every ten years.
> Who found the money?
>
> So many statements.
> So many questions.

Then a new kind of poem, more personal and domestic, began to emerge from his homes in Denmark and California, setting everyday pleasures against the distant rumblings of war. Natural observation enters his poetry for the first time, and even the word 'I'; and a new tug between the poetic and the didactic begins to make itself felt:

> I realize: only the happy
> Are liked. Their voice
> Is good to hear. Their face a delight.
>
> The crippled tree in the yard
> Accuses the poor soil, and yet
> Passers-by blame it for being a cripple and
> Rightly so.
>
> The green hulls and the sparkling sails in the sound
> Go unseen. Of the whole
> I see but the fisherman's tattered net.
> Why do I only record
> That a cottage woman of forty is misshapen?
> The young girl's breasts
> Are as warm as ever.

99

> In my poetry a rhyme
> Would seem to me almost a presumption.
> In me are contending
> Delight at the apple tree in blossom
> And horror at the house-painter's speeches.
> But only the second
> Drives me to my desk.

But the style survives this, showing itself flexible and deeply congenial to the writer: calligraphic in its neatness, like Brecht's own carefully composed manuscripts, or the *Cent Phrases* and *Idéogrammes* which Claudel wrote under the influence of Japan. It appears repeatedly in notes and letters which were jotted down without particular thought of publication; and lends itself in the 'Buckower Elegien' of 1953 to an almost Chinese delicacy of touch.

Brecht used unrhymed verse for part or whole of each of the didactic pieces; for the songs of *Die Mutter*, for *Lucullus* and *Antigone*; for the terse, epigrammatic satires which he wrote for the German Freedom Radio;[1] for the narration of *The Caucasian Chalk Circle* and the 'heightened' monologues of the *Good Person of Szechwan*. Here, for instance, is the announcement of Pavel's execution from *Die Mutter*:

> But when he went to the wall where they intended to shoot him
> He went towards a wall which had been built by men of his own kind
> And the rifles they aimed at his breast, and the bullets
> Had been made by men like himself. Merely absent
> Were they therefore, or dispersed; but for him were still there
> And present in the work of their hands. Not even
> Those who were ordered to shoot him differed from him or were for ever
>   incapable of learning.
> It's true that he still went bound with chains, which had been
> Forged by his comrades and laid by them on their comrade; yet
> Closer grew the factories; as he passed by he could see them
> Chimney on chimney, and since it was early dawn
> For it is at dawn that they normally bring them out, there was
> Nobody there. But he saw them crowded full
> With that huge throng, whose numbers had always grown
> And still grew.

And Shen Teh's scene with the airman who is attempting suicide:

> SUN: Why do you want to hack me down, sister, as a matter of interest?
> SHEN TEH: It frightens me. I'm sure you only felt like that because the
>   evening's so dreary.

[1] A station which operated in the later 1930s, ostensibly from inside Nazi Germany but in fact from Czechoslovakia or, for a time, Spain. It was organized by an independent committee to which various anti-Nazi parties and organizations contributed.

> In our country
> There should be no dreary evenings
> Or lofty bridges over rivers
> Even the hour between night and morning
> And the whole winter season too, that is dangerous.
> For in face of misery
> Only a little is needed
> Before men start throwing
> Their unbearable life away.

So it became his standard medium for passages (or whole plays) that were expository, dignified, formal; or in any other way coolly remote.

The writing was meant to be broken and asymmetrical, and such was the style of delivery which it demanded. 'How were the verses to be spoken?' asks the commentary to *Antigone*.

A. The essential was to avoid that revolting convention which demands that the actor should tackle any fairly long verse passage by, as it were, pumping himself full with some emotion which will roughly cover the lot. There should be nothing 'impassioned' either before or after speech and action. We move from verse to verse, and each must be carved out of the character's *Gestus* (or underlying attitude).

Q. How is this managed technically?

A. At the end of each line there must be a caesura, or else the start of the next line must be emphasized.

Q. How do you treat the rhythm?

A. By applying the syncopation common to jazz. This brings an element of contradiction into the flow of the verse, and allows the regular to prevail against the irregular.

Q. Is this new?

A. On the German stage Frank Wedekind tried something of the sort. The actor Steinrück took it over from him when he played Büchner's Woyzeck.

Thus in the end it would correspond not only to the austere aesthetics and sharp political argument of the early 1930s, but also to the deliberately stumbling 'dialectics' of Brecht's late plays.

*   *   *

We have concentrated on Brecht's most distinctive styles because they correspond so closely to all that is most typical in his work. But the real essence of his writing lies in the continually varying resourcefulness with which he would mix his methods. Parody (often of Goethe – a deeply uncongenial writer to him), pseudo-Shakespearean blank verse, classic hexameters,[1] pantomimic rhymed couplets, formal prologues and epilogues, popular songs old and new: all were at his command, to be drawn into a play wherever needed. *St Joan of the Stockyards* begins with a short scene outside the slaughterhouses, where Brecht puts a discussion about prices between two meat-packer kings into Shakespearean terms; it ends with a climax of parody – of Schiller, of Goethe, of Salvation Army hymns – over the tragically dead body of Johanna herself. The *Good Person of Szechwan* ends on the contrast between Shen Teh's long outburst in irregular unrhymed verse and the rosy Goethe-like verses in which the gods dodge all responsibility; the unresolved problem being summed up in a mock eighteenth-century epilogue. A further element of variety lies in the persistence of earlier styles, not only because, like the Kiplingesque and the Lutheran, he could not bear to discard them, but also because any play may contain fragments of much earlier work. The 'Solomon Song' from *The Threepenny Opera* recurs with three fresh verses in *Mother Courage*; the rousing song 'All or None' of the 1930s is included in the post-war *Die Tage der Commune*; 'Let them not deceive you' in Scene 11 of *Mahagonny* dates from about 1918. If Brecht was, as he himself claimed, a thief, he also stole from the drawers of his own desk.

And his prose has many of the same features. Here, too, there is a certain formality, even in naturalistic or colloquial dialogue; here, too, he uses proverbs and dialect to provide a popular anchor; here, too, the language is cut to essentials. The same models recur: Rimbaud in *Im Dickicht der Städte*, the Bible in *Trommeln in der Nacht*:

MANKE: The linen is folded, but the bride does not come.

ANNA: My linen has been bought, I have laid it piece by piece in the cupboard, but now I need it no longer. The room has been rented, and the curtains hang ready and carpets are not lacking. But he has come who has no shoe and only one coat and the moths are in that.

– and the dispassionate style of the Nō plays in the didactic works. That is not all: there is also the influence of Jaroslav Hašek[2] to be seen not only in *Schweik* but also in *Mother Courage*; even perhaps in *Mann ist Mann*.

[1] In the commentary to *Antigone*, and in his unfinished version of the *Communist Manifesto* (*Gedichte* 6). The model here is Lucretius, and a Lucretian 'didactic poem on the nature of men' was to form a framework for the *Manifesto*; the surviving fragments are in *Gedichte* 9. There is also a short story of Brecht's where Lucullus and Lucretius quote hexameters at each other, some of them Lucretius's and some Brecht's.

[2] An unpublished note of Brecht's says: 'If anyone asked me to pick three literary works of this century which in my opinion will become part of world literature, then I would say that one of them was Hašek's *Adventures of the Good Soldier Schweik*.' (In conversation he also spoke highly of Silone.)

GALY GAY: . . . And they can say what they like, and it was really only an oversight, and I was much too drunk, gentlemen, but a man's a man for all that, and that's why they have to shoot him.

There is that of Grimmelshausen in the tremendously vigorous artificial seventeenth-century dialogue of *Mother Courage*. And there is the classical, almost Tacitean, prose of the 'Short Organum' and other late reflective works, with their love of antithesis and paradoxical play upon words.

The great prose satires on war: Hašek's *Adventures of the Good Soldier Schweik*, Grimmelshausen's *Simplicissimus*

Prose slides into heightened prose or irregular verse, blank verse and prose alternate; each is liable to be interrupted by rhymed or unrhymed songs. The whole mixture suits Brecht's idea of conflict and incompatibility; it gives, to the later works especially, a great richness of texture; and the liveliness of the writing will sweep the audience along, even where the construction of a play becomes confused or slack. This, certainly, is something that is not easy to achieve in translation, and all that can be given here is an approximate idea that there is something worth achieving. Yet Brecht's German does lie surprisingly close to us. Its English models – Kipling, Tin-pan Alley, Waley, the great Elizabethans, and even the common-or-garden thriller – its occasional hint of Whitman, its relation to the common continental, classical and Biblical heritage: all combine to make a strong bond such as we seldom feel with more turgid German writers. And the very un-smooth clarity at which Brecht aimed, though it is much more remarkable in German, is a not uncommon quality in our language too.

This clarity is really the essence of all Brecht's writing: the stiffening that prevents his eclecticism from becoming just a horrid jumble. It gives his work, for all his interest in words and styles and elegance, a down-to-earth quality that is not usual even in English. This is due in the end not to any literary technicalities but to the writer's concern with an un-highbrow audience: with the ordinary, easily confused people of his country, and with the proletariat in whom he pinned what little faith he had. It was always the unpretentious who interested him: who were the subject and object of his writing and, he hoped, its historical justification. 'HOW THE FUTURE WILL JUDGE OUR WRITERS' he headed a poem of 1939 in honour of the Danish novelist Martin Andersen-Nexö.

> They who sat on the golden chairs to write
> Will be asked about those who
> Wove their overcoats.
> Not for loftiness of ideas
> Will their works be examined, but
> The stray sentence which helps to establish
> Some odd feature of men who wove overcoats
> Will be read with interest, for here perhaps we have descriptions
> Of famous forebears. . . .

'The most striking characteristic of Po Chü-I's poetry,' wrote Waley in the introduction to *170 Chinese Poems*, 'is its verbal simplicity. There is a story that he was in the habit of reading his poems to an old peasant woman and altering any expression which she could not understand. . . .' Brecht reproduced these sentences with obvious approval. And he did so not because of any undue folksiness or belief in the homespun virtues, but because he wished his work to communicate ideas and attitudes, his audience to grasp them. There is nothing in Brecht's writing that is obscure.

THREE

Theatrical Influences

In 1913 the Lessingtheater in Berlin celebrated the centenary of Georg Büchner's birth with performances of his half-forgotten plays *Leonce und Lena* and *Woyzeck*. His third play, *Danton's Death*, was staged by Max Reinhardt in a memorable production in the Deutsches Theater in 1916 and again at the end of 1921 in the Grosses Schauspielhaus. These are the works that Herbert Ihering, Brecht's own earliest critical supporter, has called

> the great by-products of German literature, and if only they had stood in the middle of the main stream they might have given it a decisive twist.

For just as Heine differs from other German poets, so Büchner stands apart from the tradition of Goethe and of Schiller, from the German classical drama and also from the naturalists who followed. *Leonce und Lena* is closer to Musset; *Danton's Death* to Shakespeare; while his single prose story shows his close relation to Reinhold Lenz, a short-lived eighteenth-century admirer of Shakespeare's whose *Hofmeister* was adapted by Brecht. The unfinished *Woyzeck*, now somewhat hidden from us under the weight of Alban Berg's opera, is a wholly independent and revolutionary work: a tragic precursor of *Schweik* which was based, like *Madame Bovary* some twenty years later, on a true-life story that had been reported in the daily Press.

Büchner, like Brecht, was a medical student and a revolutionary, and his influence runs right through Brecht's work from *Baal*, which is clearly modelled on *Woyzeck*, to *Die Tage der Commune* with its evident recollections of *Danton's Death*. As Brecht later said:

> The line that seems to lead to certain attempts of the epic theatre runs from the Elizabethan drama via Lenz, early Schiller, Goethe (*Götz* and both parts of *Faust*), Grabbe, Büchner. It is a very strong line, easily followed.

It was in *Woyzeck* at Frankfurt in 1919 that Helene Weigel played her first professional part; it was Albert Steinrück's performance as Woyzeck that showed Brecht the possibilities of a restrained style of acting and the 'broken' verse delivery to which we have already referred. The short scenes, the terse dialogue, the folk-songs and the sinister poetic atmosphere which they punctuate: all these pointed to a new loose method of telling a story, which Brecht found to be used also by the great Elizabethans. Such plays could now be performed almost as fluently as they read, thanks to the develop-

Early influences. *Left:* Steinrück as Woyzeck.
Right: Frank Wedekind

ment of relatively new techniques like electric stage lighting and the revolving stage. In Reinhardt's 1907 production of *Twelfth Night* the stage rotated with the curtain up, while the actors stood in front and mimed the gist of the episode to come. In his *Danton's Death* players were scattered among the audience, and several episodes took place at once.

Frank Wedekind, the poet and singer, born of German-American parents in 1864, was the contemporary playwright most associated with this trend. Before coming to the Munich Schauspielhaus at the age of thirty-four he had worked in the scarcely respectable professions of journalism, advertising and the circus; and although he had given some Ibsen readings in Switzerland (under the name of Cornelius Minehaha) he approached the theatre with much of the freshness of the amateur. 'Unlike the naturalistic school,' wrote his friend and biographer Artur Kutscher, whose lectures at Munich University Brecht is said to have attended to the neglect of his medical and philosophical studies,

> he does not want people to forget that they are in the theatre, but he emphasizes the theatre and always keeps the public and its reactions in mind.[1]

[1] Kutscher died in 1960, aged seventy-two. His autobiography published that year makes no reference to Brecht's having studied with him, though he seems to have known both Neher and Engel. His pupil Ernst Schumacher says that he was horrified when Schumacher wanted to work on Brecht's early plays in 1945.

He claimed to know all Büchner's work, and with the Elf Scharfrichter cabaret planned to give *Woyzeck*, and *Der Hofmeister* by Lenz, as well as modern plays by himself, Hofmannsthal, Wilde and Shaw. In one play, *Musik* (1907), he tried, much like Brecht later, to follow out the structural principles of a popular ballad: a 'Sittengemälde', he called it – a moral tableau like the highly-coloured placards which the Bavarian street singers showed – 'a chronicle rather than a dramatic work'. But the real novelty of his plays lies less in their form, which was more often quite orthodox, than in their inconsequential dialogue, and the fierce conflicts and semi-under-world figures which went to make them up. He was the great Munich theatrical figure immediately before Brecht's time, and Brecht, who had sung his songs and seen him perform privately to Kutscher's class, wrote an obituary essay on him when he died in 1918.

Wedekind and Büchner (and also Carl Sternheim) are often thought of as the fathers of the Expressionist drama, and the tough, unpretentious, quick-firing style which they introduced has something in common with Brecht's first plays. But this was not the whole of Expressionism, and Brecht had good reason for disliking any of his work being classed with the rest of the school. Like him, the Expressionists proper were concerned to pursue the new formal freedom, and this led to such characteristic features of the 1920s stage as the cinematic style of production, the quick changes, the 'space stage', the plastic use of lighting and the clipped talk. But from Sorge's *Der Bettler* (1912) on, these writers often used this freedom in order to pursue high-flying utopian or apocalyptic ideas: themes relating less to Shakespeare and Büchner than to such hitherto unstageable works as *Faust Part II* and Madach's *Tragödie des Menschen*: the *Tragedy of Man*. Soon the new forms became blown out; incoherence and exaggeration started to rank as virtues; presented in the name of Mankind, self-dramatization and self-pity were inflated into a pretentious vogue. Here, a miracle of hollowness, is the final short scene from Walter Hasenclever's *Menschen* of 1918:

CEMETERY

Dawn
ALEXANDER *comes with the sack*
THE MURDERER *climbs out of the grave*
ALEXANDER *hands him the sack*
THE MURDERER: The sack is empty.
ALEXANDER *goes to the grave and gets in*
The sun rises
THE MURDERER *stretches out his arms*: I love!!

107

THE THEATRE OF BERTOLT BRECHT

Piscator.
Sturmflut (1926)
with film
background

And here, not unfairly translated, is an example from one of Ernst Toller's
political cantatas:

CHORUS ON HIGH: Trombones, proclaim it!
Unburdened is Deed!
Help Mother Nature's
Burgeoning Seed!

Thanks to writers like these, to Erich Mühsam and Johannes R. Becher and
others, such rhapsodic writing became peculiarly associated with the independent Socialists (or USPD) and with the Munich revolutionary movement. But that did not make it any more congenial to Brecht.

'Rhymed newspaper, at best,' he wrote of Toller's *Die Wandlung* in
December 1920.

> Flat visions, best forgotten at once. Flimsy cosmos. Man [Mensch] as material,
> manifesto, not as man. Man in the abstract, the singular of Mankind. His
> affairs are in feeble hands.
>   More important for the theatre: Ivan Goll's farces. Liberation of the pro-
> ducer. . . . Newspaper, ballad-singer's verses, photography: highly active
> mechanisms, poster – 'the Courteline of Expressionism'. There is good stuff
> here, childish stuff. More humanity in this than in Toller.

So if Expressionism provided the climate in which Brecht grew up it also
showed him the dangers against which to react. *Baal* was written (so Dr
Schumacher suggests) out of disgust with a play by Hanns Johst bearing the
typical title *Der Einsame* (*The Lonely One*); and when in 1922 Brecht first
met Arnolt Bronnen they 'agreed that the theatre ought to create a common,
communal feeling, as opposed to the isolationist aims of Expressionism, with
all its escapism and screaming . . .'. For he needed a stage that was less
blowsily egotistical, a style that would match the newspaper and the poster:

Piscator. *Schweik* (1928), with figures by Grosz

machine-minded, gritty and tough. Nor was it only his social sense that found the Expressionist productions so hard to stomach. They outraged his sense of humour as well.

* * *

When Brecht arrived in Berlin from Munich in 1924 there were already signs that the arts were sobering up. The deliberately shocking Dadaism of Grosz and Mehring and the Herzfeldes had given way to matter-of-fact 'Neue Sachlichkeit'; nihilism to dry political satire; 'montage' to 'reportage'. That year Erwin Piscator, a young Communist producer who had already helped to give Dadaism its 'proletarian' twist, was put in charge of the Volksbühne, where he began to apply the principles of fluidity, simultaneity and cinematic cutting to the topical, historical, factual material that was now beginning to invade the arts. This was the origin of a new, so-called 'Epic' theatre, whose first production – Alfons Paquet's documentary-style 'dramatic novel' *Fahnen* – was subtitled 'epic' by its author and staged with the help of what became identified as 'epic' methods: narrative aids based on the (silent) cinema and the magic lantern. During the prologue, photographs of the chief characters were projected on two screens either side of the stage; written titles preceded each scene to explain the plot.

Such 'highly active mechanisms' sped up the disintegration of the old naturalistic stage. Zech's 'scenic ballad' *Das Trunkene Schiff* was staged by Piscator against projected drawings by Grosz; in Paquet's Russian revolutionary play *Sturmflut* of 1926 the actors played against an actual film; at the Kammerspiele in Munich, Otto Falckenberg produced Wedekind's two *Lulu* plays against projections of Masereel's woodcuts, with verses of Wedekind's own ballads sung between the scenes; Carl Ebert used film in the Darmstadt production of *Im Dickicht* in 1927. 'The film,' wrote Brecht later, was a new, gigantic actor that helped to narrate events. By means of it documents could be shown as part of the scenic background, figures and statistics. Simultaneous events in different places could be seen together.

The example of the great Russian films was then strong, and Piscator was tempted to copy them in cases where it suited neither the period nor the play. 'A no-man's-land between the novel and the drama': so Alfred Döblin called the new form. But politically it was not so neutral, and when Piscator chose to illustrate a fifteenth-century episode with films showing Lenin and the Chinese Revolution the scandal that followed cost him his job.

For the 1927–8 season he set up his own independent company at the Theater am Nollendorfplatz. There he presented four historic productions which involved an unprecedented use of projections and of stage machinery. For Toller's *Hoppla Wir Leben* some 10,000 feet of film were shot; four film projectors were used; and the nightly dismantling of the vast 'simultaneous set' cost twice what Piscator had estimated as the production's total daily cost. Alexei Tolstoy's *Rasputin* had a hemispherical setting where three films could be projected at a time, with the actors performing in the middle of it all. *Schw,cik* adapted from Hašek's novel, had a special double treadmill stage, with projections and a cartoon film by George Grosz. Only the last play, *Konjunktur* by Leo Lania, was on a comparatively modest scale, with incidental music by Kurt Weill and a simple set. By then the company was almost bankrupt, and in the summer of 1928 it temporarily closed its doors.

Such delight in machinery, or 'electrification' as Brecht called it, was typical of the time. It had made its first and noisiest appearance before the war, with Italian Futurism; it was reflected in English Vorticism, in the metallic paintings of Léger and the Airplane Sonata of George Antheil (1922), in Corbusier's first 'functionalist' writings for *L'Esprit Nouveau* (1920–5). It was also closely identified with the Russian Revolution, through new myths like Lenin's electrification policy and also through those Constructivist artists – Tatlin, Rodchenko, Stepanova – who flourished for a few hopeful years after 1917. There is a comic photograph of Grosz and John Heartfield which shows them at the Berlin Dada exhibition of June 1920, holding up a placard to say

Art is dead
Long live
the new Machine Art of
TATLIN

For it was the Russian example, acting at first through the Dadaists, which led many Germans to interpret this as a proletarian art, matching not only the new technology but the political revolution too.

Meyerhold.
Trust D.E. (1924),
in his own theatre,
Moscow

The links between Germany and Russia were then close; a year after the Russians, Germany had had her November Revolution; and politicians like Radek or artists like Kandinsky seemed equally at home in the country of Lenin or in that of Marx. In 1923 and again in the summer of 1925 Alexander Tairoff brought his productions from the Moscow Kamerny Theatre to Berlin, where Vesnin's set for *The Man who was Thursday* (August 1925) plainly helped to inspire Piscator's production of *Hoppla*. In 1925, too, S. M. Eisenstein's shattering film *Potemkin* was first shown in Berlin, to a score by Edmund Meisel, who wrote much of the music for Piscator's productions, as also for the 1928 *Mann ist Mann*. Meyerhold himself, the most radical of all the Soviet producers, though he did not actually bring his company to Berlin until 1930, was followed with the greatest interest. He was known to be trying to mechanize his actors according to a theory of 'bio-mechanics'; for Ehrenburg's *Trust D.E.* of 1924 he projected texts on a screen above the stage; while for *Le Cocu Magnifique* and *Tarelkin's Death* he used no curtains or cyclorama, and had a wooden Constructivist mechanism in lieu of a set. Evidently Brecht saw his production of Tretiakoff's *Roar China*, for there is a note in which he disagrees with the Berlin critics, who found its treatment of the British imperialists too harsh.

The politicians had not yet laid down any rigid definition of Communist art, and it seemed logical enough to demand that it should delight in machinery as such: exposing not only the machinery of our industrial civilization but also the actual mechanisms of art. 'Meyerhold,' wrote the Soviet producer Vakhtangov in his diary in 1922, in much the same words as were applied to Wedekind above, and later to Brecht,

calls a performance 'good theatre' when the spectator does not forget for a

III

moment that he is in the theatre. Stanislavsky, on the contrary, wants the spectator to forget that he is in the theatre.[1]

So Meyerhold could use rotating scenery and semi-acrobatic actors, and expose the bare brick wall at the back of the stage; Piscator could use mechanized settings and the cinema screen; and each could claim to be attacking the bourgeois theatre in the name of the industrial proletariat. There was still nobody to admit, let alone demand, that revolutionary art should take any more conservative form.

At the same time an equally radical attack on the stock stage illusions came from quite a different direction: from Fascist Italy, where Pirandello had begun to dissect the actor himself. At the end of 1924 Reinhardt, whose rehearsals Brecht was then attending, presented his own production of *Six Characters in Search of an Author* (which had been written in 1921). A brief Pirandello craze seemed to hit Berlin, so that during 1925 there were six of his plays running there in German translation (including one directed by Berthold Viertel and one in which Helene Weigel had a part), while the author himself came with the Rome Teatro d'Arte to perform three of them in the original.[2] In plays like these the actor stepped out of his role, just as in the Russian productions they had stepped off the stage and down into the audience: supposed spectators, as in Reinhardt's production of *Danton's Death*, might suddenly begin to take part in the play. This demanded a new, self-critical acting technique: the Pirandellian actor, wrote Dr Walter Starkie in 1926,

> must not be an actor by instinct or impulse: he must for ever be able coldly to analyse his own feelings. He must be ever ready to see the character he is representing from without, as it were, in a mirror. . . . Not only the actions, the facial expression must be reasoned out, but also the diction. . . .

which had to be abrupt and 'jerky', to match the playwright's view of life as inconsistent, full of clash and contradiction. Acting here alternated with apparent non-acting, and this allowed a special concern with variations of identity: with the changes of character that are essential to acting as such.

In all this we can see the origins of Brecht's own 'epic' narrative methods, and of many of his later theoretical ideas. If in Munich he had already shown himself anxious to break through the barrier of theatrical illusion (with the placards specified for *Trommeln in der Nacht* and the silent-film scene titles

---

[1] Quoted by Joseph Gregor in Thomas H. Dickinson (ed.): *The Theatre in a Changing Europe*, Putnam, London n.d., p. 81. Compare Brecht's note on the production of *Galileo* (*Stücke VIII*, p. 210): 'The public must never lose the conviction that it is in the theatre.'

[2] See *Pirandello Ieri e Oggi* (Quaderne del Piccolo Teatro—1), Milan, 1961. L. Ferrante's *Pirandello*, Florence 1958, is mentioned there as suggesting that Brecht is a Marxist development of Pirandello.

to his own production of *Edward II*), he now wrote *Mann ist Mann* (1924–6) as much under Pirandello's influence as under Kipling's, though also with a strong element of Bavarian music-hall knockabout and of the proto-surrealist farces of Ivan Goll. In *Das Elefantenkalb*, which was designed to be played in the foyer during the interval and had a typically Pirandellian sub-title, he begged the audience to smoke, just as Erik Satie in his rather comparable 'musique d'ameublement' had begged them to talk; and the whole piece was shot through with exchanges between actors and spectators.

> The audience goes silently to the bar and orders cocktails

says one of the stage directions. So the actor has his false beard tweaked off, and in the play-within-a-play of which Brecht became so fond he is

Neher: the Elephant in Brecht's *Mann ist Mann*

forced to show himself acting. We see this device first in *Mann ist Mann* when the characters disguise themselves as an elephant called Billy Humph.

> JESSE: I tell you, Mrs Begbick, if you take the long view what is happening here is an historical event. For what is happening here? Personality is being put under the microscope; we are getting closer to the notable character. An intervention. Technology steps in. Clamped in the vice, set on the conveyor belt, the great man and the little man are the same, even in stature.[1]

The new relativity of identity, the new alternations of the actor, seem to match and reflect the elaborate motions of the machine. So in the interval Mrs Begbick proclaims that 'Tonight we take a man to pieces like a car. . . .'[2]

---

[1] Added, presumably, for the 1931 production, as it is not in the 1926 edition.

[2] The phrase 'la machine humaine' occurs in Zola's essay *Le Roman expérimental*, which also anticipates Brecht's later notion of a 'theatre of the scientific age'.

The machine civilization was also the American civilization, and until the Wall Street crash Brecht evidently associated technology less with the Five-Year Plan than with the Transatlantic myth. Here is his statement in the opening programme of Piscator's 1927–8 season:

> The great buildings of the city of New York and the great discoveries of electricity are not of themselves enough to swell mankind's sense of triumph. What matters more is that a new human type should now be evolving, at this very moment, and that the entire interest of the world should be concentrated on his development. This new human type will not be as the old type imagines. It is my belief that he will not let himself be adapted by machines but will himself adapt machines.

Piscator he came to see as 'one of the most important theatre men of all times'; and during the 1927–8 season he worked for him on the adaptations of *Rasputin*, *Konjunktur* and, most important, *Schweik*. Four of his own works were in turn considered for production: *Aufstieg und Fall der Stadt Mahagonny*, and the unfinished plays *Weizen* (i.e. *Joe Fleischhacker*), *Fatzer* and *Aus Nichts wird Nichts*.

The Threepenny Opera was written at this time, but although Piscator's influence can be seen in the use of projections the play as a whole relates rather to the highbrow satirical cabaret, and its chief formal significance for Brecht lay (as the next chapter shows) in the singing and the music; the play itself was Gay's. *Mahagonny*, performed in an embryo version in 1927 and in full at the beginning of 1930, was much closer to Piscator's style, for it was headed 'epic' by its author, and a 'Sittenschilderung' (like Wedekind's *Musik*), and produced with placards, sub-titles, projections of Caspar Neher's drawings, and even film and sound effects. But it was perhaps the writing of *Joe Fleischhacker* that was the most important step for Brecht, because it taught him the value of the Marxist analysis and showed how this applied to the drama: how, as Feuchtwanger put it in his article on Brecht of 1928, 'to observe the mechanism of an event like a car'. Not only the human machine, as in Pirandello, but the social machine too could now be taken down and inspected; so that in this unfinished work dialectics became associated at once with 'epic' or mechanized staging, and with the Chicago background against which the story was set. All these new ideas were absorbed by Brecht with a certain sense of proportion, and here he differed from such innovators as Piscator himself and the composer George Antheil, whose opera *Transatlantic* was produced at Frankfurt in 1930 with gangsters, lifts, an ocean liner, and about thirty scenes in the last act alone. In Brecht's case the real novelty and force of his plays lay in the words, which simply could not stand such top-heavy staging. Where he used Piscator's methods he used them on the small scale.

A number of Piscator's actors later became closely associated with Brecht: Ernst Busch, Leonard Steckel, the late Alexander Granach, Leopold Lindt- berg, Friedrich Gnass, Curt Bois. Hanns Eisler wrote the music for Piscator's later production of Walter Mehring's *Kaufmann von Berlin*; Grosz and John Heartfield did a number of his settings. Nor did all his collaborators think it necessary to strive for ambitious mechanical effects. In 1928 his 'Studio' under Steckel staged a play called *Heimweh* by the eccentric Dadaist- Communist Franz Jung where the author claimed to be

> attempting to loosen the traditional rigid transference to the spectator of the emotional content represented on the stage. Tension and relaxation must work on him directly, without having necessarily to be prepared by means of a 'plot'. This is furthered by the use of new means of representation (Chinese acting rather than German) and a mainly rhythmical delivery emphasized by means of pantomime, music, etc.

Brecht himself had not yet formulated his theoretical ideas, but this detached and quasi-Oriental approach seems to anticipate his next move. Artistically as well as economically, it was time to move on from Piscator's 'epic theatre' to Brecht's.

*　　*　　*

Claudel-Milhaud:
*Christophe
Colomb* (1930),
with film
background

In 1927 Paul Claudel left Tokyo after six years' service as French Ambas- sador, and was asked by Reinhardt to write him a *spectacle* or film which could be set to music by Richard Strauss. This was the origin of the 'opera' *Christophe Colomb*, which was rejected by Reinhardt, set to music by Claudel's more normal collaborator Darius Milhaud, published during 1929, and first performed at the Berlin State Opera the next year. 'This work,' says Claudel's introductory note is like a book, which one opens in order to deliver the contents to the audience. The latter, through the chorus, cross-examines the reader and the actual actors of the story. It demands explanations. It associates itself with their sentiments. It supports them with its advice and approbation. It is like a Mass in which the public takes incessant part.[1]

A new function had been found for the theatre, harking back at times to Pirandello, but most obviously to the Nō plays which its author had come to know in Japan.

The Nō actors often address their remarks to the audience direct; they have a chorus which interrupts and comments, and at times even speaks for them; and in this highly stylized manner the dramatist will tackle the greatest moral problems with a wonderful simplicity and detachment. Strongly founded in Buddhism, the Nō drama is indeed not unlike a religious ritual, or at least like one of the Bach Passions. '. . . a storehouse of history,' Fenollosa called it,

> and a great moral force for the whole social order of the Samurai. Its popularity was connected with the Japanese *penchant* for the disciplined and the difficult. . . .

– a penchant certainly shared by the Germans too. Claudel was apparently the first to see how close this lay to the anti-illusionism of the 1920s, or to the 'epic' theatre's concern with new means of narration. *Christophe Colomb* was accompanied by film sequences, and even by one or two projected titles; and at the première in May 1930, so a critic reported, one member of the audience shouted 'Piscator!' – 'the worst of all bourgeois terms of opprobrium'.

This work, long unperformed in France, closely coincides with Brecht's first essays in the 'Lehrstück': a special kind of didactic drama, quite distinct from the later didactic element in his work. The origin of the 'Lehrstück' in Germany was musical, as we shall see in the next chapter, and the form itself a kind of ritual, designed to teach certain broad social and communal virtues,

---

[1] Claudel: *Christophe Colomb*, Edition Universelle (i.e. Universal-Edition), Vienna and Leipzig, 1929, p. 7, Note sur la mise en scène. Compare Mayakovsky's poem 'Christopher Columbus' of July 1925. The opera *Transatlantic* by George Antheil was written during 1927–8 and first performed in Frankfurt in May 1930. There is also Ghelderode's *Christophe Colomb* of 1927 (in *Théâtre II*, Gallimard, Paris, 1952), which is back on the level of *Mann ist Mann*. E.g.

> COLOMB *à voix forte*: Whisky! *Il sort de sa poche un flacon plat.* Very bon whisky!
> O consolation des clowns et des navigateurs!

This work ends up with a Lutheran chorale, sung by an American, a Ballet Dancer and Buffalo Bill.

According to Brecht's collaborator Elisabeth Hauptmann he took a certain interest in Claudel's plays around 1927. An interview in *Exstrabladet* (Copenhagen), 20 March 1934, quotes him as calling Claudel 'a severe and reactionary writer' but 'an original dramatist of great stature'.

not so much to an audience as to those taking part. Hindemith and Kurt Weill, both of them friends of Milhaud's, were the chief sponsors of the new cantata-like form, and for the 1929 Baden-Baden festival they composed the *Badener Lehrstück* and *Lindberghflug* to two interrelated texts by Brecht. The Japanese influence is not directly felt in these first works, but their similarity with the new Claudel-Milhaud opera is plain. Not only do *Christophe Colomb* and *Lindberghflug* deal with contrasting aspects of the transatlantic myth – the discovery of the New World in the name of the old religion; the re-discovery of the Old World in the name of the new technology – but they are formally closely akin. Thus Claudel:

> CHORUS: Cross the boundary! Cross the boundary with us.
> COLUMBUS *crossing and taking the place prepared for him*: I have crossed the boundary.

And Brecht:

> THE RADIO: Here is your machine
> Climb in
> Over in Europe they are awaiting you
> Fame is beckoning.
> LINDBERGH: I am climbing into the machine.

See also the use of sub-titles to the sections: 'Christopher Columbus lays siege to the king.' 'Off Scotland, Lindbergh at last sights fishing-boats.' Or the double figure of Columbus, the visible orchestra, the criticism of the play itself by members of the audience, and the basic attitude of 'delivering the contents'. The *penchant* is the same, even if the ideology is different: 'This exercise,' says Brecht in his notes, 'is an aid to discipline, which is the basis of freedom . . .'. Both works are meant to be rites, and in each case the notion of a disciplined movement seems to lie behind.[1]

'I am a teacher,' says the teacher at the opening of Waley's translation of *Taniko* (which in 1930 became the Brecht-Weill 'school-opera', *Der Jasager*)

> I keep a school at one of the temples in the City. I have a pupil whose father is dead; he has only his mother to look after him. Now I will go and say goodbye to them, for I am soon starting on a journey to the mountains.

'I am the merchant Karl Langmann,' says the merchant in Brecht's *The*

---

[1] This peculiar parallel between Brecht and Claudel would be worth a proper study. Both were influenced by Rimbaud, and the Bible and the Nō drama; both used the theatre for didactic ends; both set their plays in fantastic or remote surroundings; both liked to break the theatrical illusion; both found it hard to make their characters come to life. They collaborated with composers who were themselves close friends. And they both diverged from their national tradition: Claudel because he used French to express hazy ideas, Brecht because he used German for precise ones.

Brecht's
Die Mutter.
Design by Neher.
Minimal set,
with projected
background

Exception and the Rule, written the same year. 'What can I do,' asks *Die Mutter* two years later: 'Pelagea Vlassova, forty-two years old, a worker's widow and a worker's mother?'[1] The whole problem of explanation and establishing the characters is got over as easily as'that. In *The Exception and the Rule* Brecht uses the Nō technique to tell a social parable, and winds up with a judicial inquiry; in *Die Massnahme* (1930) he sets his four Communist agitators to act out a variety of situations in this expository way, and his chorus to cross-examine and judge them. These works were all short and economical in scale, designed for the concert platform or the lecture hall rather than for the orthodox stage. The tension came not from a plot, but from the excitement of abstract logical demonstration, heightened by the pressure of outside political events.

'For some years,' wrote Brecht in 1936,

> I tried, with a small staff of collaborators, to work outside the theatre ... we tried a type of theatrical performance that could influence the thinking of all the people engaged in it. We worked with different [i.e. fresh] means and with different [fresh] strata of society. These experiments were theatrical performances meant not so much for the spectators as for those who were engaged in the performances.[2]

First produced in 1932, *Die Mutter* was the last and longest of this batch of didactic semi-amateur plays, and with it certain of Piscator's methods return. It was meant to be performed in a very simple 'simultaneous setting' by

[1] There is a very similar technique of self-introduction at the beginning of Labiche's *Le Voyage de M. Perrichon*.

[2] See also *Stücke V*, p. 276, where Brecht lists his didactic plays (less *Lindberghflug*) and points out that 'this label only applies to plays that are instructive for the *performers*. They do not therefore need an audience'.

Neher, consisting of plain canvas or sacking stretched on a metal framework. At the back there was a big cinema screen for the projection of photographs, sub-titles and slogans. But the economy of the scenes, their punctuation with songs and an occasional chorus, the whole dispassionate approach: all these things took it far from the commercial theatre – which included Piscator's – and made it in fact simpler to produce without setting, action or costumes than on the ordinary stage. When the Berlin police insisted that so subversive a play could be given as a reading only, it was immensely effective; when it was produced in the orthodox way in a New York production three years later Brecht found that the producers were missing the point.

> Comrades, I see you
> Reading the short play with embarrassment.
> The spare language
> Seems like poverty. This report, you reckon
> Is not how people express themselves. I have read
> Your adaptation. Here you insert a 'Good morning'
> There a 'Hullo, my boy'. The vast field of action
> Gets cluttered with furniture. Cabbage reeks
> From the stove. What is bold becomes gallant, what's historical normal.
> Instead of wonder
> You strive for sympathy with the mother, when she loses her son.
> The son's death
> You slyly put at the end. That, you think, is how to make the spectator
> Keep up his interest till the curtain falls. Like a business man
> Investing money in a concern, you suppose, the spectator invests
> Feeling in the hero: he wants to get it back
> If possible doubled. . . .

We shall find that these objections are fundamental to Brecht's theoretical essays of the 1930s. They sum up the whole difference between the new didactic platform technique and the conventions of the normal stage.

Similar methods persisted in Brecht's work throughout his exile in Denmark and even later; wherever the scale was too economical or the message too undiluted for the orthodox theatre to cope. The lessons of the Lehrstücke and of the cabaret language evolved with Weill were now driven home by the impossibility of getting his plays performed on any grander scale. From 1933 to 1940 only one of Brecht's new works was produced by the ordinary professional theatre, and in general their strong anti-Nazi flavour restricted them to the exiles' improvised cabarets or to politically-conscious groups of amateurs. This is very much the level of didactic entertainment known in Communist jargon as 'agit-prop'; and it led Brecht to look afresh at sketches like those of Juschni's 'Blauer Vogel' company, at the satirical works of

Auden and Blitzstein and Gustav Wangenheim, and in general at the literary revue. Here, he found, 'the linear story has been thrown on the scrap-heap: the story itself as well as its line', for such 'loosely linked sketches' 'have no story; hardly even a connecting thread'. So the concise, but consequential scenes of *Die Mutter* are followed by the independent short sketches of *Furcht und Elend*; the detached didacticism of the radio-play *Lucullus* by the satirical anti-Nazi pantomime of *Arturo Ui*; while even after the war there are traces of the same political, amateur, low-level strain to be found in his work.

* * *

The didactic spell lasted roughly from 1929 to 1934, and covered, with one exception, all the works from *Lindberghflug* to the semi-mimed *Die Horatier und die Kuriatier*, which was written in exile. The exception was *St Joan of the Stockyards*, a major play in Shakespearean form which represents a mixture of Shaw's *St Joan* -- another play staged by Reinhardt while Brecht was working for him – with certain themes from Upton Sinclair's *The Jungle* and the remains of the unsuccessful *Happy End*. With this work, and with the unfinished plays which heralded it, Brecht seemed to be returning to the Elizabethan models which he had studied in his Munich days. The use of the unrhymed irregular verse of *Edward II* now led to the use of the Shakespearean historical form, the 'chronicle', as Wedekind had called *Musik* and as Brecht later called *Mother Courage*: the 'epic' play as it had been before Piscator cranked it up. In 1927 he adapted *Macbeth* and in 1930 *Hamlet* for the Berlin radio; he planned a production of *Julius Caesar* with Piscator; then in 1931 he was commissioned to adapt *Measure for Measure* for the Volksbühne; and this formed the basis of *Die Rundköpfe und die Spitzköpfe*, which he completed in Denmark about 1935. Thus even while he was engaged on the 'Lehrstücke', at the height of the political struggle for power in Germany, he was turning to 'this dynamic idealistically-orientated drama, with its interest in the individual' (as he called it in 1930 in *The Three-penny Opera* notes), and looking at it afresh in 'dialectical' terms. Here, in more disciplined form, were the rich conflicts and shambling gait of his own fantastic early plays.

Unlike such contemporaries as Karl Kraus, Gide, Pasternak, Brecht saw Shakespeare's verse and the psychological interest of his characters primarily as functions of the story. The apparent barbarisms and clumsinesses which to some producers seem to mar plays like *Hamlet* were to him simply part of a feudal whole. Thus his sonnet of about 1940 'On Shakespeare's Play Hamlet':

> Here is the body, puffy and inert
> Where we can trace the virus of the mind.
> How lost he seems among his steel-clad kind
> This introspective sponger in a shirt!

Till they bring drums to wake him up again
As Fortinbras and all the fools he's found
March off to win that little patch of ground
'Which is not tomb enough . . . to hide the slain.'

At that his solid flesh starts to see red
He feels he's hesitated long enough
It's time to turn to (bloody) deeds instead.

So we can nod when the last Act is done
And they pronounce that he was of the stuff
To prove most royally, had he been put on.

Similar means, he thought, could be used to express the barbarisms of our own time: the bloodthirsty competition of the Chicago meat market in *St Joan of the Stockyards*, or the inhuman racial policy of the Nazis in *Die Rundköpfe und die Spitzköpfe*, both set against the general background of the class struggle which Brecht now saw as determining all our movements.

Such conflicts could be made either to lead to clear didactic conclusions or to illuminate our own problems while remaining more or less unresolved.

> Shakespeare's great solitary figures, bearing on their breast the star of their fate, carry through with irresistible force their futile and deadly outbursts: they prepare their own downfall; life, not death, becomes obscene as they collapse; the catastrophe is beyond criticism. Human sacrifices all round! Barbaric delights! We know that the barbarians have their art. Let us create another.

This Brecht set out to do in his exile, writing in *Galileo* and *Mother Courage* two works modelled on the Shakespearean 'history' which take a great sweep across time and space in order to show how the problems of intellectual honesty on the one hand and chaotic war on the other cut across the (class-determined) self-interest of two immensely live and human characters. These are a great change from the bloodlessness of Johanna Dark or the rather tedious puppets of *Die Rundköpfe und die Spitzköpfe*, and their background has a new authenticity. But after the marvellous compression of *Die Mutter* (and of many of the sketches in *Furcht und Elend* too) the actual construction of the plays seems slack.

It is deliberate, for the rambling methods of the Elizabethan theatre fitted Brecht's conception of the Marxist dialectic. Argument, clash, contradiction: the 'mechanism of an event' could be shown in slow motion; one scene following shapelessly on another so as to lead to a cumulative rather than a conclusive effect. His project of the 1950s. for instance, for staging his own translation of *Coriolanus* was not designed simply to lead to a clear solution.

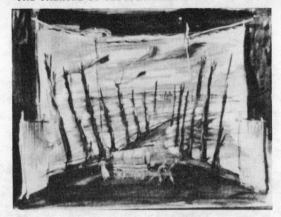

Mother Courage. Design by Teo Otto (1941)

P.: Is it for the sake of these perceptions that we are going to do the play?

B.: Not only. We want to have and to communicate the fun of dealing with a slice of illuminated history. And to have first-hand experience of dialectics.

P.: Isn't the second point a considerable refinement, reserved for a handful of connoisseurs?

B.: No. Even with popular ballads or the peepshows at fairs the simple people (who are so far from simple) love stories of the rise and fall of great men, of eternal change, of the ingenuity of the oppressed, of the potentialities of mankind. And they hunt for the truth that is 'behind it all'.

So Brecht linked Shakespeare on the one hand with dialectical materialism, and on the other with 'the "Laughable Adventures" of the old popular epics'; the traditional unhurried Bavarian narrative forms.

'Perhaps the poetry should lie more in the actual situations,' he wrote of Auden and Isherwood's plays, 'and less in the reactions of the characters who are confronted with them.' 'The truth is concrete': 'Die Wahrheit ist Konkret', he inscribed in large letters on his Danish and Californian homes. This was for him exactly the merit of Shakespeare: no speculation, or hints, or cheap 'psychology', but

. . . all these great and small conflicts thrown on the scene at once: the unrest of the starving plebeians together with the war against their neighbours the Volsci; the plebeians' hatred for Marcius, the people's enemy – together with his patriotism; the creation of the people's Tribunes – together with Marcius's appointment to a leading post in the war. How much of that do we get in the bourgeois theatre?

Actual events, actual relations, clearly-defined actions, a sort of running

*The Caucasian
Chalk Circle.*
Drawing by
Karl von Appen
(1954)

fight in which each successive issue is plain: Brecht had aimed at such goals in Munich days, and in Shakespeare he saw them attained. In Shakespeare, but not in the average Shakespearean production.

So Brecht's later plays represent something of a return to the orthodox theatre, even though they were written with little idea when that return might in practice take place. That does not mean that he had discarded any of the various elements in his style, however revolutionary, or that Shakespeare's influence was in any way exclusive. We can still see one line – the line of jungle warfare – running from *Im Dickicht der Städte* through *St Joan of the Stockyards* to *Arturo Ui* and *Turandot*. One can trace the documentary line from Piscator through *Die Mutter* to *Die Tage der Commune*. One can follow the didactic thread from *Lindberghflug* to *Antigone* and the *Herrnburger Bericht*; the Elizabethan itself from *Edward II* to the unfinished *Coriolanus* project, and also in the persistent influence of Büchner and Lenz. None of these lines can be said to have been exclusively the right track for Brecht; there are good and bad works along each one, and there are first-rate plays like *Puntila* which seem to stand outside. But each brought him something different. Büchner and the Elizabethans gave him the example of a loose sequence of scenes of great geographical and chronological scope; Piscator showed him how to speed and amplify the story by mechanical means; the Japanese, through Waley, taught him to cut narrative corners, and 'deliver the contents' in a forceful yet unemotional way. These and other influences seemed to fit logically together; the wild dynamics of his youth to reappear quite properly as the 'dialectics' of his big exiled plays. And so from about 1940 on they often seem inextricably mixed.

The Caucasian Chalk Circle, to take one example, can be traced back to the *Kreidekreis* which was written by Carola Neher's husband Klabund and produced by Reinhardt in October 1925. Luise Rainer, the film actress, who knew and admired Brecht's poetry, and had played in *The Threepenny Opera*, commissioned Brecht in Hollywood to write a play on the same Chinese theme. He took a story which he had called *Der Augsburger Kreidekreis*, added a contemporary prologue, shifted the scene to the Caucasus and grafted on to it the independently-evolved figure of the disreputable judge. The plot and some of the language are Biblical; the 'Song of Chaos' Egyptian; the technique of narration and comment Japanese; the construction cinematic; the conclusion didactic; the wedding scene a reflection of the Marx brothers' *A Night at the Opera*; the soldiers an apparent recollection of *Mann ist Mann*; the atmosphere a cross between Brueghel and the pseudo-Chinese; the framework a commonsense, non-political issue debated in modern Georgia. . . . And several of the later plays have a pedigree as complicated as this.

It brings us back yet again to the same point: that Brecht was receptive to a number of influences, and never rejected what he had once absorbed. He developed three or four quite individual dramatic styles, yet perhaps nothing was so individual as their continually varying mixture. This was not just wilful, or mere wayward picking up of scraps: every strong influence which he underwent seemed proper to the state of his own development at the time, and in each case it is previously suggested in his own work. Piscator's 'epic' methods are foreshadowed in *Edward II*, just as the Nō drama is suggested in the two 1929 cantatas and the Shakespearean narrative in the first plays of all. It must be remembered that there were several obvious directions in which Brecht did not develop: the naturalistic play, for instance, or the psychological drama, or the poetic mystery, or the whimsical and elusive fantasy, or any return to the French, Italian or even German classic tradition. Magpie as he was, his preferences were clear, and if it is at all reasonable to compare him to Shakespeare it is just in this: that he remains overwhelmingly himself despite the use of many models. 'Shakespeare?' he said. 'He was a thief too. . . .'

FOUR

The Music

Brecht was no trained musician, but far more than most writers he had musical ideas at the back of his mind, and his work is full of musical implications. This began with his early settings of the 'Legende des Toten Soldaten' and other poems to his own tunes, where 'actual delivery' became bound up with questions of intelligibility and of verbal punch. For the first few plays he assembled his own music in the same rather rudimentary fashion: for *Baal*, for *Edward II* and *Trommeln in der Nacht*. Then for *Mann ist Mann* and even for *The Threepenny Opera* he sketched rough drafts of the songs that Edmund Meisel and Weill actually composed; and from then on he found that he could collaborate with certain composers so closely and effectively as to realize many of his own musical aims. More than most playwrights, more even than the majority of poets, he has become known by the musical settings of his works. *The Threepenny Opera* lives mainly by its songs, *Happy End* by nothing else; *Mahagonny* and *Lucullus* are highly original operas; while the whole group of didactic pieces or Lehrstücke has a special part in the musical life of the time. Kurt Weill, Paul Hindemith, Hanns Eisler, Paul Dessau, Rudolf Wagner-Regeny: all the composers with whom Brecht worked are figures of some importance, and the particular movement with which they became linked – the socially-orientated music promoted by the publishers Schott and Universal-Edition, and tried out at the Donaueschingen and Baden-Baden festivals – is among the most interesting and most neglected aspects of recent musical history. Like Jean Cocteau, Brecht had a strong influence on the form, orchestration and general approach adopted by his collaborators, but this was exercised by practice rather than by any public whip-cracking or polemics. It was just that poetically, as well as dramatically, he seemed to think in near-musical terms.

The musical movement in question developed out of that with which Cocteau was associated, for it started by reflecting many of Stravinsky's and Satie's ideas, while Darius Milhaud played a personal part in it from quite early on. Its objects were a new lightness and clarity after the heavy and uneconomic works of Mahler and Strauss; its methods a return to classical models and, much more closely bound up with this than we now realize, an exploitation of the trenchant, lively and still uncorrupted language of jazz. Stravinsky had set the ball rolling with the chamber opera *Renard* of 1915:

Stravinsky's
*L'Histoire du
Soldat*. Setting
for the Berlin
production
of 1925

a work of 'predominantly dry timbre and bouncing resonance'[1] which was
intended 'to be played by clowns, dancers or acrobats, preferably on a trestle
stage with the orchestra placed behind'. With Ansermet, Ramuz and the
painter René Auberjonois he then planned to found a travelling (wartime)
theatre on the same scale: a scheme whose sole realization was in *L'Histoire
du Soldat*, written for narrators, dancer and seven musicians, and produced
on a trestle stage (with podium either side), in Lausanne on 28 September
1918. This work showed the first influence of the jazz pieces which Ansermet
had brought back from America the previous year: an influence openly
admitted in Stravinsky's *Ragtime* of 1918 for eleven instruments, and in the
Piano-Rag-Music of 1919.

In 1918 Cocteau, some nine years senior to Brecht, wrote his essay *Le Coq
et l'Harlequin* advocating a clear and popularly-based musical style. A year
before, his ballet *Parade* to Satie's music had been given by Diaghileff in
Paris; (it was repeated more successfully in 1920). Here was music 'like an
inspired village band',[2] with a 'Rag-time du Paquebot' and slogans shouted
through megaphones; here were novel characters: the Chinaman, the Little
American Girl, the Acrobats. In 1919, again with Cocteau, Darius Milhaud
wrote his *Boeuf sur le Toit* for an orchestra of twenty-five, which was given
three performances that winter with the Fratellini and other clowns. This
work was set, writes Milhaud, 'in a bar in America during prohibition. With
some very typical characters: a Boxer, a Negro Dwarf, an Elegant Woman,
a Red-head dressed as a boy, a Bookmaker, a Gentleman in Tails. . . .'[3] Its
alternative title was in English: 'The Nothing Doing Bar'.

---

[1] Eric Walter White: *Stravinsky*, John Lehmann, London, 1947, p. 65.

[2] Cocteau: *Cock and Harlequin*, translated by Rollo H. Myers, The Egoist Press, London,
1921, p. 57.

[3] Milhaud: *Notes sans Musique*, Julliard, Paris, 1949, p.116. Another interesting French
anticipation may be seen in the productions staged by the Autant-Laras' *Art et Action*

These are the obvious ancestors of Kurt Weill's *Mahagonny*; and the younger French composers continued exploring along these lines. Cocteau's *Mariés de la Tour Eiffel*, with more megaphones and a rowdy score by his friends 'Les Six', was given on 19 June 1921; a Milhaud shimmy called *Caramel Mou* was performed by a negro dancer that May; *La Création du Monde*, his negro ballet with book by Cendrars and settings by Léger, was produced by de Maré's Swedish Ballet in 1923. ('I followed the example of Harlem and had an orchestra of seventeen soloists, and freely used the language of jazz, which I combined with a classical feeling.') Jean Wiéner, that interesting composer and pianist who has long operated in the gap between 'serious' music and jazz, sponsored a series of concerts in 1922 which included *Pierrot Lunaire* and *Mavra*, Stravinsky's other chamber opera; Milhaud met Cole Porter and recommended him to de Maré for a ballet; 1924 saw the first (American) performance of Gershwin's *Rhapsody in Blue*. Ravel himself, with whom Cole Porter took lessons, wrote his *Enfant et les Sortilèges* 'dans l'esprit de l'opérette américaine': a kind of sung ballet which was produced by Balanchine in March 1925 and represented a continuation of that process of extreme 'dépouillement', or stripping-bare, which began with his violin and cello sonata of 1920.

All this means that the relations between lowbrow music and the new anti-Wagnerian aims of the younger serious composers were for a time very close: that the actual scale of performance was being cut down, harmonies clarified, melody emphasized, orchestration tightened up. An element of classical balance was being reintroduced. And for some reason this trend expressed itself not in the orthodox opera but in short and rather frivolous stage works, where the means were economical and the words themselves – as in the rhythmic recitation devised by Milhaud for Claudel's *l'Ours et la Lune* of 1918 – treated in a clear and novel way: a process that led in 1923 to the first performance of Edith Sitwell's and William Walton's *Façade*.

* * *

In 1921 a group of German musicians, most of them born between 1890 and 1900, and including Hindemith and Heinrich Burkard, launched a small annual chamber music festival under the patronage of the Prince of Fürstenberg at Donaueschingen. This became in effect Stravinsky's platform in Germany, and from 1925 on he came to the festival each year. 'Germany,' he wrote in his *Chroniques*, 'was plainly becoming the centre of the musical movement . . .'. Milhaud's friendships with Hindemith and Kurt Weill

between 1915 and 1922. The works presented included *Gulliver*, *Robinson Crusoe*, *Le Bateau ivre* and writings by Villon, Marinetti and Claudel. Masereel was one of the scene designers, and a highly stylized realism was the aim.

Milhaud's
*Le Boeuf
sur le Toit.*
Design by
Dufy (1920)

had their origins here; Weill's own reputation was made with a Quartet at the second festival in 1922; Hindemith wrote a whole series of small-scale more or less neo-classical works. Other German musicians associated with this group carried the French experiments a good deal further, both inside and outside the actual festivals, and managed to bring them to a rather wider public. Ernst Křenek wrote his jazz operas *Sprung über den Schatten* (1924) and *Jonny Spielt Auf* (1927), with its negro hero; Wilhelm Grosz (known to us as the composer of 'It was on the Isle of Capri that I met her') wrote a *Jazzband* for violin (1925) and the ballet *Baby in the Bar* (1927), and set Ringelnatz's light verse to some very original music. A jazz class was instituted at the Frankfurt Hochsches Konservatorium under Matyas Seiber, who published a *Jazz Percussion Tutor*. In 1923 Hermann Scherchen introduced *l'Histoire du Soldat* at Frankfurt with Carl Ebert as narrator, later taking it on tour with a cut-down version of Cocteau and Milhaud's short opera *Le Pauvre Matelot* (1926). It was performed at the Berlin State Opera in 1925, and in 1928 was produced there by Brecht's friend Jakob Geis, as part of the première of the Cocteau-Stravinsky *Oedipus Rex*. The Germans not only took the French ideas up; they took them seriously; and they took them to the public. And all this for more than 'purely' musical reasons.

In 1927 the Donaueschingen festival shifted to Baden-Baden and began to reflect the same social and aesthetic ideas as were current in the theatre at the time. 'Thanks to Hindemith's severe and judicious selection,' wrote Milhaud later, 'the programmes had an undeniable aesthetic pattern.' The pattern was that of 'Gebrauchsmusik' and 'Gemeinschaftsmusik', or applied music and amateur music, two terms expressing the broad social-aesthetic question: What ought music actually to do? 'What didn't they try out there?' writes Heinrich Strobel in his study of Hindemith. 'Film music, mechanical

music, potted opera, radio music, music for young people, for amateurs. . . .'
That first year they performed a batch of four chamber operas: Hindemith's
own 'film sketch' *Hin und Zurück*, whose action and music alike go suddenly
into reverse in the middle of the work; Ernst Toch's *Prinzessin auf der
Erbse*; and Milhaud's specially-written nine-minute opera *l'Enlèvement de
l'Europe* to a text by Claudel's friend Henri Hoppenot (later the Free French
representative in Washington). The fourth work was the 'Songspiel' *Mahagonny* by Weill and Brecht.

'Gebrauchsmusik', or functional music, really originated with Satie's
'musique d'ameublement' – musical furniture, to be listened to with half an
ear – and Milhaud's *Machines Agricoles* of 1919, settings of more or less
random texts from farmers' and seedsmen's catalogues. Here is the new
mechanized spirit that inspired Stravinsky's works for pianola, or Hindemith's various pieces for mechanical instruments (including the Bauhaus
Triadic Ballet) of 1926 and 1927; and it had its own aesthetic appeal.

> Affiche, crime en couleurs. Piano mécanique,
> Nick Carter; c'est du joli!

– wrote Cocteau in his *Cocardes*, to convey the garish charm of the old
silent cinema. The film indeed offered the one really new Gebrauch, or
function for music, and at the same time it challenged the modern composer's technical and mechanical ingenuity. Antheil's *Ballet Mécanique* (for
eight pianos and percussion) was fitted to a film of 1924 by Dudley Murphy
and Fernand Léger; L'Herbier's film *L'Inhumaine* of 1923 (made with the
help of Léger, Cavalcanti, Autant-Lara and the jazz-modern architect
Mallet-Stevens) included scenes of the rioting at Antheil's first Paris recital
and was set to music by Milhaud; in 1927 Hindemith wrote a piece for
mechanical organ to accompany a Felix cartoon. Film music figured at the
Baden-Baden festival of 1928 (another Felix cartoon arranged by Ernst
Toch, and a synchronization by Hindemith of a mechanical piano to fit
Richter's *Spuk der Gegenstände*) and 1929 (a recording of this on sound-
track, plus another Richter film set by Walter Gronostay, and Cavalcanti's
La p'tite Lili to music by Milhaud). Brecht was of course right when he
suggested that the invention of sound recording must knock such highbrow
experiments on the head, but for a moment the composers were encouraged
to neglect the old orchestral and operatic apparatus for an apparently new
world: a world which, like Piscator's theatre audiences, got particular pleasure
from seeing the wheels go round.

'Gemeinschaftsmusik', communal music, sprang, according to Dr Strobel's
account, from Hindemith's meeting with the singers of various youth
organizations at the Donaueschingen festival. He began writing music for

amateurs: first the instrumental *Schulwerk* (all in the first position) and *Spielmusik*, then the choruses (Op 43, No. 2) and the Sing und Spielmusiken of 1927 and 1928. Milhaud followed suit with the cantata *Pour louer le Seigneur* and various pieces now included in his *La Musique en Famille et à l'Ecole*, while at Baden-Baden in 1929 there were amateur pieces by Wagner-Regeny and Walter Leigh, and in the 1930s Hindemith's *Plöner Musiktag* and Carl Orff's well-known *Schulwerk* carried the tradition on. These were the origins of the school opera and the 'Lehrstück', or didactic piece, where the performers were meant to learn as they went, and to learn not only the notes but the technique and pleasure of working as a collective too. Both the 1929 Baden-Baden festival and the 1930 Neue Musik festival in Berlin were primarily devoted to such works. The object was as much social as musical, and the writers of the texts were driven in the direction of a corresponding simplicity of diction and clarity of sense.

* * *

Kurt Weill had already used texts by Kipling and Villon for his pantomime *Zaubermacht* of 1923, and the poems in Brecht's *Hauspostille* so impressed him that he proposed a collaboration whose first result was the primitive *Mahagonny* of 1927. 'Till then,' wrote Brecht later,

> Weill had written relatively complicated music of a mainly psychological sort, and when he agreed to set a series of more or less banal *song* texts he was making a courageous break with a prejudice which the solid bulk of serious composers stubbornly hold.

This meant rejecting the sacred dogma according to which 'folk' music is respectable and popular music not. Despite the complaints of his teacher Busoni that he was setting out to be 'the poor man's Verdi', Weill saw that

> jazz has played a considerable part in the rhythmical, harmonic and formal liberation at which we have now attained, and above all in our music's steadily increasing simplicity and intelligibility. . . .

while Brecht likewise held that it 'signified a broad flow of popular musical elements into modern music, whatever our commercialized world may have made of it since'.

Sharply orchestrated, and free from all mushiness, jazz not only fitted Brecht's conception of a down-to-earth vernacular language but also helped to establish his dramatic points.

> So-called 'cheap' music, particularly that of the cabaret and the operetta, has for some time been a kind of 'gestisch' music [i.e. one which expresses attitudes. See page 173 for an explanation of the term]. Serious music however still clings to lyricism and cultivates expression for its own sake.

Here, at a new low, economical level, the problem of the opera could be

Kurt Weill
(1900–1950)

tackled much more effectively than in the top-heavy 'Zeitoper': the modernist operas of Křenek and Max Brand (*Maschinist Hopkins*, 1928) and Hindemith himself.

> Composers who aim to put new blood in the opera are inevitably (like Hindemith and Stravinsky) brought up against the whole operatic apparatus. Great apparati like the opera, the stage, the Press, etc., impose their views as it were incognito.

Spurred by reading the libretto of the *Beggar's Opera* during the winter of 1927–8, Brecht saw the chance to undermine this apparatus as Gay and Pepusch had done two centuries earlier: by writing a 'ballad opera' in the new popular terms.

In *The Threepenny Opera*, which he and Weill wrote in a considerable hurry in the summer of 1928, the singers were primarily actors and the songs interruptions; the music was never allowed to swamp the continually lucid text. The melodies were nostalgic, the counterpoint neat and the harmonies often disconcertingly prickly, but it was scored for a band of eight musicians only, and the singers came from the world of the theatre and the cabaret, not from the grand operatic stage. 'I couldn't read a note,' writes Weill's widow Lotte Lenja, of her appearance in the first *Mahagonny*, '– exactly why I was chosen.' Such methods imposed new rules, which were outlined by Brecht in *The Threepenny Opera* notes:

> Nothing is more revolting than when the actor pretends not to notice that he has left the level of plain speech and started to sing. The three levels – plain

Brecht and
Weill's opera
*Aufstieg und
Fall der Stadt
Mahagonny*
(1929)

> speech, heightened speech and singing – must always remain distinct. . . . As
> for the melody, he must not follow it blindly: there is a kind of speaking-
> against-the-music which can have strong effects; the results of a stubborn,
> incorruptible sobriety which is independent of music and rhythm.

Music here becomes a kind of punctuation, an underlining of the words, a
well-aimed comment giving the gist of the action or the text. And this
remains its prime function in all Brecht's plays.

Happy End, with its very successful songs, was composed on the same
pattern, but the completed *Aufstieg und Fall der Stadt Mahagonny* represents
a swing towards the orthodox opera, for although it has the same lightness
and punch and the same nostalgic jazz tunes the music runs almost con-
tinuously throughout the work. The orchestra in the original version was
some forty strong, including strings (which Brecht always disliked), plus a
stage orchestra of twenty-one; the writing was less disjointed, and the bass
often less percussive and monotonous than in the two musical plays The
real innovation, never followed up by Brecht, lay in the alternation of
rhythmical and free dialogue, sometimes over the orchestra, sometimes unaccompanied, and in the ingenious combination of solos and chorus. The
words emerged as clear as ever, but the general effect, even after the work
had been re-scored for something more like a dance band, was further from
unadulterated theatre than Brecht cared to go.[1]

[1] Mr David Drew says that the re-scoring was done for the Paris performance of 1932.
An article by Günter Hartung in the *Wissenschaftliche Zeitschrift der Martin-Luther
Universität Halle-Wittenberg*, June 1959, p. 659, suggests that Weill had misgivings about
Aufricht's (or more likely Brecht's) insistence on using cabaret and operetta singers for
the 1931 Berlin production. See also Aufricht's own *Erzähle, damit du dein Recht beweist*,
Ullstein, Berlin, 1966, for an account of the differences between Weill and Brecht, who
called his friend a 'phoney Richard Strauss'.

The Baden-Baden festival, 1929
Left to right: Weill, Hardt, Hindemith, Flesch, Brecht

In the notes which he and Suhrkamp wrote on this work about 1930 he admitted that it was what he called a 'culinary opera', whose different elements are cooked into a common mush, even though it is also a 'Spass'; a piece of fun, which a guilty conscience has stopped its authors from making too easy to swallow.

> The opera 'Mahagonny' pays conscious tribute to the idiocy of the operatic form. The idiocy of opera lies in the fact that rational elements are employed, solid reality is aimed at, but at the same time it is all washed out by the music.

So he returned to the principles of *The Threepenny Opera*: clear division of songs from dialogue; no illustrative or 'psychological' element in the music; an orchestra of not more than thirty; and the singer as a 'reporter' whose private feelings must remain a private affair. He now classed *Mahagonny* with the new opera of Hindemith and Křenek: an attempt to modernize the content and mechanize the form of the opera without querying the 'apparatus' or the social function which it performed. He himself set out 'more and more to emphasize the didactic at the expense of the culinary element'.

The close connection of these works with the experiments being conducted at Baden-Baden was recognized by the serious critics and stressed by Weill himself:

> The *Threepenny Opera* takes its place in a movement which today embraces nearly all the young musicians. The sacrificing of 'art for art's sake', the playing down of the artist's individuality, the idea of film music, the link with the

musical youth movement, and arising from these the simplification of musical means of expression – they are all stages along the same road.

Two new steps in this direction were taken at the 1929 Baden-Baden festival, which was devoted to the didactic cantata and to works specially written for radio. For this Walter Goehr composed a setting for Feuchtwanger's pseudo-American poems *Pep*; Hanns Eisler wrote his cantata *Tempo der Zeit*; while Brecht provided the text for two pieces: *Lindberghflug* (for radio) with music by Hindemith and Weill, and the *Badener Lehrstück* to a score by Hindemith alone. The second work started with the final chorus of the first.

Unfortunately the collaboration with Hindemith was not entirely successful. 'Every word can be understood,' wrote Heinrich Strobel of Kurt Weill's part of *Lindberghflug*.

Brecht and Hindemith's *Badener Lehrstück* (1929). The large clown is about to be sawn in half. Projected title behind. Brecht himself is seated at the table on the left of the picture

Hindemith's music is much more atmospheric: it uses precisely the same means of characterization as his stage works have made familiar.

At the same time Brecht pushed the conception of the Lehrstück a good way further than Hindemith wished to go, writing that

> The Lehrstück, product of certain musical, dramatic and political theories, all of which envisage the collective practice of art, is designed to clarify the ideas of the authors and of all those taking part, not to provide anybody with an emotional experience.

Hindemith wanted his work to be played by any instrumentalists available, and left them free to omit whole sections if they wished ; Brecht was concerned with the instructive aspects of the text as a whole. The question at issue was whether 'Gemeinschaftsmusik' was to teach the writer's ideas, or to restrict itself to teaching music, plus the simple social pleasure of performing together. It was with this purely musical didacticism that Brecht so disagreed: 'The cellist in the orchestra, father of a numerous family, now began to play not from philosophical conviction but for pleasure. The culinary principle was saved.'

The performance of the *Lehrstück*, with Hindemith conducting an audience that included Gide and Gerhardt Hauptmann, and the words of the choruses projected on a screen, caused a major scandal at Baden-Baden, thanks largely to the gratuitous and, on paper, laboriously unfunny scene for the three clowns. (This, according to Dr Strobel, was the reason why the festival had to shift the following year to Berlin.) Brecht then added further sections to his text, which he had not regarded as complete, but Hindemith refused to set them to music, with the result that each refused to let the work be performed except in his own version, and it became impossible to perform it publicly at all. The irresistible poet had met the immovable musician, and they had arrived at a stalemate: a great pity, because Hindemith's score was judged to be one of his finest achievements:

> Without in any way sacrificing his individual point of view Hindemith has simplified his style to the point of universal intelligibility. His music has an unsentimental dignity: powerful and serious. . . .

It was also, says Dr Strobel, 'the only occasion on which Hindemith collaborated with a writer of real importance.'

At the festival in 1930 further Lehrstücke (like *Das Wasser* by Döblin and Ernst Toch) were followed by the first 'school opera', written on very similar principles. 'The practical value of a school opera,' wrote Weill, 'consists precisely in the learning of it.' He and Brecht had turned, as we saw, to the Nō drama, and found there the material for the school opera *Der Jasager*. *Lindberghflug*, henceforward given with Weill's music only, was rechristened 'a radio Lehrstück for boys and girls'. Other school operas followed: Hindemith's *Wir bauen eine Stadt* (1931), Milhaud's *A Propos de Bottes* (1932); but *Der Jasager* was one of the most successful of them all, and was widely performed in German schools before 1933. It was arranged, according to Weill,

> in such a way that all the parts (chorus, orchestra and soloists) can be performed by school-children. . . . The score is laid out to suit the resources of a school orchestra: a basic orchestra of strings (less violas) and two pianos, with *ad lib* three woodwind (flute, clarinet, saxophone), percussion and plucked instruments.

He emphasized the instructional value of the text, and also the possible emergence of a new musical market. This he saw not only in the schools but also in 'the working-class movement'.

Yet when at the end of the year Brecht came into contact with this movement it was through another composer; and although there was no break between him and Weill the really productive period of their collaboration ends at this stage. It was in a sense logical, for it was a turning point in Brecht's work, and Weill's music was becoming too light and nostalgic; apt even, with its very genuine charm, to 'wash out' the new-found roughness of Brecht's verse. On Weill's side too there was a new urge to compose freely ('sich ausmusizieren') which he could gratify in his subsequent opera *Die Bürgschaft* to Neher's libretto. It was, says Lotte Lenya, 'a kind of relief after the restraints of writing for untrained singers, children and the special needs of Brecht'. They worked together on the 1931 productions of *Mahagonny* and *Mann ist Mann*, for which Weill wrote fresh incidental music; they planned a number of works, including an opera called *Der Moabiter Pferdehandel*; and later in America they discussed the music for the *Good Person of Szechwan* and an operatic version of *Schweik*. But all that has so far come down to us of these plans is some isolated songs, and their one major work after 1930 remains the ballet *Die Sieben Todsünden* (*Les Sept Péchés Capitaux*) of 1934, which the late Constant Lambert regarded not only as Weill's best stage work but as 'the most important work in ballet form since *Les Noces* and *Parade*'. Whatever the truth of this judgment it was a quite conscious regression on Brecht's part. He never cared to print the songs which he wrote for it, and it seems a plain attempt to earn money in exile by recapturing the spirit of his greatest success.

* * *

Hanns Eisler, five months younger than Brecht, and a pupil of Schönberg and Webern, had come from Vienna to Berlin in 1925. He was an austerer composer than Weill; his sister Ruth Fischer and his brother Gerhard Eisler were both prominent Communist Party officials; and he had already become well known as a composer of Communist songs. As such he was prepared to do what Hindemith evidently would not, and give a certain supremacy to the text. Thus although *Die Massnahme*, the Lehrstück which he and Brecht wrote for the 1930 festival, was in one sense a logical continuation of the two pieces of 1929 and a natural companion to the *Jasager* (whose essential theme it repeated in Communist dress), the whole work had a strong political flavour, and Eisler's songs were revolutionary in their impact. Hindemith and the other directors of the Neue Musik objected to this. *Die Massnahme* was not performed at the festival; and Brecht's connection with the bulk of the new movement now ceased.

He and Eisler turned instead to the Socialist-Communist workers' choral societies, one of which (the Gemischte Chor Berlin) had originally been conducted by Hermann Scherchen, just as Anton Webern in Vienna had conducted the Arbeiter-Sinfonie. The didactic aim now became narrowed to these left-wing singers:

Hanns Eisler (1898-1962)

As there are half-a-million working-class singers in Germany, the effect on the singer is at least as important as that on the hearer.

So Brecht thought. But when three of the Berlin societies agreed to perform *Die Massnahme* at the end of 1930 the unfortunate effect was to split this whole movement; and in the end it was only the converted to whom Brecht was left preaching. In these circumstances the Baden-Baden principle of actual participation no longer seemed so important. Two years later *Die Mutter*, the last of the Berlin didactic works, was played mainly by professional actors, with the chorus relegated to a very minor role. And from then on Eisler's position in the partnership was a good deal less prominent than Weill's had been: at least, so far as the major works were concerned, though Brecht also supplied the words for individual choruses of a more or less rousing kind, such as Eisler had already been composing for some years.

Eisler was exactly the right composer for Brecht's mature poetic style. He had none of the faintly cheap nostalgia that haunts much of the work of Weill: he is an even more skilled (and in many ways highbrow) composer, who used his gifts like Brecht himself to make the meaning simple and clear. Like Brecht he used ecclesiastical (the Lutheran chorale) and popular models (folksong, popular ballads and jazz), and made of them something in no way imitative or spiced-up but recognizably his own. 'What is essential in modern music?' he asks in an article of 1949.

137

Brecht and
Eisler's
'Lehrstück',
Die Massnahme
(1930). Projected
text behind

It is not the increased resources in discordances or in new colours, but the
dissolution of the conventional musical language as handed down to us. A
piece which is full of discords can be perfectly conventional in its approach,
and one which uses relatively simpler material may, if the means are applied
in an individual way, seem completely advanced and new.

This is true of most of his settings of Brecht's words: their originality consists in the chamber-music orchestration and lively counterpoint, in those
changing rhythms that match Brecht's irregular lines, in the dry flavour and
the persistent yet slightly unexpected melodies, at once logical and fresh.
Eisler's music for *Die Mutter*, wrote Brecht,

can by no means be called simple. Quâ music it is relatively complicated, and
I cannot think of any that is more serious. In a remarkable manner it makes
possible a certain simplification of the toughest political problems, whose
solution is a life and death matter for the working class.

It underlined the words and interrupted the story, exactly as Brecht had
demanded in *The Threepenny Opera* notes.

During 1931 Brecht and Eisler collaborated on a third work: the semi-
documentary film *Kuhle Wampe*, which culminates in the singing (by Ernst
Busch) of the well-known Solidarity Song. They next worked together on
the songs for *Die Rundköpfe und die Spitzköpfe*, which was staged during
Brecht's exile in Denmark; then in 1937 Eisler emigrated to the USA, where
Kurt Weill had already gone. Among the various theatrical and film figures
whom Brecht listed for membership of his proposed 'Society for Theatrical

Science', or Diderot Society, that year, Eisler is the only composer mentioned; and it is plain that Brecht relied on his opinions where much more than the music was concerned. They worked together again in Hollywood in 1942 on Fritz Lang's film *Hangmen Also Die*, then on Brecht's own play *Simone Machard*, while for *Galileo* in 1947 Eisler wrote a long *Moritat*-like ballad and twelve short songs for boys' voices to go between the scenes.

These boys' or women's choruses, sometimes unaccompanied, recur in the incidental music which he wrote after 1949 for some of the productions of the Berliner Ensemble; but Brecht and he never again seem to have collaborated on any work of major interest, and most of these pieces are very slight. There are also a great number of individual songs by Eisler, and these range from the more private and esoteric settings of Brecht's exiled poems to the disappointing banalities of the children's poems and other 'positive' political songs written after Brecht's return home. The East German Academy's edition of Eisler's collected songs and cantatas embraces something like 150 songs to texts by Brecht.

But if it was Brecht who gave Eisler much of his sense of words and of the stage, his own ideas of music (as outlined in his essay 'Über die Verwendung der Musik fur eine epische Bühne' of 1935) were very largely Eisler's work. Thus they are not always easy to reconcile with the musical settings of his third major collaborator Paul Dessau, or even with the amusing Weill-like songs which Rudolf Wagner-Regeny wrote for *Trumpets and Drums*. Both these composers had made their mark in the same school as the others: Dessau with some 'thin, pathetic' film music at Baden-Baden in 1929, and two school operas in 1932: Wagner-Regeny with three short operas (one of them called *Moritat*) staged at Essen in 1929 in sets by Neher, and three full-scale 'culinary' operas to Neher's librettos, of which *Der Günstling* became well known during the Nazi period. But it was only in America that Dessau came to work with Brecht,[1] and Brecht never gave his name as a 'Mitarbeiter'. Evidently he did not play the same part as Weill and Eisler at the planning stage; and it is perhaps for this reason that his scores for the big late plays – *Mother Courage* (1946), the *Good Person of Szechwan* (1947–8), *Puntila* and the semi-operatic *The Caucasian Chalk Circle* all tend to be brittle rather than clear. They may respect Brecht's ideas of instrumentation:

---

[1] Dessau wrote the music for the first productiou of *Furcht und Elend des Dritten Reiches*. By his own account however (in the symposium *Erinnerungen an Brecht*, Reclam, Leipzig, 1964) what inspired Brecht to suggest their working together was Dessau's singing of his own setting of a song from *St Joan of the Stockyards* in New York in 1942. In Santa Monica they discussed the *Mother Courage* songs; the tune for the introductory song (also used in *Hauspostille*) being Brecht's choice. At that time Brecht wanted *Lucullus* made into an opera, and asked Dessau to suggest the idea to Stravinsky, who refused. Dessau himself took the job on in 1948.

Brecht and Dessau's opera *Die Verurteilung des Lukullus* (1951)

they may have been worked out in close consultation with him: they may be a fair illustration of the plays. But time and again they blur the text, and the music seems exotic where it ought to be precise.

Dessau's settings of Brecht's words represent a reversion to the gingered-up folk or pseudo-folk style of the early Stravinsky. Thus the *Mother Courage* songs, he writes,

> based on the folk-song, extend it by enriching it with rhythmical and harmonic multiplicity

– that is to say, by abruptly-changing rhythms, ragged discords, and the insertion of tin-tacks in the piano hammers. This is certainly not ineffective: the bitter, sometimes violent orchestration gives the play a distinctive flavour, and the self-conscious 'modernism' of the method is less specious than it seems at first. But the general effect is to underline Brecht's own mannerisms – an affected orientalism or a deliberate tattered squalor. The music is basically atmospheric; and except in the *Mother Courage* songs it fails to bring out, or even to let through, the sense. Both *The Caucasian Chalk Circle* and, still more, the opera *Die Verurteilung des Lukullus* represent a return to the despised 'culinary' approach. *Lucullus*'s score is in many ways brilliantly exciting, but the critic is right who complained that the music 'is bogged down in illustrative externalities', and the opera remains within the orthodox framework because the composer is heading in a quite different direction from Brecht's austerely didactic verse. No doubt Brecht could have checked this if he had wished, and perhaps one can read a certain disillusionment with didactic methods into his new tolerance of the 'idiotic' operatic form. But for all his surface innovations Dessau is not an opponent of the 'apparatus', and when Brecht in the 1940s returned to the orthodox theatre this collaboration helped him to adopt a more orthodox attitude to the opera as well.

In England today we seem once more to be getting interested in the origins of this whole musical movement. We are reviving the small-scale works of Stravinsky, like *Mavra* and *Renard* and *L'Histoire du Soldat*; we see some connection between these and the economical, almost chamber form of opera evolved at Aldeburgh by Benjamin Britten; but we tend to forget what came between. The German social-musical developments of the 'twenties have remained in the shadow since 1933; to imply that music has any social aspect at all is now rank bolshevism; and the part played by Brecht and his collaborators is wholly ignored. Yet surely there was a quite continuous process, to which such works as the Honegger Concertino or the Falla Harpsichord Concerto or Auric's score for *A Nous La Liberté* all contributed, as well as neglected pieces like Křenek's Little Suite for Piano (Op. 13a) or Wilhelm Grosz's Ringelnatz songs (Op. 31) or Kästner's and Edmund Nick's charming satirical cantata of 1931, *Leben in dieser Zeit*.

It all represents a certain deflation of the pompous, difficult, uneconomic approach to music. And once we no longer look only at Stravinsky and Britten, the two extremities, we see that this is bound up with a new, largely social urge towards intelligibility, and a corresponding need for composers and writers to have something definite to say. Nowhere is this so clear as in *Die Mutter*, but the movement continues through Gershwin's and Kaufmann's *Of Thee I Sing* and later, American, works by Weill such as *One Touch of Venus* or the 'school opera' *Down in the Valley*, to bring fresh sense and artistry also to the popular musical show. 'Its effect on the stage,' said the citation by Columbia University, who in 1932 gave *Of Thee I Sing* the first Pulitzer Prize to be gained by a lowbrow work,

> promises to be very considerable, because musical plays are always popular, and by injecting genuine satire and point into them, a very large public is reached.

Compared with *The Threepenny Opera*, or even with Antheil's *Transatlantic*, which it in some ways resembles, the Gershwin work was pure Gilbert-and-Sullivan. None the less, this suggestion proved true. In America at least (where Stravinsky, Bartok and Milhaud all wrote works during the 1940s for musical-comedy kings or dance-band leaders)[1] the lowbrow media have remained open to the highbrow artist, with the results that we saw in *Oklahoma!* and Leonard Bernstein's ballet *Fancy Free* and many other good and successful works. And Marc Blitzstein rightly dedicated his *The Cradle Will Rock* (one of the landmarks in this particular story) to Brecht. For the combination of accessibility, artistry and solid content is fundamental to Brecht's ideas.

[1] Stravinsky wrote works for Paul Whiteman, Woody Herman, Billy Rose, and Barnum and Bailey's Circus. Bartok wrote the *Contrasts* for piano, violin and clarinet for Benny Goodman. Ravel is supposed to have given lessons to Cole Porter and Duke Ellington, and was himself responsible for the dance-band arrangement of his *Bolero*.

FIVE

Theatrical Practice

When Brecht was a student at Munich he began to write criticisms of the Augsburg municipal theatre, and these essays, recently rediscovered, show his early doubts not only of Expressionism but also of the German classical style and of the very basis of the existing stage. 'Ach, it's good enough for Augsburg,' his friends would say in answer to his attacks,

> And all the time they are treating themselves as exceptions. But let me tell you, dear readers: there is nothing to stop one from filling theatres with the exceptions. . . .

This he at once set out to do. Leaving the university, he became a 'Dramaturg' at the small Munich theatre known as the Kammerspiele, and early in 1922 persuaded the young author Arnolt Bronnen to make him responsible for the single Berlin production of his play *Vatermord*. Here for the first time he tried to prick the inflations of Expressionism, repeatedly bringing the actors back to the exact sense of their lines. They were players of some eminence (Agnes Straub, for instance, and Heinrich George),

> and in came this thin, rather undersized Augsburger and told them in dry, clearly articulated syllables that all their work was so much crap. There were fearful explosions. . . .[1]

Such explosions indeed that Berthold Viertel was asked to take the production over, and there were resignations from the cast.

It was nearly two years before Otto Falckenberg, the director of the Kammerspiele, put Brecht in charge of his first proper production. The plan was that he should produce *Macbeth*, but after consultation with Lion Feuchtwanger he arranged to substitute a less well-known play of the same period, which the two writers could adapt with a freer hand. This was Marlowe's *Edward II*, for which his school friend Caspar Neher designed the scenery and costumes. 'We wished,' he later wrote,

> to make possible a production which would break with the Shakespearean tradition common to German theatres: that lumpy monumental style which the Spiessbürger so love.

The few photographs and accounts that have survived suggest that in this

---

[1] The play was finally performed on 14 May 1922 in the Deutsches Theater, with a cast including Elisabeth Bergner and Alexander Granach.

Brecht's first
production:
Edward II
(1924)
On the right a
'Moritat'-singer
with a
hurdy-gurdy

production Brecht was anticipating his later work, just as his language was anticipating his unrhymed verse of the 1930s. 'Sawing gently at the nerves,' said Marieluise Fleisser, and Herbert Ihering (writing in 1926):

> He did not analyse the characters; he set them at a distance. . . . He called for a report on the events. He insisted on simple gestures. He compelled a clear and cool manner of speaking. No emotional tricks were allowed. That ensured the objective, 'epic' style.

It seemed truly to be a turning point in German classical production, and Ihering sees it as leading to Erich Engel's *Coriolanus*, and even to the Stravinsky-Cocteau *Oedipus Rex*, whose première in 1928 was in Berlin.

Trommeln in der Nacht, the first of Brecht's own plays to be produced, had been staged by Falckenberg at the beginning of the previous season in what seems to have been an unduly Expressionist style. It was quickly followed by *Im Dickicht*, which Engel produced while Neher designed the sets; and from then on these two were closely associated with Brecht's work, both in Berlin (where Reinhardt engaged them) and again after the war with the Berliner Ensemble. A third Munich figure who had a strong influence on Brecht was the dialect comedian Karl Valentin, on whose sketches he modelled three of the early one-act plays. Here was the same 'vertrackte Dialektik' (or perverted logic) as he found in the surrealist farce or the films of Chaplin: the basis of the *Elefantenkalb* and the clown scene in the *Badener Lehrstück*, and of the considerable knockabout element in his work. In this comedian's relation to his public, who sat there drinking beer, 'puffing away at pipes and cigars and listening to a huge brass orchestra in the interval',[1] he seems to have sensed the possibility of a new kind of theatre: a critical but dispassionate audience, which would regard the actor in the same wide-awake spirit as it judged a sporting event.

[1] Feuchtwanger: *Success*, London, 1930, p. 199.

Brecht (clarinet, with cap) and Karl Valentin (tuba, with bowler) in a Munich sketch of the early 1920s

Carl Zuckmayer has described how he and Brecht came as somewhat erratic 'Dramaturgen' to Reinhardt's complex of Berlin theatres in 1924, engaged on the recommendation of their friend Engel. They were supernumerary, and apart from firmly rejecting Musil's play *Vincenz oder die Freundin bedeutender Männer* they did very little of a Dramaturg's work. Brecht was disgruntled at not being given a Shakespeare production, and at the end of the 1924–5 season their contracts were understandably allowed to lapse. According to Zuckmayer

> Brecht seldom turned up there; with his flapping leather jacket he looked like a cross between a lorry driver and a Jesuit seminarist. Roughly speaking, what he wanted was to take over complete control: the season's programme must be regulated entirely according to his theories, and the stage be rechristened 'epic smoke-theatre', it being his view that people might actually be disposed to think if they were allowed to smoke at the same time. As this was refused him he confined himself to coming and drawing his pay.

Luckily it was one of those moments when Reinhardt returned from semiretirement to organize a whole series of new productions; and the rehearsals which he conducted were of extreme interest for Brecht. Shaw's *Saint Joan* opened the season, with Elisabeth Bergner; the newly-built Komödie was inaugurated with Goldoni's *Servant of Two Masters*, produced in semiimprovised Commedia dell'Arte style—the actors chatting freely with the prompter and discussing their parts; while Pirandello's *Six Characters in Search of an Author* followed along the same anti-illusionistic lines. These three works (and also *Le Malade Imaginaire* with Max Pallenberg) were all produced by Reinhardt himself; and at the end of February 1925 Erich Engel

Brecht's Berlin flat about 1926. *Left to right:* Samson-Körner, the boxer, Brecht, Seelenfreund (in boxing gloves), Borchardt and Küpper (both 'Dramaturgen'), Elisabeth Hauptmann. Painting by Neher

staged *Coriolanus* at the Lessingtheater with sets by Neher and some collaboration (it seems) by Brecht, Fritz Kortner taking the title part.

Reinhardt remained based on Berlin for another year, and this saw his production of *Kreidekreis*, two more Pirandellos, a single (Junge Bühne) performance of Marieluise Fleisser's *Fegefeuer in Ingolstadt* with Helene Weigel (whom Brecht was soon to marry), an Edgar Wallace play at the Deutsches Theater with Oskar Homolka, Engel's *Lysistrata* with Camilla Spira and Curt Bois, and a successful visit to the Komödie by Juschni's 'Blauer Vogel' troupe. It was, as Brecht later realized, a wonderful period in the German theatre, and he himself was able to get wonderful actors for his plays: Fritz Kortner, Oskar Homolka, Ernst Deutsch, Alexander Granach; later Peter Lorre – to mention only those players who are internationally known. Yet although the productions of the time had an obvious influence on him, they were far removed from the 'smokers' theatre' of which he had begun to dream. Red plush, half-darkness, evening dress: the cosiness of the middle-class theatre was not for him.

Instead, he became interested in sport, with its hard seats and bright lights, and at the beginning of 1926 he wrote an article which he called 'How to apply the principles of good sports promotion to the theatre': a conception which to some extent underlay the writing and first production that year of *Mann ist Mann*. The producer, Jakob Geis (a 'Dramaturg' at the State Theatre in Munich when Brecht was at the Kammerspiele), aimed, he wrote,

Caspar Neher, about 1930

to show the play's underlying sense by making the surface meaning as clear as possible. In other words: no implications, secrets, ambiguities, half-lights; but: facts, brilliant illumination, light into every corner, absence of feeling, no 'laughing with a catch in the throat'. The theatre considered as craft rather than art: avoidance of private affairs – these should make a secondary appearance, emerge as self-evident.

The stage was being brought closer to the boxing-ring, and at Frankfurt Melchior Vischer, who produced Brecht's one-act farce *Die Hochzeit* there at the end of 1926, claimed to 'see sport as the central rallying-point of the theatre – a new theatre'. (He wrote a play that year called *Fussballspieler und Indianer*: Footballers and Red Indians: a title perfectly expressing the current Anglo-Saxon vogue.)

Piscator's season at the Theater am Nollendorfplatz followed in 1927–8, and that same winter the actor Ernst-Josef Aufricht took over the Theater am Schiffbauerdamm, with Engel and Caspar Neher as his chief collaborators. Here Brecht was concerned not only with the production of *The Threepenny Opera* and of *Happy End*, but with Geis's production of Marieluise Fleisser's *Pioniere von Ingolstadt* too, while he himself produced *Mahagonny* elsewhere for the same management in 1931. Looking back later, he felt this to have been the theatre where his characteristic methods were worked out, though some of them in fact had appeared in embryo earlier. Already in

Munich he suggested that slogans on placards be put in the auditorium for *Trommeln in der Nacht*; sub-titles had been shown between the scenes in *Edward II*; in *Baal* in 1926 Twardowsky had introduced the scenes as a kind of compère; there had been a half-height linen curtain and a song sung verse by verse during scene changes in Geis's production of *Mann ist Mann*. But only now did these link together with the use of projections for song texts or drawings, with the visible lights and formal interruption of the text by songs, to make a completely distinctive style which, in Brecht's view, imposed special demands on the actor as well. The climax came at the Berlin Staatstheater in 1931, when Brecht staged the most completely original of his productions in the ordinary theatre: *Mann ist Mann*, with Helene Weigel and Peter Lorre. Here the acting was deliberately impersonal and disjointed; the scenery was fragmentary, the costumes fantastic and Neher's projections enormous caricatures. (See the photographs on pp. 171 and 173.) 'Giant soldiers,' reported the Russian playwright Sergei Tretiakoff,

> armed to the teeth and wearing jackets caked with lime, blood and excrement stalk about the stage, holding on to wires to keep from falling off the stilts inside their trouser legs.

And again: 'The performance produced a tremendous impression on me, second only to Meyerhold's *Rogonosetz*' (i.e. *Le Cocu Magnifique* by Crommelynck: a famous production which marked the high point of Constructivism on the Soviet stage).

Almost concurrently, from 1929 to 1932, Brecht was producing his more didactic works in the concert hall, first at Baden-Baden and then in Berlin. Here was an even severer contrast to Piscator's commercially-organized West End theatre, whose most revolutionary technical and political experiments depended finally on middle-class interest and capitalist support. Ruling out all but a minimum of make-up, costume or setting, Brecht now made the concert or lecture platform as unemotional and unhypnotic as the boxing-ring; it became impossible for the actors to do more than demonstrate and illustrate; the audience could no longer be 'carried away'. It seemed like the first trial skeleton of a completely new theatrical framework, which might well be confirmed by the impending social revolution; but events turned out otherwise. Yet this is what gave Brecht his interest in working with the left-wing amateur actors and singers with whom he came into contact during his exile: the Danish Revolutionary Theatre, for instance, or the Theatre Union of New York. It compelled him, moreover, to develop methods which might have been very hard to stomach for the commercial stage. 'Forget about settings,' he told Mordecai Gorelik before the production of *Die Mutter* in New York:

Brecht, Eisler (*left*)
and Dudow;
about 1931

Let's have a platform, and on this platform we'll put chairs, tables, partitions – whatever the actors need. For hanging a curtain give me a wooden pole or a metal bar; for hanging a picture a piece of wall. And I'll want a large projection screen. . . . Let it all be elegant, thin and fine, like Japanese banners, flimsy like Japanese kites and lanterns; let's be aware of the natural textures of wood and metal. . . . We'll place two grand pianos visibly at one side of the stage; the play must have the quality of a concert as well as that of a drama. . . . And we'll show the lighting units as they dim on and off, playing over the scene.

In 1936 Brecht helped stage *Die Rundköpfe und die Spitzköpfe* in Per Knutson's tiny Copenhagen theatre, again with visible pianos and lights; in 1937 *Senora Carrar* was produced in a Paris lecture hall by Slatan Dudow, in 1938 Brecht staged *Furcht und Elend*. He produced nothing in the professional German theatre from before his exile until after the end of the war.

But a number of the best anti-Nazi actors and producers – Therese Giehse, for instance, Leorard Steckel, Wolfgang Langhoff and Leopold Lindtberg – had gravitated to the Zurich Schauspielhaus, and here in Switzerland between 1941 and 1948 they gave the premières of four of Brecht's big new works: *Mother Courage, Galileo,* the *Good Person of Szechwan* and *Puntila* (that of *Lucullus* having been given in 1940 by Radio Berne). Brecht himself was in America during nearly all this time, so that he had little say in the solution of the enormous practical problems which such plays presented, with their dozen or so scenes and huge casts; and, perhaps as a result, ordinary practical or economic questions came to count for less and less in his later work. Only during his last two years in America did Charles Laughton's interest make it possible for him to work on a Hollywood production of *Galileo*, and the leisurely atmosphere in which its preparation took place was very different from the crises and tensions of the old Berlin days, or from the economies and topicalities which the anti-Nazi struggle had imposed.

> We used to work in Laughton's small library, in the mornings. But often L. would come to meet me in the garden, running barefoot in shirt and trousers over the damp grass, and would show me some changes in his flower-beds, for his garden always occupied him, providing many problems and subtleties. The gaiety and the beautiful proportions of this world of flowers overlapped in a most pleasant way into our work.

Here too was a stimulating collaborator:

> In a most striking and occasionally brutal way L. showed his lack of interest in the 'book', to an extent that the author could not always share. What we were making was just a text; the performance was all that counted. Impossible to lure him to translate passages that the author was willing to cut for the proposed performance, but wanted to keep in the book. The theatrical occasion was what mattered, the text was only there to make it possible; it would be expended in the production, would go off like gunpowder in a firework. Although L.'s theatrical experience had been in a London which had become thoroughly indifferent to the theatre, the old Elizabethan London still lived in him, the London where theatre was such a passion that it could swallow immortal works of art greedily and barefacedly as so many 'texts'.

It was in several ways a new and important experience, and it was fresh in Brecht's mind when he came over to Zurich at the end of 1947. Here he wrote and staged his *Antigone* with Helene Weigel and with Neher's settings, then worked with the Schauspielhaus company on *Puntila* and completed the 'Short Organum', a summary of his theoretical views which seems as detached and reflective as *Galileo* itself. He had not worked with Caspar Neher for sixteen years; he had not seen his wife act for ten. But he now had nine major plays which he wanted to produce; and he was determined to return to Berlin and put them on.

In a divided (and from June 1948 blockaded) Berlin, Wolfgang Langhoff had come from Zurich to take over the Deutsches Theater in the eastern half of the city, now operating once more under Max Reinhardt's name. Early in 1948 he produced *Furcht und Elend* here and staged a special ceremony in honour of Brecht's fiftieth birthday; and it was understood that

Brecht and Helene Weigel would join him in order to produce *Mother Courage* themselves. Their move was delayed by the permit troubles that were typical of those times, but at the end of October they arrived by a roundabout route in Berlin, and immediately set to work with Erich Engel once more as joint producer, and the Deutsches Theater company and staff. The impact of this historic production allowed them, with Langhoff's support, to form their own Berliner Ensemble, which split off as a semi-independent body, taking some of the Deutsches Theater's younger players, recruiting others from theatres, amateur companies or cabarets, and sharing the Deutsches Theater's stage and all its technical resources.

Round this nucleus the old team began gradually to reassemble, from America, from Switzerland, from Austria and from Germany too. Neher, Engel, Elisabeth Hauptmann, Hanns Eisler joined the directing board, together with Dessau and Ruth Berlau from the years of exile (but without Margarete Steffin, who had died). Emil Burri was in Munich; Slatan Dudow reappeared as an East German film director. Actors from Brecht's early days (Paul Bildt, G. A. Koch); actors from Piscator's and Brecht's own political productions (Busch, Gnass, Steckel, Bienert, Curt Bois): these came to form the experienced, though by no means permanent, core of a company that drew also on Zurich and Munich (Giehse, Gaugler and the scene designer Teo Otto) and on such old associates as John Heartfield and Wieland Herzfelde.

At the beginning of 1954 it expanded into a full-blown East German State theatre, moving a few hundred yards to that same Theater am Schiff-bauerdamm where *The Threepenny Opera* had been staged twenty-six years before: a sign of continuity that was certainly important to Brecht. For no-where else in the arts, except perhaps in the work of such composers as Blacher and Orff, was the connection with the pre-Nazi tradition so effectively and fruitfully re-established as here. The gap that is still so obvious in German painting, if not in German writing too, was bridged in the theatre by Brecht and his wife. Here at least the return to old-style modernism did not divert the new generation from its own tasks, but seemed to lead on to something fresh.

* * *

So, after some thirty years of unorthodox, if not always unsuccessful work in the theatre, Brecht was finally able to form his own team and set up his own theatre, equipped, as he put it,

> with good actors and all the necessary machinery, where I can try out various ideas with a number of mainly youthful collaborators, while around me on the tables lie '*Modell*-books' with thousands of photographs of our productions,

Mother Courage. *Left*: Lindtberg's 1941 production at Zurich with Therese Giehse. *Right*: Brecht's and Engel's 1949 production at the Deutsches Theater, with Helene Weigel

together with more or less precise descriptions of the most variegated problems and their provisional solution. So I have every possibility. . . .

This was not just the 'theatrical laboratory' for which he had pressed at the outset of his career, 'where actors, writers and producers can work for their own amusement, with no particular end in view'. The principle of fun (*Spass*) was still very much there, and Brecht repeatedly brought it home to his disciples; but he had also a number of aims. One was to prepare and perfect the staging of the big plays which he had brought back from exile. Another was to revive a German theatre whose degeneration under the Nazis had 'passed unnoticed, because it was accompanied by an equally vast degeneration in the capacity to judge'. The third was to train the young.

The primary principle which he taught his collaborators was that of the *Fabel* or story. The chain of events must be clearly and strongly established not just in the production, but beforehand in the actual play. Where it was not clear it was up to the 'Dramaturg' to alter the text, in order to cut unnecessary entanglements and come to the point. The play itself might be by Farquhar or Gerhart Hauptmann, Lenz or Molière, but 'the writer's words are only sacred in so far as they are true'. This went for Brecht's own words as well, and his plays were subject to continual small changes even in the course of a single run. Atmosphere and 'psychology' did not matter as such; everything would emerge given a clear and credible sequence of concrete events. 'Each scene,' says a writer in *Theaterarbeit*, is subdivided into a succession of episodes. Brecht produces as though each of these little episodes could be taken out of the play and performed on its own. They are meticulously realized, down to the smallest detail.

The chain of events had become his substitute for the tidy, comprehensive 'plot'. Thus the 'Short Organum':

> As we cannot invite the public to fling itself into the story as if it were a river, and let itself be swept vaguely to and fro, the individual events have to be knotted together in such a way that the knots are easily seen. The events must not succeed one another indistinguishably but must give us a chance to interpose our judgment.

'Playing according to the sense', the Ensemble calls it; and the sense is what Brecht tried to get clear in any play, first for himself and his collaborators, then for the audience too.

Hence, for example, his emphasis on that side of Shakespeare's work which is so often neglected: the actual story. 'It is a long time,' he found, 'since our theatre played these scenes for the events contained in them; they are played only for the outbursts of temperament which the events allow.' His analysis of *Hamlet* concludes:

> These events show the young man, already somewhat stout, making the most ineffective use of the new approach to Reason which he has picked up at the University of Wittenberg. In the feudal business to which he returns it simply hampers him. Faced with irrational practice, his reason is utterly unpractical. He falls a tragic victim to the discrepancy between such reasoning and such action.

Coriolanus, which he planned for four years with the Ensemble, was carefully gone through in order to establish the chain of events:

R.: So really the plebeians have not become united at all?

B.: On the contrary. Even the Second Citizen joins in. Only neither we nor the audience must be allowed to overlook the contradictions that are bridged over, suppressed, ruled out, now that sheer hunger makes a conflict with the Patricians unavoidable.

R.: I don't think you can find that in the text, just like that.

B.: Quite right. You have got to have read the whole play. You can't begin without having looked at the end. Later in the play this unity of the plebeians will be split up, so it is best not to take it for granted at the start, but to show it as having come about.

W.: How?

B.: We'll discuss that. I don't know. For the moment we are making an analysis. Go on . . .

Actors in Brecht's post-war productions. Angelika Hurwicz in *The Caucasian Chalk Circle*; Hans Gaugler as Läuffer in *Der Hofmeister*

In such conferences Brecht would get his colleagues to make a written or verbal précis of the play, and later they would have to write descriptions of an actual performance. Both were practice in distilling the incidents that count.

The casting of a production followed very different principles from those current in the British and American theatres. In Germany, Brecht found, 'a whole generation of actors had been chosen by false standards and trained on false doctrines', and so he preferred to work with inexperienced young players who had something of the freshness of the amateur. Even off stage such players seem to look like ordinary people: the stereotyped actor's or actress's face is conspicuously lacking, together with the stereotyped charm of its stage expression. The immense gain in reality is reinforced by Brecht's views as to these people's employment:

> Parts are allotted wrongly and thoughtlessly. As if all cooks were fat, all peasants phlegmatic, all statesmen stately. As if all who love and are loved were beautiful. As if all good speakers had a fine voice.
>
> It is pure folly to allot parts according to physical characteristics. 'He has a kingly figure.' Do all kings have to look like Edward VII? 'But he lacks a commanding presence.' Are there so few ways of commanding? 'She seems too respectable for Mother Courage.' Have a look at the fishwives.

For Brecht saw a character in terms that he regarded as unpsychological: as an inconsistent bundle of conflicting motives and interests, as inconsistent as himself, or as the world in which we all live. Such characters are never 'rounded': they have to be presented as a jagged mass of broken facets, clear and hard and often transparent, offering many irrelevancies and distortions to the eye.

'At rehearsals,' say (presumably Brecht's) notes to the *Courage* 'Modell-buch', 'it is in fact difficult to satisfy the impatience of the actors, who are used to trying to carry the audience with them, and to work out the details thoroughly and inventively one after the other, according to the principles of epic acting.' Of course the need for a cool and intelligent expository approach by his actors had long been present to Brecht's mind, and he always demanded a certain degree of detachment, a conscious interest in showing the audience the successive links of the story and the various aspects of each part. But this does not mean, as is often supposed, that he insisted on some artificially chilled style of acting. Laughton, for instance, whom he often held up as a model, was not by any means an unemotional actor; still less is Brecht's old friend Ernst Busch, as seen in his roles of Azdak and Galileo and the cook in *Mother Courage*. It was just that the ranting and emotional wallowing of the German stage had become aggravated during the Third Reich:

> Poetry had declined into declamation, art into artificiality; surface glitter and fake profundity were trumps. In lieu of the exemplary we had the symbolic; instead of passion, temperament.

And with the new players as with the old hands of the 1920s this forced him to use special means to cool the actors down.

One such means, which he used in the rehearsals for Lenz's *Hofmeister*, was to make the actors rehearse their parts in indirect speech; thus –

LISE: When she came back with his pot of coffee she found that he had bolted the door. Why was he locking himself in? No undesirable could cross their threshold at that time of night. Here is your hot drink, she said.

LÄUFFER: Thank you, said Läuffer; would she hand it to him? He pushed her quickly out of the room.

'The note sounded in these texts,' wrote Brecht, 'was that of the eye-witness report'; and this was the note which he wanted to hear persisting throughout the finished performance. Another method was to get each actor to use his own local dialect in the rehearsals, so that the real text would keep

a certain freshness, although its content was familiar. Yet another was to make the actor change the tenses in his part, to add 'the man said', 'she said', at the end of each speech, or to try and imagine each sentence in terms of 'not . . . but' – thus: 'he told her not to take the coffee away but to hand it to him' – so as to make it clear that each sentence has its unspoken ('dialectical') alternative. All these were so many aids to the actor's understanding, reflecting Brecht's conception of 'how one must rehearse; that is, carefully, listening to oneself when speaking, and making ready for observation by the audience human characteristics which one has oneself observed'.

At rehearsals there was, as in other German theatres, a prompter reading the text aloud, so that the actors learned as they went. A secretary noted the producer's suggestions on another copy; and during his last year or two Brecht started to have tape-recordings made as well. He himself did not believe that the producer should try to 'mould' the actors, or interrupt their rehearsals too freely. He 'is not one of those producers,' wrote a colleague, 'who know everything better than the actors. *Vis-à-vis* the play he takes up a position of "ignorance": he waits to see what happens. One gets the impression that Brecht doesn't know his own play: not a single sentence.' That meant that he was open to any suggestion, so long as it could be shown to him on the stage. 'Don't talk about it,' he would say. 'Act it to us.' In this way discussion was cut down, and the actor himself was made quickly aware if his proposal fell flat.

Brecht was extremely sensitive to groupings and gestures, which in all the early rehearsals were designed simply to tell the story, in an almost silent-film way, and only later became refined and polished up. In this he depended often on his old friend and associate Caspar Neher, who would not only design the setting and the costumes but in dozens of sketches would suggest the

Neher's sketch and
Brecht's realization:
'Herr Puntila
in the bath'

action too: Puntila having his bath, for example, or Matti haranguing a broom as he sweeps out the yard. We can leave aside Neher's contribution to the theatre in general: to the Deutsches Theater of the 1920s, for instance, or to Oskar Fritz Schuh's productions in West Berlin in the 1950s, or to opera at Salzburg and Glyndebourne and throughout the world. In all these fields his achievement is well known. But in Brecht's theatre he played a decisive part from school-days on, providing him with drawings and projections and teaching him to use the elements of scenery as if they were simply properties on a bigger scale. In his kind of setting every item that matters to the play is as authentic and tangible as it can be made, and all else is merely indicated: a real door, a real fence, a real street-lamp, standing solid and fit for use on an otherwise almost empty stage. 'He is a great painter,' wrote Brecht (and the reproductions of Neher's early work show that there may be something in this),

> But above all he is an ingenious story-teller. He knows better than anyone that whatever does not further the narrative harms it.

And again. 'In his designs our friend always starts with "the people themselves" and "what is happening to or through them". . . . He constructs the space for "people" to experience something in.'

The actual appearance of Neher's stage (and, following him, of Teo Otto's, Heinrich Kilger's and Karl von Appen's), with its firm, rough, well-worn details and subdued greyish colours, was very congenial to Brecht's idea of visual beauty. This idea seemed sometimes to verge (like Brecht's own clothes) on the merely drab: the dustbin romanticism of his youth, with its beggars and tarts and melancholy waste spaces. But it was not simply squalor-mongering or affectation. More than most people he looked for a certain tactile element in the visual and applied arts; and his chief pleasure

The beauty of work

came not from gaiety and colour but from materials that bore the evidence of long contact with the labour of human hands: pewter, for instance, or old leather or well-polished wood. Thus –

> Of all works my favourite
> Are those which show usage.
> The copper vessels with bumps and dented edges
> The knives and forks whose wooden handles are
> Worn down by many hands: such forms
> To me are the noblest. Likewise the flagstones around old houses
> Which have been trodden smooth by footsteps, ground away
> With tufts of grass between them: those
> Are happy achievements.
>
> Taken into use by the many
> Frequently altered, they improve their shape, become special
> By general application.
> Even fragments of sculpture
> With their sliced-off hands are dear to me. They too
> Seem to have lived. They were dropped, and yet they were carried
> They were hacked down, yet they never stood too high.
> Dilapidated buildings
> Again seem like half-completed
> Enormous projects: their fine proportions
> Can already be inferred; yet they still need
> Our understanding. At the same time
> They have served their purpose, been sloughed off. All this
> Delights me.

In the visual arts proper Brecht took remarkably little interest. The theatre used the Picasso doves—symbols of peace—for its curtain and its posters,

Visual austerity. Brecht's work-room in his flat in East Berlin

and fought many accusations of 'Formalism' on their behalf. But his own rooms in Berlin and Buckow held only some masks, a carving or two, and a few unframed Chinese wash drawings. There was no colour, no modern paintings; and his collaborators followed suit, so that in room after room in their Berlin flats one sees books, pewter, the simplest modern or Biedermeier furniture, bright lighting and bare white walls.

It was an austere visual-tactile aesthetic, whose only contact with gaiety was in the paintings of the elder Brueghel. And it meant in effect that Brecht judged every inanimate aspect of a production for its human interest. 'Furniture and properties,' says a note to *Galileo*,

> must be realistic (including the doors) and must above all have a social-historical appeal. The costumes must be individually distinguishable and must show signs of wear.

Properties naturally developed a special importance, as can be seen from the poem on 'Weigel's Properties', to be found in his *Poems*. For the basis of this aesthetic is work, and work itself was given special attention in all Brecht's productions. The jobs done by his characters, whether plucking a chicken or mending a motor-tyre or scrubbing a man's back in the bath, always had to be done properly, as if they had a life-time's practice behind them. They could never be allowed to degenerate into 'business': a botched-up imitation of activities which to Brecht were at once beautiful and socially important.

But Work has also a semi-comic reflection in Money, and Brecht delighted to emphasize the sordid financial details which nicer-minded producers would have skipped. In his writings, in his productions and even in his private talk, he adopted the same uninhibited attitude towards money as the orthodox theatre now pretends to adopt towards sex. Thus Helene Weigel as *Mother Courage* would bite a coin to see that it was genuine (just as one of the characters in the 1932 *Die Mutter* had done), then stow it away in an old purse which opened and shut with an extra loud click. This was quite deliberate, and reflects both a genuine fascination with money's mechanics – the comic attitudes to which it leads men – and a lively concern with its moral and social implications. Similarly Samuel Butler, so Brecht wrote in an early review of *The Way of All Flesh*,

> is one of those bourgeois writers who can be counted on the fingers of one hand: those in whose work money occupies the place which it does in bourgeois life. With the others (and one can list five of them by listing the five most successful writers of our day) the fact that money-making is never the subject of their work makes one suspect that in their case it may be the object instead.

'People treat Business as tedious but inevitable,' says his note to *Mother Courage*, 'like the scenic descriptions in a novel. The "business atmosphere" is simply the air which we breathe, and take more or less for granted.' Any method of breaking this peculiar barrier was welcome. Even by quite crude means, the actor must try to show the economic basis of his role.

*   *   *

All this implies an immense care for detail, with a consequent slowing down of the whole tempo of Brecht's work. The Ensemble's productions of *Galileo*, *Tage der Commune* and *Coriolanus* were already being planned when *Theaterarbeit* (the illustrated account of the company's work) was published in 1952. Of these the first was in rehearsal at the time of Brecht's death four years later; the second was staged in October 1962, the third not till September 1964. For a single production might demand between sixty and a hundred rehearsals, and there was no economic pressure to compel any tightening-up. The rush and tension of *The Threepenny Opera* in 1928, or even of the Swiss *Antigone* in 1948, seemed very remote; the old electric atmosphere had gone. And yet the knotting-together and presentation of all these details (of acting, of setting, of properties, of music and sound effects) had to be on the same clear-cut, dispassionate, episodic lines as Brecht had always preached.

A clear, brilliant light must be thrown on the finished article, so that the audience might judge it as keenly as 'an acrobatic turn on the music-hall stage. Bright spotlights extinguish the features. Shadows, if only relative, hamper the dialogue that issues from them. . . .'

A song in
*The Threepenny
Opera* of 1928.
Projected title,
visible lights,
visible organ-
pipes, placards,
curtain-wires

Give us some light on the stage, electrician. How can we
Playwrights and actors put forward
Our view of the world in half-darkness. The dim twilight
Induces sleep. But we need the spectator's
Wakeful-, even watchfulness. Let them
Do their dreaming in the light. The short night-time
We now and then require can be shown by moons
Or lamps, likewise our playing
Can make clear what time of day it is
Whenever needed . . .

The analogy of the boxing-ring still to some extent held good. And so did
the 'epic' methods which Brecht had derived on the musical side from the
Beggar's Opera and on the technical partly from Piscator: the low white
curtains, for instance, running on visible steel wires stretched across the
proscenium opening –

        on them
You shall project the titles of the events
To come, for the sake of tension and that
The right thing may be expected. And please make
My curtain half-height, don't cut the stage off.
Leaning back, let the spectator
Notice the busy preparations being so
Ingeniously made for him, a metallic moon
Comes swinging down, a shingle roof
Is carried in; don't show him too much
But show something. And let him observe
That this is not magic but
Work, my friends.

A scene-change
in *Die Mutter* of
1951. Projected
title on the
half-curtain,
with background
projection visible
above

1916. Unermüdlich bekämpfen die
Bolschewiki den imperialistischen Krieg

– the musical instruments lowered from the flies in *Mother Courage*; the
titles and formal presentation of the songs:

> Cut away the songs from the rest!
> By some symbol of music, by change of lighting
> By titles, by pictures now show
> That the sister art is
> Coming on stage. . . .

It had become a theatre of significant, laboriously polished fragments, where
the labour itself came first and the audience second. But the presentation
was still that of the sport- and machine-minded theatre of the 1920s, and, to
a great extent, of the didactic platforms that followed.

The perfect solution for each play, once arrived at, had to be fixed; and
so the Ensemble began to compile 'Models': collections of photographs which
made a complete record of a production. These were designed partly as a
check: 'to test the sense and beauty of our dispositions', writes Ruth
Berlau, to whom this development was mainly due. But at the same time
they were meant to be a permanent guide for other producers who wished
to stage Brecht's big plays – *Mother Courage*, *Puntila*, *The Caucasian Chalk
Circle*, and also the earlier *Die Mutter* – whether with the Ensemble itself or
elsewhere. Probably no other producer has ever used photography to such
an extent, or been able to standardize the interpretation of his plays; and
the results were uneven. Some producers would make a flat copy of the
'Model', perpetuating Brecht's mannerisms without showing their *raison
d'être*. Others followed his principle that 'the main effect of studying the
solution of certain problems should be to make one aware of the problems
themselves', and changed Brecht's solution wherever another answer

The half-curtain in *Puntila* of 1950. A verse of the 'Puntila-lied'
being sung between scenes

seemed to suit their actors and their audience better. When Brecht himself
produced *Mother Courage* at the Munich Kammerspiele in 1950 he used his
own 'Model' yet tried to approach each problem afresh. The actors there,
says a writer in *Theaterarbeit*, found that 'Model or no Model, they could
show what they liked. If it was good it was accepted at once'.

It was this remarkable combination of freshness and care that made the
special force of Brecht's company, rather than any particular recipes which
they employed. Every small-part player and stage hand could feel that he
was contributing, and that his suggestions would be seriously entertained.
Such qualities are less easy to pin down than superficialities of style, and so
in Western Europe at least it is largely by the latter that the Ensemble has
become known. This is unfortunate, because there are several respects in
which Brecht's example is dangerous, and might be fatal if followed on the
non-German stage. Where an imitation Stanislavsky production, for instance,
can be very satisfactory in its way, an imitation Brecht production might
easily become tinged with affectation, and dated at that. Yet something
turned the Berliner Ensemble almost from the first into one of the finest
companies in the world, and it was not merely Helene Weigel's gifts as an
organizer and leader. It was not the individual talents of its members, for,
if one excepts Helene Weigel herself and Therese Giehse, these were no
greater than those of many other permanent or *ad hoc* groups. Nor was it
even the very generous material support which the East German Government gave. The Ensemble's distinctive strength lay in a common interest,
a common keenness and a common desire for perfection, which allowed it
to play together as a brilliant and apparently happy team. And these were
undoubtedly traceable back to Brecht.

They sprang not from Brecht's methods as a producer so much as from
the company's confidence in him as a great playwright, and from the per-

sonal authority which he therefore enjoyed. Here, in a time of the greatest artistic, political and social confusion in Germany (and in the world at large), was a writer who used a fresh, individual dramatic language to say something both intelligible and serious. Here was an artist who recognized the social content and impact of his work without letting that recognition knock all the guts out of him. Here was an exceptionally obstinate man who was prepared to defend these qualities to the last against the rival pulls of Western and (as we shall see) Eastern orthodoxy. Such characteristics were only indirectly connected with the strengths and weaknesses of his production methods, and though he did also stamp these methods on his players the chief strength of his example lay in his attitude towards life and art. Like their own liveliness and sense of purpose, his influence on them was not confined to the stage.

SIX

The Theory

So far we have dealt with Brecht's practice and his intentions without reference to his dramatic theory, simply because it has so often been a cause of confusion. In Western Europe and the United States it is better known than either his plays or his actual methods of production, and for this reason it is often wrongly assumed that these merely follow the lines which it – or its interpreters – lay down. Words like 'Gestus', 'Gestisch', 'Epic Theatre', 'Alienation', 'Estrangement', the 'V-Effect' (or E-Effect, or A-Effect, according to the translator's whim; the innocent reader gets the impression that there is a whole stock of these alphabetical horrors) are taken as describing sacred principles of the Brechtian Theatre, so that almost anything, down to and including errors and accidents, can be interpreted in their murky light. It becomes simpler and more entertaining for the critic to write about the theory, which he can find discussed by a dozen other critics in his own language, than to tackle the plays themselves. As a result, the Ensemble's productions get treated as examples of a new theoretical approach, when they ought to be judged primarily as realizations of the playwright's work.

The basis of Brecht's theoretical writings is his strong dislike of the orthodox theatre, and especially of the ranting and pretentious German classical stage. 'With us,' wrote Brecht of his fellow-Germans,

> everything easily slips into the insubstantial and unapproachable, and we begin to talk of Weltanschauung when the world in question has already dissolved. Even materialism is little more than an idea with us. Sexual pleasure with us turns into marital duty, the delights of art subserve education, and by learning we understand not an enjoyable process of finding out but the forcible shoving of one's nose into things.

On the stage this is reflected in an empty, synthetic 'temperament' which

> is worked off in artificial or unnecessarily noisy declamation, and tries to blanket the emotions of the personage with the emotion of the actor. There is little chance of hearing any genuine human voice, and one gets the impression that life must be exactly like a theatre instead of the theatre being just like life.

So many critics who do not understand the language have dismissed Brecht as a typical German that it is important to get this straight. Certain of Brecht's theoretical recommendations can only be understood in terms of the particular German (and Austrian) tradition against which he was revolting. They may confuse anyone who tries to apply them in a theatre where this tradition no longer holds.

This does not mean that his general objection to the orthodox theatre is not valid for other countries too. From America to Russia, the theatre has designs on the spectator's emotions which tend to prevent him from using his head. The audience is drawn into the 'plot' and made to identify itself with the characters; the means by which this is achieved falsify the picture of reality; and the audience is too contentedly hypnotized to see that it is false. However brilliant the production, its effect (if not its object) is to put us in an uncritical frame of mind. 'Let us enter one of these establishments,' says Brecht's 'Short Organum' of 1948,

> and see the effect which it has on the spectators. . . . True: their eyes are open, but they stare rather than see, just as they listen rather than hear. They look at the stage as if in a trance – an expression which comes from the Middle Ages, the days of witches and priests. Seeing and hearing are activities, and can be pleasant ones, but these people seem relieved of any activity and like men to whom something is being done. This detached state, where they seem to be given over to vague but profound sensations, grows deeper the better the work of the actors, and so we, as we do not approve of this situation, should like them to be as bad as possible.

And the next paragraph:

> As for the world portrayed there, the world from which slices are cut in order to produce these moods and fluctuating sensations, its appearance is such, produced from such slight and wretched stuff as a handful of cardboard, a little miming, a bit of text, that one has to admire the theatre folk who, with so feeble a reflection of the real world, can move the feelings of their audience so much more strongly than does the world itself.

A synthetic emotional tension wrecks the sense, and 'the incidents proper to the play disappear like meat in a cunningly mixed sauce with a taste of its own'.

This is just what many theatre-goers want: in fact, 'the majority', suggests Brecht in a poem of 1934. They prefer neither to see the real world on the stage nor to get to grips with it:

> . . . Exhausted
> By the unceasing struggles of their daily life they await with greed
> Just what repels the others. A little massage
> For their flaccid spirits. A little tautening
> Of slackened nerves. Easy adventure, a sense of magic hands
> Bearing them off from a world they cannot master
> And have to give up.

Of course the orthodox theatre can fulfil this task, and it is no part of Brecht's argument to suggest that it does not. But the task itself seems morally and intellectually degrading (and politically contemptible too) because it makes it harder for the audience to understand the world in which it really lives. Even the world of the past becomes falsified when it is presented to the emotions in this way; psychologically as well as physically, the classics then come to be played in fancy dress. 'Our theatres no longer have either the capacity or the wish to tell these stories, even the relatively recent ones of the great Shakespeare, at all clearly: i.e. to make the connection of events credible.' Again, 'the sensations, insights and impulses of the chief characters are forced on us, and so we learn no more about society than we can get from the "setting" ' 'That is the sort of theatre', concludes the relevant section of the 'Short Organum', 'which we face in our undertakings, and so far it has been fully able to transmute our optimistic friends, whom we know as the children of the scientific era, into a cowed, credulous, hypnotized mass.'

He began setting down such ideas on the theory of the theatre soon after he moved to Berlin in the mid-1920's. There his supporter Herbert Ihering was in charge of the theatre section of the *Berliner Börsen-Courier*, which not only kept Brecht busy with invitations to join in various slightly factitious public discussions ('What do you imagine your public wants of you?' 'How ought the classics to be performed nowadays?' and so on) but offered him a platform for anything he cared to write. At first his essays there, like all his public statements of the time, were fairly aggressive: attacks in the name of 'the younger generation' on virtually every feature of the established German theatre. Thus in 1926 he was contrasting the 'elegance, lightness, dryness, objectivity' of any sporting manifestation with the synthetic and exaggerated passions of the theatre, and lamenting the latter's lack of *fun*: of *Spass*, a concept which always remained important to him. He was determinedly rationalistic and anti-emotional, if we can believe the very interesting interview printed in *Die literarische Welt* the same year; empathy – the whole process of identification of actor with part and audience with actor – seemed to him just to confuse the public's understanding of the play. 'I don't let my feelings intrude in my dramatic work', he is reported as saying, and again: 'I appeal to the reason.'

This rationalism was one element in his concept of the epic theatre, which was now beginning to take shape. Brecht was neither the first nor by any means the only person to apply this phrase to the avant-garde theatre of the 1920's, but he gave it a distinctive sense, identifying it with three specific concerns of his own: the unemotional (or *sachlich*) approach, the new economic and social subject-matter of such plays as *Joe P. Fleischhacker* and Leo

Lania's *Konjunktur*, and also 'playing from memory':[1] acting, as it were, in quotation marks and from foreknowledge, without ever pretending that cast and producer are unaware what is about to happen. By 1927 he was calling for the establishment of 'a great epic and documentary theatre', and if the phrase itself originated in the traditional antithesis of 'epic' and 'dramatic' this first public proclamation of Brecht's concept clearly owes something to his experience of Piscator's professedly epic theatre, with its use of documents and projections. 'To expound the principles of the epic theatre in a few catchphrases', he wrote that November,

> is not possible. They still mostly need to be worked out in detail, and include representation by the actor, stage technique, dramaturgy, stage music, use of the film, etc. The essential point of the epic theatre is perhaps that it appeals less to the feelings than to the spectator's reason. Instead of sharing an experience the spectator must come to grips with things. At the same time it would be quite wrong to try and deny emotion to this kind of theatre.

Strictly speaking, 'epic' is an Aristotelian term for a form of narrative that is 'not tied to time', whereas a 'tragedy' is bound by the unities of time and place. It is the same loose linking-together of events as we find in the Shakespearean history or the picaresque novel, and it is in this sense that it was used by the eighteenth-century German writers – by Goethe and Schiller, for instance, in their correspondence, or by Büchner's predecessor Lenz. Where English criticism uses the term to convey heroic scale, more or less irrespective of the type of work, and Romain Rolland in France could refer to his revolutionary dramas as 'tout un théâtre épique' in German its primary meaning is a particular narrative form.

In this sense it was plainly applicable to the kind of theatre which was developing out of the old close-knit naturalism of Ibsen and Hauptmann: from Reinhardt's Shakespearean productions in the early years of the century, through the Büchner revival and the fluid, if flabby, construction of many Expressionist plays. It applied to the new narrative technique of the cinema: of Chaplin and Keaton, Tom Mix and Douglas Fairbanks; as well as to the methods of men like Griffith and Eisenstein whom we know as 'epic' directors in the English sense. It was applied in literature not only to the purely picaresque novel like *Schweik* but to any breaking down of the old conventions of the 'plot': whether by the new 'reportage' or in the novels

---

[1] A diary note of Elisabeth Hauptmann's for 23 March 1926, says 'Brecht has found the formula for 'epic theatre': playing from memory (quoting gestures and attitudes) ...' This suggests that he had been aware of the phrase before deciding its meaning.

of Joyce and Dos Passos and Alfred Döblin. This is the basic meaning of 'epic' even in Brecht's use of the term: a sequence of incidents or events, narrated without artificial restrictions as to time, place or relevance to a formal 'plot'. But the very fact that it was annexed by this particular group of writers at this particular time – by Bronnen about 1922 or 1923;[1] by Piscator and Alfons Paquet in 1924; by Brecht apparently in 1926 – meant that it came also to be associated with the new formal means which they then evolved: with Piscator's use of film, for instance, or Brecht's scene titles and half-curtains; even, as we have seen, with his general campaign against a turgid, ranting, over-emotional style. 'This intermediate form,' wrote Döblin in 1929,

> always arose (and arises) wherever the coldness of the author's feelings stops him from associating himself intimately with the fate of his characters or the development of the plot. . . .[2]

This definition was not true of Homer or Shakespeare or Hašek. It was not true of Chaplin and Cecil B. de Mille, and it would have made nonsense to Aristotle, from whom the term arose. But it did seem in tune with the 'new matter-of-factness' of the machine age; and when it was made it was roughly true of Brecht.

So 'epic theatre' had become a somewhat confused term, narrowed down to cover certain fashionable trends, anti-Reinhardt and anti-Expressionist, even before Brecht started writing his major theoretical essays. These did not start to appear at all systematically until 1930, when he had already ended his association with Piscator and was following *The Threepenny Opera* with the first of his musical-didactic works. In that year, when the end of the Weimar Republic was already in sight, he added the first notes to his plays and issued the first of a new series of publications: the grey paper-bound volumes called *Versuche*, or 'Attempts' (as had been Lessing's plays). They open with this slightly aggressive announcement:

[1] According to *Arnolt Bronnen gibt zu Protokoll* (Rowohlt, Hamburg, 1954), p. 144, the word was applied to Bronnen's plays *Excesse* and *Katalaunische Schlacht*.

[2] Alfred Döblin: 'Vom Bau des epischen Werkes' (1929), quoted in Piscator: *Das Politische Theater*, Berlin, 1929. Döblin's own novel *Berlin Alexanderplatz*, Berlin, 1929, is broken by formal narrative captions, summarizing the story to come, that are closely akin to the sub-titles used in Brecht's productions. E.g. before Book 1: 'Here, at the beginning of the story, Franz Biberkopf leaves Tegel prison, whither he had been led by his previous aimless existence. He finds it difficult to re-establish himself in Berlin, but none the less he succeeds in the end. This makes him happy, and he now takes an oath to lead a decent life.'

Compare also the chapter headings to Erich Kästner's *Fabian*, Stuttgart, 1931.

The publication of the *Versuche* takes place at a moment when certain works are intended less as individual experiences (with the character of finished works) than as a means of using (transforming) certain institutes and institutions (i.e. with the character of experiments) and with the object of continually illuminating by their coherence each of the very varied operations undertaken.

The notes of 1930 to *The Threepenny Opera* and *Mahagonny*, in other words, appeared as part of Brecht's general war on the theatrical and operatic apparatus of the day: a 'continuation by other means' of the new form of drama which he was simultaneously starting to establish outside.

The working out of a new apparatus on the basis of a new society is something not covered by the Aristotelian use of 'epic', and it is a good deal more radical than the particular technical methods for which Piscator had adopted the term. But Brecht had these meanings in mind even while starting to use the slogan 'epic theatre' in a way that more and more restricted it to his own 'attempts'; and this accounts for many of the inconsistencies in his theory. 'Modern theatre is Epic theatre,' he proclaimed in number 2 of the new volumes, in the notes to *Mahagonny*; then went on to show in schematized (and often-quoted) form the 'shift of balance' or 'shift of accent' which this theatre demanded:

Dramatic form of Theatre	*Epic form of Theatre*
Plot	Narrative
implicates the spectator in a stage situation	turns the spectator into an observer, but
wears down his power of action	arouses his power of action
. . .	. . .
the human being is taken for granted	the human being is the object of the inquiry
he is unalterable	he is alterable and able to alter
eyes on the finish	eyes on the course
one scene makes another	each scene for itself
growth	montage
. . .	. . . [1]

Lantern-slide sub-titles, projections, Weill's music are all counted as part of the new system, which emphasizes the 'direct, didactic' aspect of the text. 'Feeling' is opposed to 'Reason', and the whole object is summed up at the end of the notes: 'Thus to develop the means of entertainment into an object of instruction, and to change certain institutions from places of amusement into organs of public communication.'

[1] Only eight out of the nineteen points are quoted here.

Epic Theatre, 1931.
Brecht's production
of *Mann ist Mann*
in Berlin

'Narrative' rather than 'plot', and 'each scene for itself' are true picaresque principles, while 'montage' was a fashionable 1920s word. But all the other points are new, and they change the meaning of 'epic' not only to exclude all idea of entertainment but to rule out the traditional conceptions of 'catharsis' and 'empathy' as well. One need only look at Brecht's plays of this time – at *Mahagonny* itself, to start with – to see how little he really believed that entertainment must be scrapped. But the Aristotelian theory of catharsis, or purging of the emotions by self-identification (empathy) with those of the actor, was an essential part of the hypnotic, anti-critical theatre which Brecht so loathed; it meant 'carrying the audience with one', 'losing oneself in the play'. So in the essay on the *Dreigroschenprozess*, also written in 1930, he began to set up the idea of a 'non-Aristotelian drama', although 'epic' was itself an Aristotelian term: and later he wrote *Senora Carrar*, the least typical of all his plays, as a piece of deliberately 'Aristotelian, i.e. empathy-, drama'. A good many of his notes on the plays were presented in the *Versuche* under this general heading of 'On a non-Aristotelian drama', though at first he seemed to prefer the title 'On a dialectical drama' which was announced at the back of the first *Versuche* volume but only survived as a group of notes among Brecht's posthumously published papers. Already, because empathy depends on illusion, Brecht treats the 'epic methods' of the 1920s as something more than new narrative aids; they become means of breaking the magic spell, of jerking the spectator out of his torpor and making him use his critical sense.

His third volume, containing the notes on *The Threepenny Opera*, elaborates the need for sub-titles on lantern-slides as a means of 'literarizing' the theatre. They bring it into line with other 'institutions' (i.e. presumably, the newspaper, the poster hoarding and the already defunct silent film) and encourage that boxing-ring attitude of 'smoking and observing' which Brecht wanted his audiences to have. Songs and sub-titles alike are presented as a deliberate means of interrupting the play: of taking the wind out of the actors' sails and showing the actual mechanics of the work. Visible musicians, visible lights, have to be accompanied by a deliberate breaking of the tension and disillusionment of the actor. He must 'use quite different means to draw attention to events which had previously been announced in the sub-titles, so that their substance held no element of surprise'; he 'must not just sing but show a man singing'. The new principle was that 'der Zeigende gezeigt wird': that the process of showing must itself be shown.

For Brecht believed that it is the actor's business not to express feeling but to 'show attitudes' or *Gesten*. In the accompanying essay on the *Dreigroschen-prozess* he developed this conception of the 'Gestus' a good deal further, speaking not only of individual 'Gesten' but of 'Gestisches Material' and

Epic Acting, 1931.
Peter Lorre in
Mann ist Mann

the 'Grund-' (or basic) 'gestus' of a play. This idea, closely akin to those of Behaviourism,[1] is a central part of his doctrine, but it is hard to make it so in English, for the equivalent term 'gest' (meaning 'bearing, carriage, mien') has unfortunately become an obsolete word. It is at once gesture and gist, attitude and point: one aspect of the relation between two people, studied singly, cut to essentials and physically or verbally expressed. It excludes the psychological, the sub-conscious, the metaphysical unless they can be conveyed in concrete terms. 'All feelings must be externalized,' Brecht later wrote: hence the silent-film quality of certain episodes in his plays, or the very individual kind of acting which he demanded of Peter Lorre in his self-styled 'epic' production of *Mann ist Mann* in 1931. This led him to defend Lorre against critics who felt that the actor had not given a 'powerful' enough performance, and objected to his apparently mannered speech. The fragmentary, episodic style of acting, wrote Brecht in reply, was meant to show a man not as a consistent whole but as a contradictory, ever-changing character whose unity comes 'despite, or rather by means of, interruptions and jumps'. The delivery of the lines was broken to show successive 'Gesten'; and the whole sequence of attitudes shown demanded a leisurely timing. It was up to the spectator himself to see that they hung together.

It must be remembered that Brecht was applying this method of production to, and speaking with such solemnity of, an early play which had

[1] Behaviourism itself was sometimes seen as a 1920s phenomenon. 'If dadaism is the last word in art, if jazz is the omega in music, why may we not have a similar transvaluation in psychology?' (A. A. Roback: *Behaviourism and Psychology*, Cambridge, Mass., 1923, p. 27.)

many frivolous and even silly features, and little relation to what he was writing in 1931. Its Anglo-Indian setting, as Feuchtwanger pointed out, 'is in every respect the invention of an Augsburger; the soldiers are a quite childish derivation from Kipling; and the central point of the story is an exceptionally feeble gag with an artificial elephant'. It is misleading to treat this play itself as the first 'epic', as some interpreters do, for it is formally no more epic than *Baal*. But the production was of great importance to Brecht and to his theory, for not only was it in other respects new and compelling, but it marked a deliberate attempt to hold the spectator at arm's-length, so that he would keep his critical judgment throughout. In terms not unlike Claudel's Brecht asked the audience for 'an attitude corresponding roughly to the reader's method of thumbing through a book and checking back'; while the actor was advised, much as in Pirandello, 'not to make the spectator identify himself with individual sentences and thus get caught up in contradictions, but to *keep him out of them*'. This apparently new technique may reflect some of the methods which Seami had recommended to the Japanese Nō actors: the notion, for instance, that the actor only tires the audience by trying to 'carry them with him', and ought to hold himself back so as to give them a breathing-space; or the idea that he should confront them with 'an emotion which they do not expect'.[1] But such precedents were unknown to Brecht when he actually wrote this play; or even *The Threepenny Opera* and *Mahagonny*; and his whole picture of the 'epic theatre' seems then to have been in a very sketchy state. It is only with the didactic works of the 1930s that the new theoretical requirements are clearly posed and met.

The notes on the chief of these, *Die Mutter*, were published in 1933 and show an increasing concern with the spectator's detachment. The actor must 'make himself observed standing *between* the spectator and the text'. The spectator must be stopped from 'losing himself'; he must be split from his fellow-spectators; he must not congeal with them in a quivering emotional jelly. Here Brecht pointed to the example of Helene Weigel, who in the Nō-style opening of the play spoke

> the sentences as if they were in the third person, and so she not only refrained from pretending in fact to be or to claim to be Vlassova, and in fact to be speaking those sentences, but actually prevented the spectator from transferring himself to a particular room, as habit and indifference might demand, and imagining himself to be the invisible eye-witness and eavesdropper of a unique intimate occasion.

[1] Arthur Waley: *The Nō Plays of Japan*, London, 1921, pp. 44, 47. About this time, Elisabeth Hauptmann wrote a radio play expounding and discussing Seami's ideas.

Epic Acting, 1951. Helene Weigel in the
opening scene of *Die Mutter*

At the same time he gave the first proper definition of the 'non-Aristotelian drama',

> Just as it refrains from handing its hero over to the world as if it were his inescapable fate, so it would not dream of handing the spectator over to an inspiring theatrical experience. Anxious to teach the spectator a quite definite practical attitude, directed towards changing the world, it must begin by making him adopt in the theatre a quite different attitude from what he is used to.

In this sort of play the theory seems to have a creative, not merely an explanatory part; for here is the new, cool, socially-orientated theatre at which Brecht was aiming. The earlier plays had often been critical of our world, but there is no sign that they ever inspired anybody to want to change it. *Die Mutter* not only fired its audiences with revolutionary ideas but was outside the scope of the established theatre, which, short of re-writing the whole work, has always found it too tough a play to 'theatre down'.

The Nazi triumph of 1933 put a stop to any immediate hope of transforming the theatrical apparatus, and cut the ground from under Brecht's new didactic stage. But so far as the theory was concerned he went on building on the existing basis, even though it no longer seemed so much to dictate the actual forms of his plays. The pseudo-Shakespearean *Die Rundköpfe und die Spitzköpfe*, for instance, 'unlike *Die Mutter*, is addressed to a "wide" public and takes more account of purely entertainment considerations'. It is cast in more or less orthodox form, and the topical, political element in it is not deeply ingrained in the work but superficial, as if grafted on. None the less, Brecht still demanded the same unorthodox style of production when the play was staged in Denmark in 1936. Once again (so his notes show) the lights were visible; the mechanism of the two pianos was displayed; the actors addressed the audience direct; a nun brought in a gramophone and placed it on the stage; and there were deliberate parodies of Shakespearean acting and the French eighteenth-century conversation piece. In an exaggerated outburst of 'lofty and passionate' acting the actors were made to carry modern umbrellas, in the hope that

> the spectator, having had his attention drawn to the outmoded nature of such conduct, went on to notice that lofty speech is bound up with the individual problems of the upper class.

– which is perhaps one of the oddest apologies ever to have been made for an ordinary 1920s joke. 'I am the Einstein of the new stage form,' he told Mordecai Gorelik about this time: an ambition which must have helped to compensate for his practical isolation. In the 'Society for Theatrical Science', which he was then planning to form, he hoped that Auden, Burian, Eisenstein, Okhlopkhov, Piscator, Tretiakoff and a number of others would join him in pooling experimental methods and discussing their results.[1]

By now he had formulated a concept which had already been anticipated in other terms in his earlier writing but seems none the less to have been something of a revelation to him, first subserving, then supplanting, the 'epic theatre' in his interests. This was the famous 'Verfremdung' – estrangement, alienation or disillusion in English; dépaysement, étrangement or distanciation in French: a wide choice of equivalents, none of which is exactly right. With 'Verfremdung' went the 'Verfremdungseffekt', where 'Effekt' corresponded to our own stage use of the word 'effects': a *means* by which an effect of estrangement could be got. Both these new words have a single object: to show everything in a fresh and unfamiliar light, so that the spectator is brought to look critically even at what he has so far taken for granted. Thus –

> To see one's mother as a man's wife one needs a V-Effekt; this is provided, for example, when one acquires a stepfather. If one sees one's form-master hounded by the bailiffs a V-Effekt occurs: one is jerked out of a relationship in which the form-master seems big into one where he seems small.

'Verfremdung', in fact, is not simply the breaking of illusion (though that is one means to the end); and it does not mean 'alienating' the spectator in the sense of making him hostile to the play. It is a matter of detachment, of reorientation: exactly what Shelley meant when he wrote that poetry 'makes familiar objects to be as if they were not familiar', or Schopenhauer when he claimed that art must show 'common objects of experience in a light that is at once clear and unfamiliar'. The value of this conception for Brecht was that it offered a new way of judging and explaining those means of achieving critical detachment which he had hitherto called 'epic'. It did not, so far as the outsider can see, lead him to change those means or introduce new ones, or even to make the overdue distinction between them and 'epic' narration proper; for 'Verfremdung' and 'Episierung' seem to have been used by him to mean exactly the same thing.[2] But it gave a rational basis to conclusions at which he had already arrived.

Brecht took over this phrase and applied it to his own work in the notes on

---

[1] Others mentioned in Brecht's papers are Per Knutzon, Per Lindberg, Nordahl Grieg, Per Lagerquist, Slatan Dudow, Karl Koch, Georg Hoellering, Hanns Eisler, Fritz Kortner, Max Gorelik, Archibald Macleish, Jean Renoir, Léon Moussinac, Christopher Isherwood and Rupert Doone. Nothing seems to have come of this scheme.

[2] Compare the two examples given on pp. 155-6 above. The former is given by Brecht under the heading of 'Episierungen', the latter under that of 'Verfremdung'.

The Chinese actor.
Mei Lan-fang
(from a book in Brecht's
possession)

Die Rundköpfe und die Spitzköpfe, where he suggests that the three or four chief incidents in each scene ought to be treated

> as self-contained scenes and raised – by means of inscriptions, musical or sound effects and the actors' way of playing – above the level of the everyday, the obvious, the expected (i.e. estranged).

Its obvious derivation is from that 'Priem Ostrannenija', or 'device of making strange' (or 'Verfremdungseffekt') of the Russian Formalist critics which will be discussed in more detail in the next chapter; and it seems significant that conception and catch-word alike only enter his work after his first visit to Moscow in 1935. There in the Chinese actor Mei Lan-fang, whom he saw perform without make-up, costume or lighting, he had found an actor who seemed to stand aside from his part and 'makes it quite clear that he knows he is being observed'.[1] This fitted Brecht's preference for any performance that exposed the technique and the process of 'showing', and he described Mei Lan-fang's methods in his first essay on the means by which the actor could secure a 'V-Effekt'. Later essays, like 'Die Strassenszene' and 'Neue Technik der Schauspielkunst' (both of 1940), out-

---

[1] A photograph reproduced in *Brecht on Theatre* (Methuen, London, and Hill & Wang, New York, 1964) shows Mei with Eisenstein, Tairoff and Tretiakoff. Brecht said it was 'a room full of specialists' and Tretiakoff was a friend of his, thus the photograph is some indication that these men, who certainly knew all about the Formalist doctrines, could have been in the audience with him.

lined a whole range of methods by which such detachment could be achieved. The actor must demonstrate like a bystander describing an accident; he must remember his first reactions to the character whom he represents, and keep them fresh; must view him from a socially critical angle; must show his own point of view; must treat the story not as 'broadly human' but as historical, unique. The aim was the same as before: as in *Die Mutter* the actor must stand between the audience and the part; as in *Mann ist Mann* he must keep the spectator out; as in Pirandello he must coldly analyse his feelings; as in *Edward II* he must achieve a clear, cool, objective style. The point was simple. It was for the author and the producer to present the world in an unfamiliar light. It was the actor's responsibility not to take the edge off that unfamiliarity by losing himself in the play.

Theoretical notes and essays of this type are something of a snowball: a statement is made, then another statement has to follow to explain what the first statement means, and in the end a whole agglomeration seems to have set itself in motion, without the direction followed always being what its author wants. Already Brecht had had to qualify certain of his ideas; to insist, for instance, that 'renouncing empathy in no way meant renouncing the emotions, however badly abused they had been', or to point out that 'the actual practice of the V-Effekt is not half so unnatural as its description'. The rational aspect of the theory had been overstressed, its aesthetic implications hardly touched, its relevance to an impending social and theatrical reorganization taken for granted. But since *Die Mutter* the social-cum-aesthetic situation had altered; there was less and less logical connection between the snowball and the type of play which Brecht was actually writing; and where he tried to establish it it seemed forced. In *Senora Carrar* and in the individual scenes of *Furcht und Elend* he had returned to certain principles of the naturalistic stage; in *Galileo* and *Mother Courage* he had written 'epic' plays in the old picaresque sense. In all these works the entertainment aspect was, if not more important, at least much more plainly obvious than the didactic, and convincing major characters were at last beginning to emerge. Accordingly he set to work about 1937 to write a large-scale theoretical work in dialogue form, where four or five characters would discuss and resume all his ideas about the theatre together with something of his own practice. He called this plan *Der Messingkauf*, after the story of the man who buys wind instruments not for the music they make but for the brass they are made of. Unfortunately it was never completed, and all that has come down to us is a group of lively and stimulating fragments together with a number of much later poems on the theatre which Brecht classified under the same title. He wrote few theoretical notes or essays (so far as we know) in America, and it was not until his return to Europe after the war that he again

Epic Theatre, 1951. Three scenes from Brecht's
production of *Die Mutter*

took up the idea of a wholesale reconsideration of his principles, basing himself on the now abandoned *Messingkauf Dialogues*.

*   *   *

The 'Short Organum for the Theatre' was finished in 1948. This beautifully-written study, with its Aristotelian title and its paragraphs on the apparent model of the *Poetics*, takes the existing edifice of Brecht's theory and shifts it on to new foundations. 'The battle was for a theatre fit for the scientific age,' he says of his earlier theoretical writings (for since the writing of *Galileo* he had begun to interpret his own work in scientific rather than political terms).

> And yet what we achieved . . . was not science but theatre, and the accumulated innovations worked out during the Nazi period and the war – when practical demonstration was impossible – compel some attempt to set this kind of theatre in its aesthetic background, or anyhow to sketch for it the outlines of a conceivable aesthetic.

No longer is instruction the object, and the transformation of society, theatre and all, the only criterion: Brecht's theatre is now to be justified as entertainment. 'Let us therefore cause general dismay,' the introduction concludes,

> by revoking our decision to emigrate from the domain of the merely pleasant, and even more general dismay by announcing our decision to take up lodging there. Let us treat the theatre as a place of entertainment, as is proper in an aesthetic discussion, and try to discover which type of entertainment suits us best.

The theatre's moral and ritual implications take second place; pleasure becomes its 'noblest function'. 'Even when people speak of higher and lower degrees of pleasure, art stares impassively back at them; for it wishes to fly high and low and to be left in peace, so long as it can give us pleasure.'

Yet this change means less than at first appears. For the newly-admitted aesthetic pleasure is treated as comparable with that of the scientist: it is the pleasure which comes from seeing a beautiful and efficient piece of mechanism, or piece of reasoning, or piece of social analysis. 'Science and art meet on this ground, that both are there to make men's life easier . . .'; and science itself embraces the science of society, so that only a theatrical representation which squares with the latter – i.e. with the Marxist analysis, which is all that the science of society seems to have meant to Brecht – can have this particular appeal. The old social and critical attitude is still there, absorbed into the new aesthetic, and all the rest follows: 'Verfremdung'; the emphasis on attitudes; all the essentials of the 'epic theatre' except the name; even such favourite details as titles, projections and a special lighting for

Stanislavsky,
1902

songs. The basis of the argument has been changed to correspond with Brecht's real beliefs; the flavour of the writing has become reflective rather than polemic; he has halted the snowball and tried to put it on a permanent plinth. But not a single specific recommendation has been dropped.

A new theatre is still envisaged, but it is now to be distinct from other 'institutes and institutions', and it is only vaguely sketched. The right scientific, sceptical spirit is to be found, Brecht thinks, among the industrial workers, and so the theatre must go

> straight out into the suburbs where it can stand, as it were, wide open, at the disposal of those who live hard and produce much, so that they can be fruitfully entertained there with their great problems. They may find it hard to pay for our art, and immediately to grasp the new method of entertainment, and we shall have to learn in many respects what they need and how they need it; but we can be sure of their interest.

There will be no 'theatre of the scientific age' unless these people bring it to birth.

Thus the 'Short Organum' is something of a compromise between the old didactic aims for which the theory was first evolved, and the more orthodox (but by no means wholly undidactic) theatre of Brecht's middle age. It was also something of a liability to Brecht himself. For when he returned to a more active theatrical life in 1948 he found that the workers were not all that scientific and sceptical any more than they had been under

Brecht,
1951

Hitler; and the audience which he demanded was slow to come forward. Apart from occasional factory performances in its early days, his company played in the centre of Berlin, and as for the theory itself, it was hardly put into effect there at all. 'Admittedly,' says a writer in *Theaterarbeit*,

> one or two practical indications from these works were followed for particular plays, but in Brecht's view the present condition of the theatre does not allow their full application.

In the Ensemble, theory was seldom mentioned; visitors found it hard to get Brecht to discuss it. The titles, projections and other mannerisms survived, but he plainly found it a continual nuisance to explain why he was not following all his former recommendations to the letter. 'There is no purely theoretical approach to Epic Theatre,' he said; and once again 'It is not true . . . that epic theatre . . . proclaims the slogan "Reason this side, Emotion that" '; finally, 'I cannot rewrite all the notes to my plays.'

'I have been brought to realize,' he wrote in *Theaterarbeit*,

> that a lot of my remarks about the theatre are wrongly understood. I conclude this above all from those letters and articles which agree with me. I then feel as a mathematician would do if he read: Dear Sir, I am wholly of your opinion that two and two make five. . . .
>
> Most of these remarks, if not all, were written as notes to my plays, to allow them to be correctly performed. That gives them a rather dry and practical tone, as if a sculptor were writing a matter-of-fact order about the placing of

his work, where it should go and on what sort of a base. Those addressed might have expected something about the spirit in which the work was created. They would find it difficult to get that from the order.[1]

This is not really right, for the notes to the plays, though at times they do give matter-of-fact instructions, undoubtedly owe most of their fascination to the fact that they lay down the law. They are much too full of programmatic slogans like 'Verfremdung' and the 'epic theatre' for Brecht to be able to pass as a simple practical man. What is true, however, is that when it came to the practice of the Ensemble and to the performance of the later plays there was little superficial sign of their being based on a distinctive theory. Indistinguishable from a superb Stanislavsky-trained actress', wrote Mr Sam Wanamaker of Helene Weigel's Mother Courage, while Paul Rilla (one of the few German critics whose judgment Brecht respected) considered that the play itself 'has no more epic elements than a Shakespearean history'. Quality apart – admittedly a big reservation – only certain favourite methods remained to stamp this theatre as Brecht's, and they seemed more like personal idiosyncrasies than evidence of a special theoretical approach. The careful narrative clarity, the perfection of detail, the acute observation, the concrete expression of attitudes, the emotional restraint: these were the real essentials, and they might all have been aimed at, and even sometimes achieved, by producers of a more empirical school.

By now epic narrative in its original sense had become more important to Brecht than its didactic accretions, and this allowed him to rescue one or two of the babies that had been thrown out with the bathwater in 1930. In a country where a second-hand version of the critical standards of Stalin and Zhdanov had succeeded those of Goebbels he felt it necessary to restate, in his notes to the *Hofmeister*, the ideals of poetry and artistry: that sheer attractiveness which had earlier become debased in his eyes but now seemed at once reconcilable with his conception of realism and even essential to its impact. 'Who would have thought,' he exclaimed in a similar connection, 'that I, who always attacked Art with a capital A, should now find myself acting as art's defender?'[2] Even empathy was allowed back, under strict

---

[1] See also the 'Conversation at Rehearsal' in Brecht's notes to *Katzgraben* (*Brecht on Theatre*, p. 247): 'If the critics were to approach my theatre as the spectators do, without bothering too much in advance about my theories, they might simply see theatre before them – a theatre, I hope, of imagination, humour and sense – and only when they came to analyse its effects would they notice its novelty, which they could then find explained in my theoretical notes. The cause of the trouble, in my view, was that my plays have to be properly performed if they are to come off, and so I was forced to supplement (oh dear!) a non-aristotelian drama by describing (heaven help us!) an epic stage.'

[2] Said to Wieland Herzfelde about the East German Academy's discussion of the Barlach exhibition (see page 204) and quoted by him in *Neue Deutsche Literatur* (Berlin), 1956, No. 10, p. 11.

control, in such scenes as the death of Kattrin in *Mother Courage*: that sudden eruption from the narrative flatness of the play. Thus the note (presumably by Brecht) on this episode in the 'Modellbuch':

> In reality the epic theatre is in a position to present other occurrences than excitements, collisions, conspiracies, psychological implications, etc. But it is also in a position to represent these.

'Take an example,' he tells a colleague in a 'Conversation about Empathy' of 1953:

> a sister lamenting that her brother is off to the war; and it is the peasant war: he is a peasant, off to join the peasants. Are we to lose ourselves in her agony? Or not at all? We must be able to lose ourselves in her agony and at the same time not to. Our actual emotion will come from recognizing and feeling the double process.

So the half-social, half-aesthetic position of the 'Short Organum' is followed by a compromise between empathy and detachment, and the inconsistency becomes attractive for its own ('dialectical') sake. At the same time the actual expression 'Epic Theatre' is thrown into the melting-pot in the introduction to 'Dialektik auf dem Theater' (a group of dialogues and theoretical fragments collected in 1956). For '. . . it does not of itself embrace the productivity and mutability of society'; in other words, it is too rigid for Brecht's conception of 'Dialectics'; and so 'The term must be reckoned inadequate, although nothing can be put in its place.' It is indeed clear both from Brecht's last notes (especially the 'Appendices to the Short Organum' printed in *Brecht on Theatre*) and from his collaborators' recollections that during 1956 he was thinking of proclaiming a new doctrine of the Dialectical Theatre, whose emphasis would above all be on 'contradictions' and on the chain of conflicts in the story. But he died without ever putting it forward in print.

All these ideas had to be worked out by Brecht on paper as well as in practice, but there is little doubt which of the two processes came first. None of the main features of his work seems to be traceable back to purely theoretical considerations; again and again he appears to be intellectualizing a choice of methods or of models which had originally been made on half-conscious aesthetic grounds. But given that this process was essential to him it is a pity that Brecht allowed it to bulk quite so large in the public picture of himself and his work. It stimulated interest, as new aesthetic recipes always do, particularly when they depend on unfamiliar key words. Much of it is set down in a marvellous prose style. But it did not always illuminate the particular plays referred to; it ignored or concealed many of Brecht's own qualities; and it put the sceptics off. Once the shock of novelty has gone the magic words have little real point: *Gestus* becomes a mock-scientific term for what Mr Auden calls 'those aspects which individuals reveal to each other through their deeds, their words and their looks'; *Epic Theatre*, a high-sounding phrase of the 1920s made to embrace any kind of play that Brecht wrote – taut or loose, realistic or fantastic, didactic or amusing – and some quite ephemeral mannerisms as well; while *Verfremdung* not only sums up the need for an original outlook and a detached judgment but opens the way to pure freakishness of a distracting kind. The theoretical writings are at their best where they are analysing the world, or the classics, or the existing theatre. As a blueprint for the future they are only too likely to mislead.

Jargon is nearly always inexcusable, a cover for unclear thought. Its fascination, like that of the self-contained systems which it is made to serve, is dangerous, and it is incredible that the author of *Galileo* did not know this to be so. The theory may illuminate his own methods of production, but without some knowledge of these it is a bad guide, easily leading the producer into affectation or tedium. 'Seriousness, fire, jollity, love of truth, inquisitiveness, sense of responsibility' are among the essentials which Brecht confessedly took for granted, and there are many abuses which would have horrified him, though according to the letter of the theory they are legitimate enough. 'In most cases,' Dr Schumacher recollects him as saying, during the summer of 1956,

> all that remains of the 'Verfremdungseffekten' is the 'effects', stripped of their social application, stripped of their point.

Of course the theory remains worth studying, and it is full of suggestive ideas for anyone who understands Brecht's work. But all that is essential in it is apparent from Brecht's own practice in the theatre, and to a producer of any intelligence it must emerge still clearer from the actual plays. The point can be grasped without the theory. It cannot be grasped from the theory alone.

SEVEN

Politics

If Brecht's work is largely known to us through his theory, its most obvious feature is its reflection of a consistent social and political point of view. This appears in the themes with which he deals, in his didactic method of approach, and in that continual concern with the spectator's understanding which distinguishes his teaching from ordinary emotional propaganda. Where other politically-minded artists show their attitude only in the 'message' of their work, or even in public gestures to which their work bears no special relation, with Brecht it seems to go deep into his writing, his theories and his productions, and to shape them down to the last small detail. Opulence of setting, sloppiness of emotion, looseness of language, or the wasteful irrelevance of a lush musical score: features like these, which were (and still are) encouraged by the whole 'apparatus' or social organization of the arts, seemed by his standards not just aesthetically but morally wrong. They were fit only for an un-selfcritical society which, like the Church in *Galileo*, was scared to apply its intellect for fear of change.

The bitter conflicts of Weimar Germany, from which this attitude arose, are mirrored with extraordinary sensitivity in the changing forms and subjects of Brecht's plays: 'Brecht', wrote Herbert Ihering of *Trommeln in der Nacht* in 1922, 'has his blood, his nerves soaked in the horror of our time.' And indeed the parallels between Brecht's evolution and the history of his country were for many years remarkably close. The wild plays of his Munich period coincide with the post-war inflation, ending with Hitler's beer-cellar putsch. The less hectic years dominated in politics by Stresemann result in a group of frivolous but savage satires, where American financial and technical aid seems unconsciously mirrored in the Anglo-Saxon myth. Then from the autumn of 1929 (failure of *Happy End*) on, the spreading of the economic crisis and the revival of the Nazis are matched in Brecht's work by the development of the didactic Lehrstück and the return to the stronger language and methods of *Edward II*. In exile he tries to discredit triumphant Nazism by all the means in his power; then with the approach of war he begins to look further ahead. *Mother Courage* anticipates many of the situations that the war will bring, *Galileo* the problems that are going to face not just the scientist but the whole spirit of free inquiry in a regimented state. Up to this point Brecht is not so much moved by history as moving with it; and if his knowledge of the details of political events often seems shaky, the

The Background

subject of politics becomes so natural and congenial to him that he can use it imaginatively as another poet might use landscape, often striking the same brilliant perceptions.

Outwardly, he was for nearly thirty years an orthodox Communist. But he was never a party member, or even a party journalist or speaker, for in principle (so he told the Un-American Activities Committee in 1947)

> it was the best for me not to join any party whatever . . . I think they [i.e. presumably the German Communists] considered me just as a writer who wanted to write the truth as he saw it, but not as a political figure . . . I found out that it was not my business.[1]

Today, where the Soviet Communist Party has become so widely criticized, not only on intellectual and aesthetic but above all on moral grounds, our

---

[1] House Un-American Activities Committee: *Hearings regarding Communist infiltration of the motion-picture industry.* Eightieth Congress, first session, 20–30 October 1947. See entry for 30 October (here corrected from a recording).

As against this, Ruth Fischer (Hanns Eisler's sister) says in her book *Stalin and German Communism* that 'Brecht joined the Party in 1930'. If she were correct one would expect some other evidence to bear her out, but to this writer's knowledge there is none. Werner Mittenzwei in his *Bertolt Brecht* (Aufbau, E. Berlin, 1962) quotes an inquiry of 2 September 1932 from the Munich police, who had been 'confidentially informed that Brecht is a convinced Communist and as such has been active in writing on the German Communist Party's behalf'. The Berlin police answered eleven days later that Brecht's name was widely known in the Communist movement, but could say nothing about party membership.

judgment of the hard social core of Brecht's work largely depends on what we imagine to be its relation to the official doctrine and the official line. Unfortunately it is not yet possible to investigate this properly, for Brecht's collaborators feel that the whole subject is best left alone, and by no means all his later political poems and essays can be seen. On the one hand he has been presented as a supporter of the anti-Stalinists in East Germany, on the other as a man with 'an unshakable positive relationship to the workers, to the party and to the Soviet Union', whose slogans are beginning to be quoted almost like those of Marx or Lenin. The problem of his political views cannot just be left there, for whereas Pirandello's supposed Fascism has little bearing on his plays, with Brecht the social element is as important as any of those which we have so far discussed. No creative artist's politics were ever less independent of his work, and we have to try and indicate what they were.

* * *

Drums in the night. Spartacist riflemen in Berlin
in January 1919

In a speech in Moscow in 1955 Brecht recalled the Bavarian revolutionary movement of 1918–19.

> I was a medical orderly in an Augsburg military hospital. The barracks and even the hospitals became empty. The old city filled suddenly with new people, coming in great processions from the suburbs, with a liveliness unknown in the streets of the officials, the merchants and the rich. For a few days working-class women got up and spoke in hastily-improvised councils, berating young workers in soldiers' overalls; and the factories heard the workers' commands.[1]

[1] Pasternak translated this speech for Brecht. According to Gerd Ruge he was reluctant to do so, not caring for what he knew of Brecht's poems. He was later converted by seeing the Berliner Ensemble perform *Mother Courage*.

Grosz's famous cartoons of April 1919. *Left:* The counter-revolution.
Right: 'K.V.' ('A.1.')

It is difficult to believe, as has sometimes been suggested, that the young Brecht took any active part in this movement, but about this time he was writing his first critical articles for the Independent Socialist (subsequently Communist) *Augsburger Volkswille*, and he always claimed to have learned much from Wendelin Thomas, its editor, who in due course became a Communist Deputy in Berlin. The revolutionary influence can be felt in many of his early works, with their interest in the underdog and their bitter hatred of war; though it led at first to a kind of cynical and destructive anarchism, where the Communists seemed admirable above all because they were tough and disillusioned: followers not of Marx but of Rimbaud and Villon. 'Freedom, my children, never came,' says the early and long-suppressed 'Song of the Soldier of the red Army' with its deliberately loutish ending:

> And with our body stiff from storms
> And with our spirit scarred by ice
> And with our bloodstained empty hands
> We come grinning into your paradise.[1]

[1] *Hauspostille*, p. 15. Omitted from some later selections, despite (or because of) its obvious applicability in 1945. It does not figure in the 1951 reprint or in the first volume of *Gedichte*, where Elisabeth Hauptmann notes that Brecht decided to 'expunge it for good' soon after the *Hauspostille* appeared. It has, however, been included in *Gedichte* 8.

Savage and aimless kicking against the pricks was the central theme of Brecht's first plays: of *Trommeln in der Nacht*, for instance, with its hero drunkenly taking part in the fringes of a working-class revolt; of *Im Dickicht der Städte* or *Edward II*. 'In those days,' he later confessed, 'my political knowledge was disgracefully slight.'

He first began to study Marxism after moving to Berlin, but it was not until about 1927 that he began systematically to take private Marxist lessons, attending lectures notably by two independent figures: first Fritz Sternberg, whom he met that spring, and later Karl Korsch, a former Communist deputy who had been expelled from the party for 'left' deviations in 1926. The immediate impulse came from the researches which he undertook for the unfinished play *Joe P. Fleischhacker*: from the discovery that the wheat brokers themselves had very little idea of the principles on which their business worked. So he found himself introduced to a close-knit, all-embracing system of thought which took his instinctive feelings and interests, and seemed to justify them and link them together in realistic, concrete terms. 'What attracted Brecht above all was the humanism of Marxist theories (as he often expressed it),' writes one close friend.' But humanism is based on principles rather than on theories, and the distinctive feature of Marxism is more that it offers a clear, yet ever-moving mechanism, which assumes these principles and a steady technological progress, and allows history, society and the individual alike to be stripped down 'like a car'. 'Dialectical economics,' says Lindbergh in the first of the didactic pieces, 'which will change the world from the bottom up.' And the end of the *Badener Lehrstück*:

> Accepting that all will be changed
> Mankind and the world itself
> Above all, the disorder
> Of human classes, for there are two kinds of man
> Ignorance and exploitation.

'Changing the world', the chorus concludes, 'transform yourselves! Yield yourselves up!'

A deliberately impersonal quality marks much of the art of that time, as the words 'Neue Sachlichkeit' themselves imply. But nobody played down

---

[1] Sternberg, in his brief reminiscences of Brecht (*Der Dichter und die Ratio*, Sachse & Pohl, Göttingen, 1963) says that the turning point in Brecht's attitude to Communism came on May Day 1929 when the Berlin police shot at demonstrators. On many points, he says, Brecht was extremely critical in his attitude to the German Communist Party, but on many others he kept silent—partly, no doubt, because the policies of the German Socialist Party did not strike him as offering an adequate alternative.

his individuality so consistently as Brecht, who was in many ways the most individual artist of them all. This was what Feuchtwanger meant when he wrote that his fictionalized Brecht

> really suffered from his own personality. He wanted to escape from it, he wanted to be only one atom among many. Always some part of him projected beyond the others. He wanted to be rid of that; that must go.

Such a sacrifice of one's personality, Brecht wrote in 1927 in an introduction to the broadcast of *Mann ist Mann*, was a 'lustige Sache', a delightful affair; and with the critical conflict between Communists and Nazis he came to put it in the even more drastic language of *Die Massnahme*:

> Who are you?
> Submerge in the filth
> Embrace the slaughterer, but
> Alter our world: that's urgent!

It was not just a question of rating communication above self-expression, or simply of artistic detachment and self-control. For the last three years before Hitler came to power there was a revolutionary situation in Germany, where a man could sink his individuality and even his standards for an apparently attainable end.

'We all know,' says the foreword to *Galileo*,

> how fruitfully men can be influenced by the conviction that they are standing on the threshold of a new epoch. They find their surroundings quite un-finished, open to the most gratifying improvements, full of unknown and undreamt-of possibilities, like malleable raw materials in their hands. They feel themselves as fresh as the dawn: strong, well-rested, full of ideas. . . .

The very terms in which this is written show how that conviction must have ebbed during the middle 1930s, together with Brecht's sense of an impending transformation of the German stage. From now on, as he put it on the eve of the war,

>   the goal
> Lay in the far distance
> It could be clearly seen, although it was
> Hardly to be reached by me.

And with this recognition he seemed to become less concerned to teach the immediate political lessons of Marxism than to explore its wider implications as an account of human conduct and as an embodiment of that spirit of detached scientific inquiry in whose importance he increasingly believed. He told the Un-American Activities Committee that

> I, of course, had to study Marx's ideas about history. I do not think intelligent plays today can be written without such study. . . .

and during his American exile he began to put Marx's *Communist Manifesto* into verse:

> History deals with the acts of men that were larger than life-size;
> The ebb and flow of their fate, advance and retreat of their armies;
> Or with the pomp and destruction of empires. But, for the Marxist
> History's prime concern is describing the wars of the classes
> This is a theory of peoples divided in classes and fighting
> With themselves. Patricians and captains, slaves and plebeians
> Nobles, artisans, farmers; now proletarians and bourgeois
> Keep the gigantic machine in motion, so as to turn out
> And to distribute all our basic essentials, meantime
> Fighting a war to the knife, the age-old struggle for power.

From about his fortieth year on he dealt less with current political issues than with those shifting mechanisms which the dialectical view of history seemed to reveal.

Such 'dialectics' are essentially a method of expressing 'the flow of things'; of showing that history, science and all human life can never be treated as static but are continually developing: that all causes, all effects, all relations are dynamic; that the time element must never be left out. It was a conception which had been expressed in the nineteenth century in terms of a never-ending series of clashes, or 'contradictions' between opposing forces. '. . . life itself,' wrote Engels in *Anti-Dühring*,

> is likewise a contradiction which is present in actual things and events, continually posing and resolving itself. . . .

So different forces will tug a man (or a family, or a society) in different directions, and out of this 'contradiction' some movement will come; then new forces will come into play, and so on, and on. It is easy to see how this analogy must have fascinated Brecht. He cited Mao Tse-tung's pamphlet, 'Über den Widerspruch', as the most interesting book of 1955; and such 'contradictions' become at once the motive force and the social-aesthetic justification of his later work. They determine the plan and the means of expression. They can be put into 'Gesten'. They take the place of a plot.

Unfortunately it is easy for those committed to this method to confuse verbal, logical contradiction with a genuine tug of opposing forces; and the 'thesis, antithesis' formula leads them to class such forces in pairs of apparent

The heightened antithesis. Shen Teh and Shui Ta

opposites where in fact there are many forces at work. Often in Brecht's writing there seem to be only two sides to any question: indeed, *Senora Carrar*'s actual moral is that there can be no more. So he came during the 1930s to lump Capitalism and Nazism on one side and Communism on the other (just as Evelyn Waugh conversely lumps Communism and Nazism together and opposes them to Guy Crouchback's crusading Catholic ideals), concluding that 'Fascism can only be fought by treating it as capitalism'; that the only difference between the Fascist and the capitalist countries was that in the latter 'the butchers wash their hands before bringing in the meat'; and that to believe that capitalism could have survived without turning into Fascism was itself 'a Fascist point of view'. This accounts for the profound misconception which runs through *Die Rundköpfe und die Spitzköpfe*: that anti-semitism was only a political weapon, and that in due course the Nazi leaders and the rich Jews would combine against the working class, irrespective of race. The doctrine of the class war, which in Marx's hands was an illuminating theory to explain admitted facts, here becomes a strait-jacket into which the facts have to be crammed. Whatever does not fit has simply to be discarded or suppressed.

As we have seen, theories can have their own peculiar attractions, and there seems to be a pleasure in thinking in politically ruthless terms, which encourages its addicts to go on even where the thinking no longer corresponds with life. So Marxism often degenerates into a means of stylizing the actual course of events, facing the reader with gross over-simplifications, and leading to awkward intellectual shuffles whenever what was White (e.g. in Brecht's case, the once 'progressive' Lindbergh)[1] has abruptly to be reclassified as Black. This is the danger for the artist, and it was particularly evident in Brecht's productions, where the heightened contrasts and the caricatured villains were often so patently artificial as to make the play lose all touch with the world outside. Yet so far as the actual structure of the play goes a certain clarification of conflict can be a good thing, and it is just this that is offered by Mao Tse-tung's long essay, with its conception of a 'main contradiction' on which the politician (or the producer) must lay his finger, however confused the apparent situation: of a single overriding conflict which dominates and determines all the rest. Few dramatists or producers would think of putting it in this way, but in practice such theatrical 'dialectics' are more usual than they sound. The occasional crudities to which they led Brecht as a writer are certainly no more disturbing than the antitheses and deliberate inconsistencies of Pirandello, and they seem disciplined enough after the grotesque unrealities of his own early plays.

So the theatre of his middle age is once again a place of sharp oppositions, where the story does not 'hang together' but moves jerkily forward along 'epic' lines; where the conflicting interests of the characters are plainly visible; where 'psychology' as such is left to emerge from their clash, and there is no need for any figure to seem round and smooth. 'If art reflects life,' says the 'Short Organum',

> it does so with special mirrors. Art does not become unrealistic by changing the proportions but by changing them in such a way that the public takes its representations as a practical guide to insights and impulses, and goes astray in real life. It is of course essential that stylization should not remove the natural element but should heighten it.

Whether the process is justifiable depends on where one looks for the truth in such works. Anybody will 'go astray' who takes them as a reliable picture of Anglo-Saxon and Oriental society, or of how capitalists and proletarians behave. But in fact the element with which Brecht is concerned lies beneath this level, in the process of action and interaction itself. This gave him a special taste for the unresolved incompatibility, a delight in contradiction for its own sake which matched both his personality and his love of play on words. 'How are we to show Agrippa's speech as ineffective and having an effect?' he asks in the very 'dialectical' discussion of the first scene of *Coriolanus*. 'Wie zeigt man die Agripparede als wirkungslos und wirkungs-

---

[1] See Brecht's unpublished letter of 2 January 1950, quoted above on page 34. *Lindberghflug*, rechristened *Der Ozeanflug*, is omitted from the collected *Stücke*.

It is, of course, easy to make too much of this. Many authors change their minds about their own earlier works, and find that they have either to discard them or to try and live them down.

German Communism
before Hitler. The
workers' sports meeting
from Brecht and Dudow's
film *Kuhle Wampe*

voll?' The 'dialectics' of Brecht's later work sometimes lie close to paradox.

Unlike Goethe or Claudel or Sir Alan Herbert, he played no part in public affairs; he was neither a conspirator like Silone nor a conference-addict like Mr Spender; and though he wrote apparently Communist works, such as *Die Massnahme*, they often conflicted with the party's views.[1] Yet in Brecht's case there were certain factors that made his relationship to the party especially close. A number of his works did have an immediate and compelling impact: thus 'when *Die Massnahme* is dead and buried in the files' said one generally hostile party criticism of this piece, '– which will no doubt be very soon – its effects will everywhere be felt by the workers' choral movement and agit-prop troops'. Many of the songs with Eisler, the short anti-Fascist pieces like *Senora Carrar* and the sketches in *Furcht und Elend*, the satires which Brecht wrote for the Freedom Radio, have become bound up in this way with the traditions of German Communism, recalling to anyone who knew them the hard times of the emigration or the purposeful days

[1] See Ernst Schumacher: *Die Dramatischen Versuche Bertolt Brechts* 1918–33, Rütten and Loening, E. Berlin, 1955, pp. 344 ff. According to him this performance 'already included improvements based on criticisms put forward by the Party' (p. 368), while the text printed in *Versuche 4* 'represents a revision on the basis of proletarian criticism of the original version' (p. 345).

German Communism after Hitler. Brecht and Paul Dessau
with the Free German Youth

before 1933. They were not just obligingly-supplied symbols, like the
Picasso dove; they were actual political achievements, influencing men sometimes towards the Communist Party, sometimes against Fascism and war.

When Brecht returned to East Germany, moreover, at the height of the
'cold war', the survivors from that period had become a small, precariously
balanced ruling group, where such old-boy links counted for much. For the
first time in his life he found himself treated as an 'Insider', a member of an
Establishment, and the fact that it was a struggling and unpopular Establishment plainly made him feel his responsibility all the more. 'When I came
back,' he wrote in a posthumous poem,

> My hair was not yet grey
> I was glad of that.
>
> The troubles of the mountains lie behind us.
> Before us lie the troubles of the plains.

1953. East Berlin demonstrators in the Stalinallee, 16 June

And again, of 'Herr Keuner, the Thinking Man', his alter ego:

> Herr K. preferred town B to town A. 'In town A,' he said, 'they are fond of
> me; but in town B they were friendly to me. In town A they put themselves
> out for me, but in town B they needed me. In town A they invited me to their
> table, but in town B they asked me into the kitchen.'

How far he was suited to the new 'positive' (i.e. constructive) tasks is another
matter. From 1949 on he concentrated on rebuilding a lost theatrical tradition rather than on writing fresh plays; he wrote a number of banal but well-
intentioned songs;[1] he made three or four public statements about the
possibility of war, sat on the World Peace Council and in 1955 was awarded
a Stalin Peace Prize. But *Turandot* is one of his weaker plays; his own efforts
to write on a contemporary East German theme came to nothing; and Erwin
Strittmatter's *Katzgraben*, on whose adaptation and production he concentrated his efforts instead, seems uncharacteristically flat beside his own
work. His two major political *pièces d'occasion*, moreover, are both feeble
works: the Lysenkoist *Erziehung der Hirse* of fifty-two verses, and the
Herrnburger Bericht, which he and Dessau wrote for the Communist World
Youth Festival of 1951 (gaining in the process a National Prize). Much of
the force went out of his writing during his last seven years, and he never
recovered those gifts of contemporaneity and anticipation which he seemed
to lose around 1939.

[1] E.g. the 'Kinderlieder' in *100 Gedichte*, the 'Aufbaulied' and the 'Friedenslied'.

1953. Rioting on the borders of East and West Berlin, 17 June

But in the schematized dialectical conflict he felt, like many Marxists, that it is imperative to choose 'sides', and that this choice is bound to involve a voluntary subordination of the individual's judgment. Thus *Die Massnahme*:

> Do not follow the right road without us
> Without us it is
> The worst of all.
> Do not cut yourself off.
> We may go astray and you may be right, so
> Do not cut yourself off.

There was in fact an equally good market for his work in West Germany and Switzerland, and many provincial and city governments there might have been proud to sponsor a company like the Ensemble. But he had made his choice, and any criticism of it, or any attack on the East German system which he had chosen, only made his loyalty the stronger. This 'contradictory spirit', quite as fundamental to his character as anti-individualism, led him gratuitously to alienate much more or less 'neutral' opinion: by telling an English interviewer that George Orwell ought to have been exterminated, for instance, or by the conclusion of his message to Herr Ulbricht, the Communist (SED) Party Secretary, on the occasion of the rioting of 17 June 1953 on the borders of East and West Berlin:

I feel it necessary at this moment to write to you and express my association with the SED. Yours, Bertolt Brecht.[1]

No single act of Brecht's caused greater resentment than this sentence published out of context, for the riots, officially interpreted in East Germany as 'the work of provocateurs and Fascist agents of foreign powers and their collaborators from German capitalist monopolies' and forcibly suppressed by Russian troops, were presented throughout Western Germany as a working-class revolt against a dictatorial and foreign-sponsored régime. They had certainly begun as a genuine and justifiable demonstration, and so in three longer statements Brecht, whose main fear had been that they would result in war, went far to qualify his first words.

The SED has made mistakes which weigh heavily on a Socialist party and have turned workers against it. I am not a member. But I respect many of its historic achievements, and I feel myself bound to it when Fascist and war-mongering riffraff attack it not for its mistakes, but for its good qualities.

So he summed up his position, concluding that 'In the struggle against war and Fascism, I stood and still stand by its side.'[2]

Especially since Krushchev's denunciation of Stalin at the beginning of 1956, a comparable loyalty has not prevented many Communists from criticizing the leaders of their party, once they felt that it was no longer the Fascism of the 1930s, nor even the current military preparations of the Western Powers that provided the sole threat to their cause. Whatever impression Brecht may have given in conversation and in unpublished writing, there is no vestige of such criticism in his published work. 'The oppressed of five continents . . .,' he wrote in 1953, 'must have felt their heart stop beating when they heard that Stalin was dead,' and again:

I praise him for many reasons. Above all
Because under his leadership the murderers were beaten
The murderers, my own country.[3]

– a sentiment that would be less exceptionable if it did not contrast so oddly with the four-line epigram on another war leader that appears set thus under a portrait cut from an illustrated paper in Brecht's book of war verses, *Kriegsfibel*:

[1] *Neues Deutschland* (Berlin), 21 June 1953. A message from Brecht's collaborator Paul Dessau, printed on 19 June, says, 'The Fascist firebugs must be stamped out lock, stock and barrel.' Further messages were printed from Wolfgang Langhoff and from Friedrich Wolf, whose car had been attacked by the crowd.

[2] Unpublished statement. See also a further letter dated 21 June 1953 and published in *Neues Deutschland* of 23 June: this speaks of the workers' 'justifiable discontent', and of 'mistakes made on all sides'.

[3] From MS. Apparently unpublished.

Gang law is something I can understand.
With man-eaters I've kept up good relations
I've had the killers feeding from my hand.
I am the man to save civilization.[1]

It was a curious kind of scepticism that allowed Brecht to dismiss all the evidence that Stalin himself was a 'man-eater' or that he came to terms with Hitler where Churchill did not; and in many other respects the picture of events presented in *Kriegsfibel* seems wildly remote from the facts. Yet the scepticism was certainly there, to an extent that must often have pained the true believers. 'My job is not to prove that I have been right so far, but to find out *if.*' So he made Galileo say, and in the last months of his life he would often interrupt a rehearsal and tell his students that this, for a Marxist, was the most important sentence in the play.

* * *

Moreover, Brecht has always represented an awkward problem for the Communist Party and for Communist critics, just because he digested Marxism in his own way instead of accepting the politicians' ready-made aesthetic line. However he might subordinate himself on political matters

[1] *Kriegsfibel*, p. 38.

he could not accept the interference of amateurs in his own field, and he was temperamentally and artistically incapable of following the recipe for 'Socialist Realism' which Stalin's lieutenant Zhdanov had laid down in 1934. This called for an 'optimistic' literature, 'impregnated with enthusiasm and the spirit of heroic deeds': the kind of art, so it proved in practice, that

'Socialist Realism.' A Stalin Prize play by Korneichuk, 1935

would make few intellectual demands and give no disquieting thoughts. Tchaikovsky and folk-music were the examples henceforward put before the composers; Repin before the painters, and the nineteenth-century novelists before the writers; while the theatre was recommended to follow the methods of Stanislavsky, the great producer of the naturalistic school. Nor were these somewhat Victorian standards valid only for Russia. After 1945 the same 'Kulturpolitik' was introduced in Central and Eastern Europe, wherever Soviet military occupation led to the imposition of a Communist regime. The one clear definition of Socialist Realism remained that with which the slogan had originally been launched: 'Socialist Realism can best be shown in those works of art which Soviet writers produce.'[1]

None of Brecht's works had a 'positive' (i.e. exemplary) hero, or led to the kind of politically happy ending that is known in the jargon as a 'positive conclusion'. They were not especially 'healthy' (i.e. optimistic), and apart from *Senora Carrar* they were heretically unconventional in form. Neither his status nor his stature could prevent the party critics in East Germany from attacking *Mother Courage* on the grounds that the old woman ends up as dependent as ever on her belief in the war, and that the whole tone is unrelievedly shabby and grey. *Puntila* was held to be socially irrelevant now that there had been land reform; the *Hofmeister*, with its setting in the period

[1] A. I. Stetsky (head of Central Committee Cultural and Propaganda Section) speaking at the First Congress of Soviet Writers.

of the 'Deutsche Misere', was held to be a 'negative' work. Satire, so Brecht had to point out (much as Erich Kästner had had to tell right-wing critics some twenty-five years earlier), does not normally deal in 'positive characters:'

> The positive element in the *Hofmeister* is its bitter anger against inhuman conditions of unjustified privilege and twisted thinking.

His production of Goethe's *Urfaust*, set against the same grey background of the same period, was attacked as a virtual 'denial of the national cultural heritage', and when Eisler published the libretto of his opera *Johann Faustus* Brecht defended him in a controversy conducted in similar terms. Even *The Caucasian Chalk Circle*, whose production was deliberately designed to be a little more colourful, was criticized by one party organization on the grounds that it had been a success in the West. It was never reviewed by the party paper at all.

'A highly gifted playwright and a talented composer,' wrote this paper, *Neues Deutschland*, of the trial production of *Die Verurteilung des Lukullus* in the State Opera in 1951,

> both of undoubtedly progressive intentions, have mistakenly embarked on an experiment which on ideological and artistic grounds was bound from the first to fail.

For Brecht's text omitted to refer to the 'world peace camp' (i.e. the Soviet system of alliances and the current Communist peace propaganda in other countries), and therefore represented 'a relapse into doubts and weaknesses such as the writer should long ago have overcome. . .'. Dessau's music was 'thin and fragmentary' and recalled the unspeakable Stravinsky's, instead of arousing the masses 'so that they enthusiastically oppose a new war of conquest'. On these and similar grounds a number of critics pressed the State Opera to drop the production rather than waste official money on a 'formalist' work of minority appeal. But characteristically Brecht fought back, exploiting his own freedom from party discipline and insisting on the validity of his contract with the Opera so stubbornly as to stall even the Council of Ministers, which spent one Saturday morning locked in inconclusive argument with him and Dessau – a situation inconceivable in a State less concerned with the arts. As a result, the production was postponed but not withdrawn; the additions to the text were slight; and Dessau's continual amendments to the score involved no change of style.[1] Certainly the final

---

[1] At the suggestion of Otto Grotewohl, the East German Premier, Brecht made one significant change in order to differentiate between offensive and defensive wars. This is set out in the notes on pp. 157–8 of *Versuche 11*, reprinted with amplifications by Elisabeth Hauptmann in *Stücke VII*, pp. 267–74. (See the Analysis of the Plays for a rough account of the differences between the various printed texts.)

According to a note by Dessau in *Leipziger Theater* (Leipzig), 1956–7, No. 19, there were already six different versions of the score.

Above: Ernst Barlach: Sleeping Russian Peasants, 1908
Right: Vera Mukhina: Collective Farm Workers, 1937

version, as played for a whole season in Berlin and at the Paris Festival in June 1958, had nothing to do with Socialist Realism in Zhdanov's sense.

Moreover, Brecht was himself prepared to go over to the attack: defending the noble modern sculpture of Ernst Barlach, for instance, against accusations of 'formalism' that recalled the 'decadence' and 'art-bolshevism' of the Nazis. 'All these sculptures,' he wrote in an article of 1952, 'seem to me to bear the stamp of realism; they have much that is essential and nothing that is not'; then, quite flatly: 'Abstract criticism cannot lead to realist art.' In two poems published the next year he satirized the 'Commissions' responsible for allotting patronage and resources for the arts in accordance with the official 'Kulturpolitik': an 'Art Commission' which had overruled an exhibition jury at Dresden, and the 'Amt für Literatur' or Literary Section which gave paper to such publications as it considered 'welcome'.

> Welcome
> Are works with ideas
> That the Amt für Literatur knows from the newspapers.
> This custom
> Considering the sort of newspapers we have
> Must lead to great savings in paper. . . .[1]

[1] This and the accompanying poem ('Nicht feststellbare Fehler der Kunstkommission') are qualified by another peom: 'Nicht so gemeint', in the *Sinn und Form* Sondernummer of 1957.

204

And in August 1953 Brecht wrote a long letter to *Neues Deutschland* to point out that the 'Marxist jargon . . . superficial optimism' and 'unaesthetic administrative methods' of these semi-dictatorial bodies were simply alienating the writers and artists, and the realists among them most of all:

> . . . Prettification and improvement are the deadliest enemies not only of beauty but of political good sense. The life of the labouring population, the struggle of the working class for a worthwhile creative life is a grateful theme for the arts. But the mere presence on the canvas of workers and peasants has little to do with this theme. Art must aim at a broad intelligibility. But society must increase the understanding of art by general education. The needs of the population have to be satisfied. But only by fighting at the same time against its need for trash. . . .
>
> For administrative purposes, and given the officials available, it may well be simpler to work out definite proformas for works of art. Then the artists have 'merely' to fit their thoughts (or those of the administration?) into the given form, so that 'all goes smoothly'. But the living material so urgently demanded then becomes living material for coffins. Art has its own regulations.
>
> Realism from a Socialist standpoint: that is a great and comprehensive principle, and a personal style and an individual viewpoint do not contradict

it but help it on. The campaign against formalism must not simply be regarded as a political task, but must be given a political content. It is part of the working class's struggle for authentic solutions to social problems, which is why fake solutions in the arts must be combated as fake social solutions, not as aesthetic mistakes.

'Politicians may be surprised,' he concluded, 'but most artists find the language of politics easier to understand than a hastily scratched-together aesthetic vocabulary, which has nothing to offer but ex-cathedra pronouncements of a nebulous kind. . . .'

This 'Formalism' of which Brecht writes has since 1934 been the abomination of Soviet cultural policy, and like all such terms it has never been properly defined. Men like Zhdanov used it to cover almost any deviation from the nineteenth-century aesthetic conventions which they were used to. With Brecht it seems to mean a striving after 'originality', or even conventional formal beauty, at the cost of the sense. Zhdanov's is certainly the commoner use of the word; it was also virtually accepted by Krushchev; and if it is taken as valid there is little question but that Brecht was a formalist himself. Thus George Lukács, probably the greatest living Marxist literary critic, could attack him for insisting on 'brand new means of expression' and praise only *Furcht und Elend* and *Senora Carrar* of his works, arguing that his theoretical writings

> pass over the [question of] social content and turn the proposed social rebirth of literature into an admittedly intelligent and interesting formal experiment.[1]

– while Brecht in turn queried Lukács's Victorian models in his 'Weite und Vielfalt der realistischen Schreibweise' of 1938: an important essay, deliberately directed 'against the tendency to restrict realistic writing by imposing limits on the formal side'.

Apart from Mayakovsky, who died young and was altogether too big a figure to pull down, this 'formalist' label has been stuck on every Communist artist who felt impelled to work out a new, systematically Marxist approach to his art: on Meyerhold, Tretiakoff, Eisenstein, the Constructivists, Piscator: precisely on those men whose work bears any relation to Brecht's. In the strict sense, moreover, Formalism was a school of Soviet literary criticism headed by Viktor Shklovskij which flourished during the 1920s and was bitterly attacked for its exaggeratedly non-political views. Zhdanov and Stalin made it the scapegoat for all offences against the new canon. But it happens to be where we find the first statement of a number of Brecht's characteristic theoretical ideas.

[1] Georg Lukács: *Skizze einer Geschichte der neueren deutschen Literatur*, Aufbau, Berlin, 1955, pp. 141–2. Lukács later modified this view, writing of Brecht in *The Meaning of Contemporary Realism* (Merlin Press, London, 1963, p. 89), as 'the greatest realistic playwright of his age'.

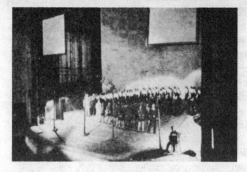

'Formalism'.
Meyerhold's
production of
*The Red
Navy Man*

For the purpose of 'Verfremdung', which Brecht launched immediately after his Moscow visit of 1935 (and only a year after Zhdanov had ordered that such ideas should be dropped), is just that which Shklovskij had given for his 'Priem Ostrannenija' or 'device of making it strange'; and if Brecht set this slogan in a more political framework that is only what Boris Arvatov of Mayakovsky's and Tretiakoff's LEF group seems also to have done. 'Braked, oblique speech' could help this estrangement, in Shklovskij's view, or a 'twisted, deliberately impeded form'.[1] There are further obvious anticipations of Brecht in Arvatov's 'militant anti-psychologism'; in the Formalist distinction between 'Fabula' ('Fabel', or narrative) and 'Sjuzhet' (an artificially imposed plot); and above all in Shklovskij's other formula of 'Obnazhenie Priema' – 'the device laid bare', or blowing the gaff – which leads the latest historian of the movement to say that

> The Formalist students were their best in dealing with what might be called quotation mark techniques – with parody and stylization, 'laying bare' the artifice and destroying the illusion of reality.[1]

This is true of Meyerhold and it is true of Brecht, whereas the officially-approved Stanislavsky method represents everything against which Brecht had chosen, in the name of Marxism, to revolt: the transfigured actors, the emotionally windswept audience, the too, too solid settings, the rigid formal framework of the plot.

In Eastern Germany this point is never raised, and since Brecht's death his aesthetic as well as his political orthodoxy has been taken as beyond dispute. But in Russia itself, although his purely political importance was granted, like Picasso's, the official 'Kulturpolitik' was for a long time hostile to his work. Tretiakoff published three of his plays in 1934, and included him in his *People of the Same Bonfire*; O. M. Brik knew his writings; Tairoff

[1] Victor Erlich: *Russian Formalism*, Mouton, The Hague, 1955, p. 216.

Brecht in Russian (1930).
Tairoff's production of
The Threepenny Opera.

staged *The Threepenny Opera* at his Kamerny Theatre in 1930 (an institution that Stalin found 'really bourgeois' and in due course closed down). But these people were themselves all arch-'formalists', and for the twenty years of the steel-hard Socialist Realist aesthetic Brecht was neither performed nor discussed. If certain of his anti-Nazi writings were published in Moscow after 1935 it was mostly in German-language editions, and for German use; and only now, with the mild but perhaps irreversible 'thaw' in Soviet cultural policy, is his influence beginning to be felt.

It is uncertain how strong it will prove to be. But when he visited Moscow in 1955 Brecht was able to persuade Nikolai Okhlopkov – another producer who had been accused of 'Formalism' – to restage Pogodin's *Aristocrats* 'in the round' as he himself had seen it at the Realistic Theatre in 1935, shortly before that establishment too was shut down.

> Brecht thought that the restaging of this play in its original version would strengthen us in our struggle against all that had been admitted to be harmful during the last twenty years in the theatre.

The Ensemble's first Russian tour in May and June of 1957 seemed to operate in the same sense, for all the performances were full; even their most conservative critics agreed in discussion that the Soviet theatre badly needed such a stimulus; and the younger theatre people were apparently enthusiastic for Brecht's ideas. Although the party leaders were still anxious to save Zhdanov's conception, the words 'Socialist Realism' and 'Formalism' were conspicuously absent from all the discussions in which the company's members took part; Meyerhold's work was once again freely and seriously referred to; and its points of resemblance with Brecht's were often picked out. In an interesting and intelligent article in *Teatr* the previous year I. Fradkin had specifically denied any relationship between Brecht's 'Verfremdung' and the Formalist doctrines, and quoted his work as showing the variations in 'Socialist Realism' existing outside the USSR. Such questions, however, were now ignored by the critics, who stuck mainly to descriptions of the plays and accounts of the acting. Some of them took exception to particular features of Brecht's style: to the masks, to the mixture of 'expressionism' (i.e. stylization) and naturalism, and to Dessau's music for *The Caucasian Chalk Circle*. Two or three concluded on the same lines as *Isvestia*, that the Ensemble ought now to decide

> which part of Bertolt Brecht's work and of his aesthetics lives, and will live for many years, and which part has faded for ever into the past.

But even then the argument was conducted on a serious level and with an honest effort to see what Brecht was driving at. Only an article in *Znamia* by Vakhtangov's former assistant, Boris Sachava, constituted something of an exception. He found it disgusting that a character should wash his feet on the stage, unnecessary that Kattrin in *Mother Courage* should be dumb instead of straightforwardly heroic, regrettable that the chance for spectacular settings had been missed. Helene Weigel, he felt, failed to 'scale the peaks of human emotion', and Brecht's whole insistence on reasoned thinking was wrong.

Within a few months of the Ensemble leaving, three theatres in the former Baltic Republics had staged plays by Brecht, and by 1960 he was once more breaking through to the Russian-language theatre proper. The first Russian book on him was produced that year – by Bernard Reich, a Munich associate of the early 1920s who had settled in Russia, been deported to Siberia and returned to live in Riga – as well as a volume of his theoretical essays; *Simone Machard* was staged at the Yermolev Theatre in Moscow; and in January 1961 the Mayakovsky Theatre there, under Okhlopkhov's management, put on a highly successful though by all accounts somewhat distorted production of *Mother Courage*, directed by Maximilian Strauch. With this Brecht seems to have become accepted: a still more enthusiastic essay in *Teatr* (by B. Singerman) claimed that it was his historic mission to 'harmonize the discoveries of Left revolutionary art in the 'twenties and early 'thirties with the artistic norms of the mid-century' – exactly what the Soviet avant-garde of the 1960s seems to be trying to do. 'In Brecht's epic theatre (as also, for instance, in Prokofiev's music and the poems of Neruda and Mayakovsky) Left art has become classical.' Even a sceptic like Rouben Simonov of the Vakhtangov Theatre, while denying that Brecht could or should have any influence on the Soviet theatre, none the less felt bound to tell foreign interviewers that Brecht was both respected and performed in Russia. Other important productions have followed – *The Threepenny Opera* at the Stanislavsky Theatre, *Arturo Ui* at the Gorki Theatre in Leningrad, and what was supposed to be an outstanding *Good Person of Szechwan* by

Moscow theatre students under Yuri Lubimov's direction. A collected edition in five volumes was announced for 1963 and 1964.

The situation in the remaining East European countries has been similar, even though Brecht seems to have made his way there independently, through the same three stages: virtual rejection, then the enthusiasm of a minority who saw here a politically tenable approach to artistic innovation, then final acceptance and a consequent slight decline in impact. Thus in Hungary and Czechoslovakia his reputation up to the time of his death rested mainly on *The Threepenny Opera* and the *Dreigroschenroman*; in 1953 the principal Czech literary publishers rejected as 'not urgent' a plan to publish his poems. But during 1957 there were productions of *Carrar*, *Mother Courage*, *Puntila* and *Simone Machard* in Prague, *Galileo* at Brno and *Mother Courage* and *The Good Person of Szechwan* in Budapest. For three or four years he was very widely played; then, in Czechoslovakia at least, he began to seem too established to offer the same stimulus to the younger theatre people. In Poland the process began rather earlier, with the Berliner Ensemble's tour of 1952, well before the Russians had opened the door. Brecht told with great pleasure how the Polish Minister of Culture of the day accused him of undoing the government's entire 'Kulturpolitik'; while a Warsaw critic wrote that the audience for *Die Mutter* arrived 'talking of Gorky only' but during the interval 'spoke only of Brecht'. Familiar arguments were of course raised against *Mother Courage* ('doubt in the value of the Human Being') and *Puntila* (why wasn't the villain 'some vassal of Wall Street'?); and the leading Warsaw producer Leon Schiller argued in a long and intelligent article that Brecht made 'too many concessions at the expense of a healthy realism', that what justified his reputation was above all his political poems, and – a familiar last word where Communist writers of any stature are concerned – that 'the leadership in his further evolution can only lie with the Party'. Two years later *The Caucasian Chalk Circle* was staged in Polish at Cracow, since when Warsaw has given the world première of *Schweik* (1957), besides a production of *Puntila* in 1958 by Konrad Swinarski, who had worked with the Ensemble in Berlin, and such other important productions as the National Theatre's *Mother Courage* of 1962 and Erwin Axer's staging of *Arturo Ui*. Nor can all this be isolated from the general attack on Stalinist aesthetic standards, or from the changes which subsequently developed in the Polish Communist régime. Generally speaking Brecht has had a liberalizing influence wherever his own proper field was concerned, and the Stalinists would not deny it. Their mistrust sprang from the realization that something of this might spill over into the political sphere.

* * *

Brecht's politics would be a complicated matter to analyse, even with full knowledge of the facts; and they are usually looked at in one of two very one-sided ways. West European Communist sympathizers will fall with uncritical relief on the work of any even mildly interesting Communist artist, all the more so (in most cases) if it differs from the Soviet mould. Against that the anti-Communists will shut their eyes to the work itself in order to concentrate on petty and often personal details which have all the inaccuracy of gossip and do not enter into ordinary critical discussion at all: the cause of Cultural Freedom would presumably suffer if a Communist artist were allowed to be any good. Between these politically-conditioned extremes it was refreshing to read the dispassionate opinion of Brecht's West German publisher and collaborator Peter Suhrkamp, who in a difficult situation spoke up with great dignity for Brecht:

> I do not share . . . the view sometimes expressed that Brecht's talents were injured by politics: I am much more inclined to see political dogma as providing the cure for the anarchy and cynical nihilism of his early plays. I remember myself, when we were working on *Im Dickicht der Städte*, how the need for social differentiation determined the shape of the language. When the poet is asked to provide songs for use in political life they are always clear-cut and plebeian: the medium demands it.

This is certainly right. The distinctive clarity and detachment of Brecht's style enter his work with his growing interest in Marxism, and it only needs a close examination of his publications of the years 1929 and 1930 to see how it all hangs together: the didactic form, the unrhymed irregular verse, the collaboration with Eisler, the start of a new theatrical theory. Scrupulously and systematically his methods were pared to fit a particular view of society, a particular method of analysis, reached in a particular sharp crisis of German history before the parties clamped down on art. Without this he might have floundered indefinitely in the old wild incoherent territory that stretches from 1918 to 1929, from *Baal* to *Happy End*. To us he would seem an 'amusing', nostalgic, greatly gifted reminder of the old Berlin decadence; and that would be all.

It is a curious case, of a consequential Marxist pursuing for some three decades methods which lead straight away from official Marxist aesthetics. If Brecht's politics make him suspect in the West, his literary originality gets him a hearing; if his aesthetics seem shaky in the East, his political reputation gets him the benefit of the doubt. None of the Russian 'Left' artists except perhaps Mayakovsky had the same chance to establish both a literary and a political position; and because Brecht combined his Marxism with the modern Western experience of new aesthetic forms he worked out a language that conveys something to East and West alike. In this lies a hope for all art, not just for the theatre. It is not only that a common aesthetic language can do much to close the wretched gap between Western and Eastern 'intellectuals'. That is obvious. It is rather that on the one hand Brecht must encourage Communists to reconsider the conceptions of 'Socialist Realism' and 'Formalism', unless a second Zhdanov supervenes. And on the other hand he has shown the Western democrat that a social, even political foundation for an artist's work is not disreputable, and need not lead him to compromise his standards so long as he believes in them himself. Which of these achievements is the more important it is hard to judge.

EIGHT

The English Aspect

The reason why the political and theoretical aspects of Brecht's works have been left to the last is that they are less important than is often supposed. His dramatic theories, and even his productions with the Berliner Ensemble, need to be seen as by-products of his writing, while although his politics inform all his work the conclusions drawn from them have often been irrelevant or false. Too many critics began by approaching Brecht, as it were, the wrong way round: they introduced him to us primarily as a Communist (or 'anti-Fascist') and/or a theoretician, whose theories are surely exemplified in the work of the Ensemble. The fact that he also wrote plays was only realized here during the last few years of his life; and in so far as they were made available to us at all, they were treated as a try-out of the doctrine rather than a major achievement on their own. As late as 1949 Sir John Gielgud could write of one of Brecht's theoretical essays that

> I did not at all care for Mr Brecht's article. It seems to be obscure, pointless and humourless.
>
> Mr Brecht presumably writes his own scripts, and it might be interesting to see a performance of one of them. . . .

And this was no untypical reaction. The very notion of a German ('Teutonic') Communist ('Stalinist') theoretician ('doctrinaire') was something that the most reasonable man might find alarming; it conveyed some kind of cross between Marx and Wagner, a party impresario who might well combine the worst features of Nazi and Soviet art.

This approach to Brecht, followed sometimes from the best intentions, but sometimes from political motives too, has been a real obstacle to the understanding of his plays. It means that they are regarded less as works of art worth performing for their own sake than as pointers to a new kind of production: part of the special secret of Brecht's Ensemble, and therefore a special challenge to us. They become exotic and rarefied where their whole essence is that they must be widely intelligible; they become mechanical where they ought to be human. The meaning is no longer, as Brecht always made it, the main thing; for sense, in this interpretation, comes second to superficialities of manner and method, while the force of the Ensemble's performances is attributed to a producer's formula, where really it springs from a conviction that the writer has something to say. To some extent this was Brecht's own fault, and his great fear of being represented abroad by unworthy productions may have defeated its own end. It gave the impression that special measures were needed over and above a real understanding of the play.

Yet, of the few productions which Brecht himself permitted in his lifetime, the enthusiastic though severely limited performances by Unity Theatre and the Royal Academy of Dramatic Art conveyed his sense and spirit much better than the more ambitious efforts of Royal Court Theatre (*The Threepenny Opera* with Bill Owen and *The Good Woman of Sezuan* with Peggy Ashcroft) and the BBC. These used Brecht's methods and collaborators, but by doing so diverted our attention too often to the mere trappings of the story, while Brecht's own insistence on eminent players, being based on insufficient knowledge of the English-language theatre, did more harm than good. Since those days there has been a certain improvement as one theatre after another has tried its teeth on his work: Sadler's Wells Opera on *Mahagonny*, the Mermaid on *Galileo*, the Royal Shakespeare Company on *The Caucasian Chalk Circle* and *Puntila*, The National Theatre, Unity and the Bristol Old Vic on *Mother Courage*, Unity again on *Simone Machard*, the Edinburgh Festival on *The Seven Deadly Sins*, the Mermaid once more on *Schweik*, and other, *ad hoc*, London companies on *Baal* and *Im Dickicht der Städte* (besides a number of productions by provincial repertory theatres). The first three of these productions were indeed surprisingly successful, conveying, despite some heavy handicaps, much of the essence of the works concerned. But the English theatre as a whole is still far from mastering Brecht; even the best of its productions have excruciatingly embarrassing moments both for the Brecht connoisseur and for the ordinary spectator; while from the box-office point of view he has of course been a disaster. Our professional theatre is anxious to tackle him all right, and he is seen by it as a challenge, an opportunity and a vast new source of ideas. But so far he has been more within the grasp of the unspoiled, and much of what has been done with his plays fully justifies those critics who see him above all else as a bore.

The moral is threefold, and it has not changed since this book first came out. It is partly that the devices which Brecht worked out for the German stage can distract or titillate the English audience, and that even where we enjoy the process, it diverts from the play. It is partly that our younger actors have more of the strength and directness needed for Brecht than their elders, however distinguished, and are much less likely to 'theatre him down'. But it is above all that, as Brecht found when the Berlin police interfered with *Die Mutter*, the real force of these plays lies in the words. The text was always his first concern in the theatre, from Bronnen's *Vater-*

mord on; and as soon as it is clearly and unaffectedly delivered the play in question has largely come to life. Stagey voices or obtrusive tricks of production are bound to destroy the point, even if they can apparently be justified in 'Brechtian' terms.

So we must cut back through the theory and the fascinating political jungle which has sprung up round Brecht; back even through the story and methods of the Berliner Ensemble; back to the poet and dramatist whom we studied in the opening chapters; to the sixteen-year-old boy who appeared to his first editor as a 'shy, withdrawn young person, who could only talk when you had wound him up. . .'.

> He was full of a real sense of life: one can almost say, possessed by a hunger for life, which he followed with all his senses alert, even though he approached everything with a certain reserve. Sentimentality was quite foreign to him. He seemed to be searching both for happiness and for truth; he could very early be seen to have a horror of baseness and a strong social feeling. Even apart from his poetic gifts he gave the impression of a definite individual with strongly personal characteristics . . . I always found it enchanting to talk to him; he gave off a kind of electric current.

There are so many different aspects to Brecht's life and work, and he represents such a close integration of normally separate fields that it is essential to start at the beginning and get this central figure distinct.

Here, in the young Brecht, are the love of movement and of our society's swift changes; and the sensitivity that made him so closely reflect them. Here are the detachment and the hatred of pretension; the resilient vitality that led him into untenable situations, with the sheer obstinacy that prevented him from giving them up. None of this has vanished in his later work, and it is only a disproportionate resentment of Brecht's supposed politics that led critics to suggest that at the end of his twenties he underwent some radical and regrettable change. The point of Communism for him was not only that it was the one rational force to oppose the rising barbarism which the more moderate parties throughout Europe were then refusing to face; it was that it seemed identifiable with scientific scepticism, with the interests of the dispossessed, with the ways of thought (and art) proper to a highly industrial age. The point of his new dramatic theory was not only that it justified certain congenial experiments but that it put the world in a fresh light and tried to stimulate the audience to see for itself what was wrong. In both these ways he was showing his 'strong social feeling' and striving for a plain, direct art in which there would be nothing false. The simplicity which he thus achieved only made his individuality more obvious: nearly all his work is unmistakable; even his conversation bore the same stamp as his verse.

Without this continual reference back to the writer it is hard to see all Brecht's aspects in perspective. His occasional ruthlessness, instead of being a deliberate renunciation of kindness for urgent social reasons, may look like cruelty; his coolness, instead of being an aid to explanation, like lack of human warmth; his hatred of the Nazis like indifference to his own country's fate. This would not matter if it were only a question of Brecht's historical role; but art involves seeing the whole picture, and deciding what is now likely to be of value to us. In this view, the important point is not that Brecht jumped too easily to ready-made Marxist conclusions; it is the scepticism which made him write: 'As for what we want to discover, we must view it, when discovered, with particular mistrust.' It is not that he believed too unquestioningly in 'the workers' and the Russians and the identification of a particular economic structure with war; it is his view that

> On no account must we yield to the desire for new beliefs that springs from the bankruptcy of the old: to men's terrible desire for blindness. . . .

It is not that he could make his characters into stylized dummies, but that

> Of course the stage of a realistic theatre must be peopled by live, three-dimensional, self-contradictory characters, with all their passions, unconsidered utterances and actions. The stage is not a hothouse or a zoological museum full of stuffed animals. . . .

Nor did the fact that his writing was explicit mean that it had to be pitched at an infantile level. For 'Art is no Land of Cockaigne, where roast pigeons fly into one's mouth'.

Such often perverse contradictions give a wide possibility of misunderstanding, but we have to see them whole. Thus beside the producer who offered the audience ready-made conclusions stood the sceptic who was ready to disbelieve all conclusions. Beside the propagandist who hammered the point home stood the rationalist who wanted each spectator to do his thinking for himself. Beside the 'epic' writer with his flat succession of carefully laboured details stood the theoretician who insisted that the audience must be kept awake. Beside the gadget-addict with his sub-titles and his tin-tack piano and his odd emblems lowered from the flies stood the ascetic who held that simplicity made for sense. In all these instances of Brecht's far-flung inconsistency it was the rational, simple side of each antithesis that was more evident from his writings, the more mannered, stylized side that appeared in his productions and has therefore seemed the more striking to us. Nobody can stage Brecht's plays in this country who is not aware of them both, and is not prepared to modify the stylization in order to suit our very different audience and stage. For the gist of Brecht's theatre is that it tries to set out the rich (and comic) complications of reality; that it uses intelligible terms and applies all the resources of the stage to furthering the sense; above all that it aims to make men think. Of course Brecht's self-contradictory nature helped to give his work depth; and it is part of his fascination as a figure. But he would not have wished it to mislead us about his basic aims.

Over-impressed with the notions of 'estrangement' and 'alienation', our producers and critics alike seem to see Brecht's work as foreign to us, and necessarily and intentionally so. They interpret it with the example of the Berliner Ensemble in mind and a novelty-seeking metropolitan audience in view; they pick on whatever appears freakish in it, overlooking those aspects that are least German, least orthodoxly Stalinist, closest to our own tradition and ways of thought. This is a pity, for technically our theatre hardly needs to try any fresh tricks; the individual competence of our actors is on the whole above that of the Ensemble; and it is no matter of 'method' but simply time and money and lack of conviction that make us fall short. What we want is writers who can bring out the best in our theatre instead of the worst; and here Brecht is a much more relevant example than is generally supposed. For he used English models, or else common European ones; he illustrated his opinions by citing Auden and Chaplin, Shelley and Swift, Hogarth and Low; he liked our traditional qualities of clarity and restraint. He worked, as we have seen, on Shakespeare and Marlowe, Webster, Farquhar, Gay and Synge; he was an addict of the English and American detective story, taking much of the tone and style of the *Dreigroschenroman* from Edgar Wallace and *Arturo Ui* from the old gangster films; even the Orientals he saw through Waley's eyes. And so his own writings ought to be much more accessible to us than to the Italians, Russians, Poles or French. We should be able to assimilate them as Lenz and Büchner assimilated Shakespeare. We do not have to treat them as 'strange' or 'alien'. Many of their lessons we can ourselves apply.

*　　　*　　　*

In a splendid essay on the Icelandic Sagas W. H. Auden defined what he calls the 'social realism' (as opposed to Socialist Realism) of these epics in terms that, without being intended for him, could well be applied to Brecht. The social realist writer, he says, must exclude himself from his narrative; he must never pass judgment on his characters, but leave them to judge one another; he must restrict his account of human nature to external signs. His heroes and villains must lie within real-life limits (so that their bravery, for instance, has to have an element of cowardice), and their speech has to be in more or less natural terms. 'It follows from this,' argued Auden,

> that, though it is possible to write social realist works in verse, provided the poet uses a mixed or middle style, prose is the natural or proper medium, and

a prose, moreover, which is as free as possible from all rhetorical schematization and metaphysical elaboration.

'Concrete and fastidious' is his phrase for this kind of writing, though he takes care not to put it forward as the only recipe for the modern writer, or necessarily the best. He sees it simply as the latest type of literature to evolve, 'and in some ways, perhaps . . . the most grown-up'.

It is certainly an approach that would be welcome in a society like ours, where so many artists have seemed to be occupying themselves with trivialities, or simply going soft. Today the tendency of many gifted writers is to become autobiographical and self-centred; they concentrate on style (or technique) to the point of affectation; they often go against the grain of our language by wrapping up their meaning or trying to pass off triviality as deep thought. There is a lack of toughness in their work, in many cases a lack of humour too, and the spark that comes from contact with a wide public is lacking. 'Anything,' as Osborne wrote, 'to avoid the odium and the bother of trying to speak to [it] in a language which you can both understand.' This is where Brecht's example can be of use, not because what he has to say is always likely to be important, but because he has worked out ways of saying things that are, and has shown us how beauty and economy can be fused with hard sense. The first English writer to learn from this example was probably Mr Auden himself, who says that he was 'certainly influenced' by *The Threepenny Opera* and *Mahagonny* and by the *Hauspostille* poems, and later translated the *Caucasian Chalk Circle* songs at Brecht's own request: thus –

He who wears the shoes of gold
Tramples on the weak and old
Does evil all day long
And mocks at wrong.

O, to carry as one's own
Heavy is the heart of stone;
The power to do ill
Wears out the will.

Hunger he will dread,
Not those who go unfed;
Fear the fall of night,
But not the light.

This instance shows Auden's characteristic lucidity, which is quite as recognizable as Brecht's; and the two poets have a number of features in common. Not only were both involved in the anti-Fascism of the 1930s, but they share the same respect for the intelligence and awareness of the sciences; and both indulge freely in parody and the use of popular forms. There is even something of 'Verfremdung' in what Mr John Lehmann has written of Auden: 'his unexpected way of looking at things, his habit of throwing light suddenly on ideas from an entirely unorthodox angle, has been one of the greatest secrets of his success'.

But one thing which is wrong with Auden's work is right with Brecht's, and that is the way in which these forms are used. There is an element in Auden's lighter verse that often turns simplicity sour: a lack of sympathy for the people to whom these forms are common, which makes their employment seem slightly mean. Where Brecht's songs and ballads can satirize without sneering, those of such English poets as Messrs Auden and Plomer are too often concerned with what are ultimately class distinctions: with jokes about places and people of lower middle-class associations: so that the medium itself becomes a piece of (formal) slumming too. Brecht's 'Jakob Apfelböck', for instance, is quite serious in its squalor –

> The light was mild as Jakob Apfelböck
> Battered his father and his mother down
> And locked their bodies with the dirty clothes
> And hung about the house all on his own.

– where Auden's somewhat similar 'Victor' of 1940 is not:

> It was a frosty December
>   When into his grave he sank;
> His uncle found Victor a post as cashier
>   In the Midland Counties Bank . . .

It is the common English disease, and it infects much of the light verse of our better poets with a deplorable highbrow facetiousness. A public form becomes a private joke, and behind it lurk the horrors of 'U' and 'Non-U'.

That, certainly, has been the great difference between Brecht and the English writers of his own generation. The latter may have shared certain common experiences; but their technical and political sophistication no longer hides signs of a certain softness at the core. Their nearest descendants, the 'Movement' poets of the 1950s, have been very much cagier about being lured into attitudes in which they do not themselves seriously believe, but as a result their work seems low-toned, reluctant to commit itself, anxious not to dabble in matters where they feel inexpert. 'Better, of course', says a poem by Mr Kingsley Amis.

> if images were plain,
> Warnings clearly said, shapes put down quite still
> Within the fingers' reach, or else nowhere;
> But complexities crowd the simplest thing.

They do indeed, and it is an undoubted weakness in Brecht that he so often ironed them out into flat antitheses. This is no reason for abandoning the effort to sort the complexities out, or for being scared of all social feeling. The poet of this group that comes closest to Brecht is Mr D. J. Enright, whose verse is not only intelligible and direct, somewhat in the manner of Brecht's unrhymed poems, but will get to grips with political or plain human issues, often in the Oriental settings which he too finds congenial. 'Good lord', exclaim the Interpreters in one of his Japanese poems,

> Good lord, if a poet really meant what he said,
> we should all be out of a job – why on earth
> would he sing of the merely real? – the papers have taken up that chorus –
> 'the agonies, the strife of human hearts?' – why, Hollywood will do that for us.
>
> The peasants have salvaged their cabbages; the block
> of flats is nearly as ready as its tenants; somewhere
> someone saves a child from a swollen river
> and really means it –

The difference here is in the tone, which is almost affectedly offhand and throw-away. This was indeed the generation known to literary journalism as the Angry Young Men; *New Lines*, the 'Movement' anthology from which these last quotations were taken, came out in 1956, the year when that ridiculous phrase was coined. It was the less academic and contained protesters that followed, however, who began to see Brecht as something of a hero and a model. Mr Christopher Logue in particular so steeped himself in Brecht's style and mannerisms that he carried over whole lines and successions of images into his own work, translating them not only into English but at times into a rather unnatural framework of self-conscious rhetoric and strained pugnacity.

The 'Movement' poets steered clear of the theatre (which Mr Amis, for one, despised for its artificiality); they liked the cinema better; they wrote no songs. No doubt they were discouraged by their precursors, who had been burdened by a dreadfully dampening conception of the verse play. According to this the poet – Eliot, for instance, or on a less awesome level Mr Christopher Fry – would rescue the language of the drama and raise its aesthetic status without apparently affecting traditional dramatic form; the fallen woman was to be saved, but to remain, ennobled, working her old West End beat. The arrival of *The Threepenny Opera*, however, at once set entirely new standards; in Mr Logue's *The Lily-White Boys* of 1960, for instance, the verse was strictly for singing: an independent element contributing to a different form of play. And this went with a new spontaneous wave of interest in the performance and public delivery of verse – in poetry to jazz accompaniment, in the narrative folk- or pseudo-folk ballad that Brecht himself so liked, in poetry readings by more or less unorthodox readers, and most recently in pure sound poems – which developed in many countries during the 1960s and produced as its most sharply intelligible practitioner here Mr Adrian Mitchell. Thus even though Brecht was very late in coming to this country, when he came it was as part of a whole series of other developments that have still not worked themselves out: not only this concern with performance but also the 'satire' movement that started in 1960 with *Beyond the Fringe*, plus a general awakening to modern German writing, much of which (the poetry especially) reflects his influence. There are now, as there were not when the the first edition of the present book was written, a number of contexts in which Brecht's poems and songs seem to us to fit naturally. It is not so hard as it was to see their relevance.

The difficulty with the English theatre in the past has been that it lacked any recognized channel by which the promising writer could get practical experience, such as the German theatre offers in the institution of the 'Dramaturg'. This has now changed considerably; Bristol has long had its resident playwright, and more recently the National Theatre and the Royal Shakespeare Company have also appointed literary managers or advisers. It is no longer uncommon for our liveliest and most promising writers to turn to the stage. Brecht's lesson here is clear: that a playwright cannot be merely literary; that he must know what he wants of actors and producer and composer and designer; and that he has to plan his work with all the elements of the combined operation in view. Unfortunately, the more eye-catching of Brecht's methods are easily divorced from his basic approach, and in so far as they have become familiar to us we may think that we have nothing more to learn. Especially in the modern American drama we have seen them reflected in a number of ways. Odet's *Waiting for Lefty* (1935), for instance, has the dry, sketch-like scenes of *Die Mutter* (which was produced in New York that year); Blitzstein's *Cradle Will Rock* is a rather thinly-written imitation of the operas with Weill; Wilder's *Our Town* and *The Skin of Our Teeth* have the deliberate breaking of illusion, the Piscator-type projections, the 'epic' shape; while Mr Eric Bentley sees Brecht's influence in Archibald Macleish and Paul Green, whose *Johnny Johnson* of 1936 with Kurt Weill seems to derive from the old *Schweik* plan; and something of the 'epic' narrative can be traced in *Camino Real* and even in *The Teahouse of the August Moon*. None of these writers seems to have got the best out of Brecht's work: the contrasts which he secures by precise cutting; the snapping-off of lines, of scenes; the continual emphasis on the hard bones of the story; the alternation of song and speech, illusion and reality, poetry and prose. Even where we have seen his methods we still have to learn how they can be combined and used.

In 1956 a great change came over our theatre. It was in every way a crucial year, for besides the first two major productions of Brecht plays and the first (and so far only) visit of the Berliner Ensemble it saw that production of John Osborne's *Look Back in Anger* from which the whole new movement in English playwriting seems to take off; Osborne himself incidentally acted the water-carrier in *The Good Woman of Sezuan*. It was also the year of the Suez and Budapest crises, which marked a certain loosening-up of political attitudes among intellectuals all over the world. These things now seem to have been related; the subsequent advance in Brecht's English reputation to have been part of a larger process in which writers like Messrs. Osborne, Wesker and Arden, producers like Joan Littlewood and Lindsay Anderson, and the emergence of such phenomena as the English neo-realist film, the Centre 42 movement, the admirable theatrical magazine *Encore* and the new satirical tradition represented by *That Was the Week That Was* and the Establishment Club all belong. In all this Brecht has been a very active influence; thus the vogue for historical plays (such as Mr Osborne's *Luther* or Mr Robert Bolt's *A Man for All Seasons*) clearly stemmed from *Galileo*, and so did the technique of their staging; the change from the naturalism of the Wesker trilogy to the lighter and bonier style of *Chips with Everything* reflected Brecht's impact on writer and producer (John Dexter) alike; while John Arden's development of an individual style of poetry-cum-realism with fierce political undertones owed something to Brecht, whether or not the debt was direct and conscious. At the same time something of Brecht has come to us through other, living, foreign influences on our theatre: through the plays of Max Frisch and Friedrich Dürrenmatt for instance, and the more recent work of Arthur Adamov, or through the productions of Giorgio Strehler in Milan and Roger Planchon in Lyon and Paris. The harsh toughness of the seventeenth century as Brecht saw it can be felt too in newer novels such as David Caute's *Comrade Jacob* and J. B. Pick's *The Fat Valley*. The film *The Seven Samurai*, which had a considerable success here, is almost like a Japanese version of *Mother Courage*.

*　　*　　*

It is worth looking at Brecht's work in this parochial, if also contemporary light, because it gives some idea of the changes that can come from assimilating him rather than from mere imitation and (more or less unsuccessful) performance. At the same time, his true value to us rests on two rather wider points, which current criticism almost entirely neglects. The first of these is that a writer, a producer or any other creative artist can be original without using novel or highly complicated means. Brecht is the proof, at a time when such people are very rare, that if an artist has the determination he will stand out most clearly from his fellows by expressing his conceptions simply and intelligibly with the means that lie to hand; and that this will give even supposed highbrows a deeper aesthetic satisfaction than any originality that is confined to the style. No man's inventiveness and creative power are unlimited: if he spends them all on the evolution of a private language he may run dry when it comes to having something to say. This is the lesson of those cases where the novelty is beginning to wear off. Under the forms of atonalism we sometimes suspect the sentiments of Brahms, under those of cubism a certain insensitive banality, under those of linguistic experimenters like Gertrude Stein – nothing much. We have run through most possibilities of fresh expression in the arts in the last fifty years and can now look at their relation to what is being expressed. Are they suitable? Is it worth while?

The satisfaction of Brecht's work lies not in the form itself, but in that command of form which can shape it to fit a content which matters. The means are often simple, familiar; the subtlety lies in their combination and choice. For as soon as anyone is moved by a communicative impulse that is stronger than himself, then he can forget about 'originality': that pathetic ideal of the arts in our time. He uses a vocabulary which people will understand, and however highly educated he is he needs all his wits and all his artistry to convey his point. In Brecht's case this impulse is due to the exceptionally close relation between art and the artist's view of our social life. The view in question is one whose political results have sometimes proved horribly wrong, but it has the great advantage of making the artist feel that he is at once a member and a useful servant of his society, living in a sphere neither above nor outside. The originality of his work will then lie under the surface; its beauty will be largely a matter of balance; the chief criterion will be how it expresses the sense. So long as it is the artist himself who determines this identification of meaning and means he will not be anyone's subordinate; the fact that some politicians would like to make him so does not have to frighten him out of the game.

This is one side of Brecht's achievement, and the other is closely akin. For it is just on this issue of intelligibility and communication that the arts have so unhappily been split. In all highly developed countries we now have highbrow art and lowbrow art, with a complicated tangle of mutual hatreds and snobberies between the two. The reason for this is not that the stuff of art is too rarefied for general circulation but that so many artists have chosen to express commonplace sentiments in a rarefied way. This is something that Brecht did not do, partly because of a social sense, partly from sheer self-control and self-denial. And yet, from *The Threepenny Opera* on, highbrows and lowbrows alike have delighted in his work, and it has influenced both ends of art, from the BBC Third Programme to the American musical stage. Behind it lies a whole Central European movement of the 1920s which is far too little recognized: a movement for taking the elements of popular and public and everyday art, and using them to make something fresh. The musical movement centred on the Baden-Baden festival, the 'New matter-of-factness' of painters and journalists and documentary writers, the light verse of the satirists, the clowning of George Voskovec and Jan Werich in Prague, the industrial art developed at the Bauhaus under Gropius: all these pointed the way to an abolition of the snob-barrier in art. And they did so not by reviving the half-dead 'folk art' of a pre-industrial society, but by using current popular forms and media for perfectly serious ends.

The Americans felt the impact of this movement more strongly than we; they absorbed several of its personalities; to a certain extent they carried it on. The high quality musical, the Balanchine and Agnes de Mille ballets, the standard of photography in *Life*, the UPA cartoons: several such examples show that highbrow and lowbrow can still interact, with extraordinarily stimulating effect. But in England, despite the examples of *New Writing* and the documentary film movement, of Mr Britten and the War Artists and the general circulation brought into the arts by the war, the temper of our culture now seems different. The highbrow artist has become scared of being contaminated, whether by commerce or by politics; it is 'reactionary' not to be 'original'; and originality is still seen as a matter of finding new and esoteric forms, most of them in fact already thoroughly explored and exhausted by the Germans or French. This is true despite the movement towards 'pop art' which swept England and the United States since the present book first appeared. Admittedly it brought a new concern with the flashier and more ridiculously commercial elements in our industrialized popular culture, which painters like Robert Rauschenberg and Peter Blake contrived to stick together in a Dadaistic or literal, *trompe l'œil* manner so as to make their own artistic language. But consciously or not this has proved to be something of a joke; because accessibility is not really the aim, pop art often conveys a flavour of smart condescension – of cultural slumming – for all its fun and individuality. Except in the one field of industrial design, highbrow and lowbrow remain held apart by jealousies, resentments and a divided communications structure that creates its own hierarchy of high and low. We are no longer quite so satisfied to accept this, but that does not mean that the cultural barriers in our society have suddenly tumbled down.

All the same they are being undermined. Not so much by the new cultural sociologists who have concerned themselves with popular culture and mass communications, for so far such researches (exemplified in Stuart Hall's and Paddy Whannel's *The Popular Arts*) have been directed to understanding mass culture as currently produced, rather than to any possibility of evolving new structures and forms. But even this concern is only part of a great social and educational transformation that has been going on in this country and seems to be revolutionizing the arts in a semi-underground way. In the sixties it was evident that the new sub-intelligentsia created by the Welfare State was making a fresh audience for the arts, particularly for serious jazz and classical music, for ballet, for factual writing and for improved visual design. Today it is clear that much more is entailed. There are all kinds of cross-connections, for instance, between jazz – and even pop music – and traditionally highbrow pursuits; there is not just a new curiosity about painting but a new sense that it ought to be *fun*; there is a revolt against the mechanical perfection of industrialized or institutionalized culture, which has created a large new public for poetry readings, for 'happenings' and even for poetry on the page. All this is something that the young now seem to see as their preserve: as an enclave of honesty, of self-expression and of profound excitement, to be defended against the dirty everyday world and developed above all on a local level – through jazz clubs, art schools, the little magazines and some of the newer provincial theatres. It would be untrue to say that Brecht was an integral part of it. For one thing the present fashion in rebellion is for something much more incoherent and nihilistic; for another the best means of access to him – his poems – remain largely closed. None the less it is a framework within which Brecht's work makes sense and could act as a fertile source of new discoveries. There is a great deal still to be got from him. In this country at least he is not a monument yet.

Bibliography

The following revised bibliography supplants that in the first two editions and like-wise the revised and shortened version given in the third (1967). The former may still be worth consulting by those seeking information about musical settings or rather ancient gramophone records, but otherwise the scholar will do better with such detailed compilations as Walter Nubel's bibliography in the *Sinn und Form* (Potsdam) Second Special Brecht number of 1957 and Klaus-Dietrich Petersen's *Bertolt-Brecht-Bibliographie* (Bad Homburg, 1968). To keep track of all the new books and articles about Brecht in many languages is probably impossible, but the publications of the International Brecht Society (see below) and the annual *The Year's Work in Modern Language Studies* (published by the Modern Humanities Research Association) do their best. So far as his own writings are concerned, how-ever, the material in the Bertolt-Brecht-Archiv in East Berlin has been most use-fully catalogued in the four volumes of its *Bestandsverzeichnis des literarischen Nachlasses*, edited by Herta Ramthun and published by Aufbau-Verlag, East Berlin and Weimar, between 1969 and 1973. The volumes cover: 1 Plays, including fragmentary and collaborative works; 2 Poems; 3 Prose, including film treatments and scripts; 4 Oddments, including source material, transcripts of discussions, tunes by Brecht and work by his collaborators. Correspondence and contracts are the main areas so far unlisted.

This archive, now part of the East German Academy of Arts, is in Brecht's old flat at 125, Chausseestrasse, 104 Berlin. The International Brecht Society is cur-rently based c/o the Department of Comparative Literature, University of Wis-consin, Milwaukee, Wis. 53201. It publishes a *Jahrbuch* from Frankfurt and quarterly *Communications* from Oxford, Ohio.

I. COLLECTED EDITIONS

Brecht's *Gesammelte Werke* were published by Suhrkamp-Verlag, Frankfurt, his principal publishers, in 1967 in two simultaneous editions, the one in seven volumes and the other, using the same setting and pagination, in twenty. Its subdivisions are *Stücke, Gedichte, Prosa* and *Schriften*, this last dividing yet again into *Zum Theater, Zur Literatur und Kunst* and *Zur Politik und Gesellschaft*. Subsequently the *Texte für Film* were added to it in the same format, and in 1974 the *Arbeitsjournal*. The edition has not been issued in East Germany.

A previous uniform edition, originated by Suhrkamp in 1955, involves many duplications and is now largely superseded in the West. Published under licence by Aufbau-Verlag, it remains the main edition in the East, where the fifth Prose volume, containing the Me-Ti aphorisms, has only recently appeared. Since its major divisions are called by the same names as those of the *Gesammelte Werke*, to reduce confusion my own references always distinguish between *Stücke, Gedichte,* etc. in the uniform edition, and *GW Stücke, GW Gedichte,* etc. in the 1967 collected works.

Two earlier collected editions, arranged on other principles and containing many variants, were left uncompleted. One was the paperbound *Versuche*, published between 1930–32 by Kiepenheuer, Berlin and from 1949–56 by Suhrkamp, who subsequently also reprinted the Kiepenheuer batch. Meant to contain Brecht's current output, each of the fifteen booklets is a mixture of his different genres. The other was the Malik-Verlag's *Gesammelte Werke*, published from Prague in 1938, of which only two volumes appeared, though two others were in course of preparation when the Nazis moved in. Only proofs have survived.

2. PLAYS

Published stage works not included in the collected editions are the first version of *Mahagonny* (Universal-Edition, 1927); the ballet *Die Sieben Todsünden* (Suhrkamp, 1959), the opera text of *Lucullus* (Aufbau, 1951) and the cantata *Herrnburger Bericht* (Freie Deutsche Jugend, East Berlin 1951). Individual poems from the ballet and the cantata have however been taken into the *Gedichte*. The major un-published works omitted are *Happy End* and *The Duchess of Malfi*, while the *Berliner Requiem* once again is divided into its component poems.

Plays have been issued in a great number of individual editions or combinations, in both Germanies. The most important for the student or director is the series of 'Materialien' volumes containing notes, background material and sometimes alter-native versions for given plays, which Suhrkamp publish intermittently in their paperback 'Edition Suhrkamp'. So far they have appeared for the following plays ('ES' number in brackets): *Antigone* (134), *Baal* (170 and 248), *Der gute Mensch von Sezuan* (247), *Die heilige Johanna der Schlachthöfe* (427), *Die Massnahme* (415), *Im Dickicht der Städte* (246), *Der Jasager/Der Neinsager* (171), *Der Kaukasiche Kreidekreis* (155), *Galilei* (44), *Leben Eduards II* (245), *Mutter Courage* (50), *Die Mutter* (305), *Schweyk im zweiten Weltkrieg* (604) and *Trommeln in der Nacht* (490). Note that the titles do not always include the word 'Materialien', and the value of the books varies.

In translation:

The *Collected Plays* are published by Eyre Methuen (London) and Random House (New York), using different translations but the same editorial apparatus. Volumes so far issued or in course of preparation are (for the UK and US editions):

1. *Baal, Drums in the Night, In the Jungle of Cities, Edward II*, the five early one-act plays (numbers 5–8 in the opening analysis, plus *Der Fischzug*) (UK and US).
2. *A Man's a Man, Mahagonny, The Threepenny Opera* (US).
5. *Galileo, Lucullus, Mother Courage* (US). This includes the Brecht–Laughton *Galileo* as well as the final version.
6. *The Good Person of Szechwan, Puntila, Arturo Ui*, the one-act plays *Dansen* and *Was kostet das Eisen?*, Practice Scenes for Actors (US).
7. *Simone Machard, Schweyk in the Second World War, The Caucasian Chalk Circle, The Duchess of Malfi* (US and UK).
9. Adaptations for the Berliner Ensemble: *The Tutor, Coriolanus, The Trial of Joan of Arc, Don Juan, Trumpets and Drums* (US only).

The earlier *Plays*, published in two volumes by Methuen in 1960 and 1962 and now out of print, contained:

1. *The Threepenny Opera, Lucullus (a), Galileo, The Caucasian Chalk Circle.*
2. *Mother Courage, Saint Joan of the Stockyards, The Good Person of Szechwan*

Galileo, The Caucasian Chalk Circle, Mother Courage, Saint Joan of the Stockyards and *The Good Person of Szechwan* have subsequently been reprinted in separate paperback editions by Eyre Methuen, London; in the same series are *Arturo Ui* translated by Ralph Manheim (1976), *The Threepenny Opera* translated by Hugh MacDiarmid (1973) and *Puntila* translated by John Willett (1977).

There is also a set of translations published by Grove Press, New York, based in some cases on early texts which under US copyright laws were 'in the public domain'. These include the *Seven Plays by Bertolt Brecht* (1961) containing:

Jungle of the Cities, A Man's a Man, St Joan of the Stockyards, Mother Courage, Galileo, The Good Woman of Setzuan, The Caucasian Chalk Circle

and the paperback volumes:

Baal, A Man's a Man and The Elephant Calf (1964), *Jungle of the Cities and other plays* (1966), *Edward II* (1966), *The Mother* (1965), and *The Visions of Simone Machard* (1965).

For translations of the other plays see the opening Analysis of the Plays.

3. VERSE

The collected *Gedichte* are arranged more or less chronologically, but they embrace as separate entities the three books of new poems published by Brecht in his lifetime: *Hauspostille* (1927), *Lieder Gedichte Chöre* (with Hanns Eisler, 1934), and *Svendborger Gedichte* (1939). They are due to be supplemented by a volume of some eighty previously unpublished poems. Other collections now superseded are as under:

Taschenpostille was the precursor of *Hauspostille*, published the previous year in an edition of 25 copies and almost identical with it in composition. It was republished by Aufbau-Verlag, E. Berlin, in 1959.

Hundert Gedichte was a selection by Wieland Herzfelde of published and unpublished poems, issued by Aufbau-Verlag in 1951. It was not published in Western Germany.

Gedichte und Lieder was a selection by Peter Suhrkamp of published and unpublished poems, issued by Suhrkamp-Verlag in 1956. It was not published in East Germany.

Kriegsfibel, included in *Gedichte 6*, were written as four-line comments to war photographs, and were published in this form by Eulenspiegel-Verlag, E. Berlin, 1955.

A number of poems or groups of poems (notably 'Aus dem Lesebuch für Städtebewohner', 'Studien', 'Buckower Elegien' and 'Gedichte aus dem Messingkauf') were originally published in different volumes of the *Versuche*. There are also various books of selections, mostly made since Brecht's death. The most notable of these (on account of its cheapness) is the *Gedichte* selected by Siegfried Streller and published by Reclam, Leipzig, in 1955. It should not be confused with the ten-volume edition of the same title. *Selected Poems* chosen for English schools by K. Wölfel was published by the Oxford University Press in 1965.

In translation:

Poems 1913–1956. A selection of about 500 poems translated by various English and American hands, and edited by John Willett and Ralph Manheim in consultation with Erich Fried. Eyre Methuen, 1976. (Excludes songs from plays.) Also available as three paperback volumes (without notes, etc.): *Poems Part I: 1913–1928, Poems Part II: 1929–1938*, and *Poems Part III: 1938–1956*.

Songs and Poems from Plays. Supplementary volume of about 170 poems, compiled by the same editors on the same principles. To be published by Eyre Methuen.

Selected Poems. (Fifty poems, with English translation by H. R. Hays.) Reynal and Hitchcock, New York, 1947. Grove Press, New York and Calder, London, n.d. (1959).

Poems on the Theatre. (Most of the 'Gedichte aus dem Messingkauf', translated by John Berger and Anya Bostock.) Scorpion Press, London, 1961.

A Manual of Piety. (Bilingual edition of the *Hauspostille*, translated by Eric Bentley.) Grove Press, New York, 1966.

4. PROSE

The *Prosa* division of the collected works includes the following: some eighty stories, of which eight had already been published, interspersed with poems, as *Kalendergeschichten* in 1948; the *Flüchtlingsgespräche*, a set of dialogues written in 1941–2 and first published in 1960; *Der Dreigroschenroman* (1934), Brecht's only completed novel, on themes from *The Threepenny Opera*; *Die Geschäfte des Herrn Julius Caesar*, an unfinished novel in diary form first published in 1957; *Me-Ti/ Buch der Wendungen*, an incomplete set of aphorisms with a Chinese setting but contemporary relevance; the *Tui-Roman*, extensive notes and fragments for a novel on the German intellectuals (relating to the play *Turandot*); and finally the *Geschichten vom Herrn Keuner*, aphorisms which Brecht had begun publishing in the *Versuche* and kept adding to.

In translation:

A Penny for the Poor. (*Der Dreigroschenroman*, translated by Desmond Vesey and Christopher Isherwood.) Robert Hale, London, 1937. Under title *The Threepenny Novel*, Evergreen Books, New York, 1956; Hanison, London, 1958; Penguin, London, 1961.

Tales from the Calendar. Translated by Yvonne Kapp and Michael Hamburger, Methuen, London, 1961.

'Die Geschäfte des Herrn Julius Cäsar.' Partial translation by Dorothy Alexander in *Nimbus* (London), February 1958.

'Meditations of Herr Keuner.' (Short selection, translated by Heinrich Fraenkel.) In *New Statesman* (London), November 3, 1956, p. 542.

5. THEORY AND PRACTICE OF THE THEATRE

The *Schriften zum Theater* division of the collected works includes the notes on plays, the theoretical essays and dialogues and the two major theoretical works, the

'Kleines Organon für das Theater' and the unfinished 'Der Messingkauf' which preceded it. Poems associated with the latter, however, are printed in the *Gedichte*. There was also, confusingly, a much shorter *Schriften zum Theater* selection published by Suhrkamp in 1957. Outside this scheme of things, and containing some additional writings by Brecht, are the following:

Theaterarbeit. (Collective account of the Berliner Ensemble's first six productions, edited by Brecht, Berlau, Palitzsch, etc., and fully illustrated.) Dresdner Verlag, Dresden, 1952; Progress-Verlag Johannes Fladung, Düsseldorf, n.d. (1955). This contains a number of important notes and fragments by Brecht, as well as work by other hands and many photographs of the Ensemble's performances.

Antigonemodell 1948. (Photographs of a production, with text of the play and special commentary by Brecht.) Henschel-Verlag, Berlin, 1955.

Couragemodell 1949. (Companion volume.) Ibid, 1958.

Aufbau einer Rolle – Galilei. (Three booklets, giving text of the play, Brecht's account of his collaboration with Laughton, and Eisler's account of Busch's performance, with photographs of the relevant productions.) Ibid, 1958.

There are many photographs of Berliner Ensemble productions subsequent to *Theaterarbeit*, with cast lists and other details, in Friedrich Dieckmann: *Karl von Appens Bühnenbilder am Berliner Ensemble*, Henschel-Verlag, East Berlin, 1971. Another relevant book is Fritz Hadamovsky's catalogue *Caspar Nehers szenisches Werk*, Brüder Hollinek, Vienna 1972, which lists this designer's extensive legacy to the Vienna National Library.

In translation:

Brecht on Theatre. (Selected notes and essays, translated and annotated by John Willett.) Methuen, London, and Hill and Wang, New York, 1964. Includes the 'Kleines Organon für das Theater' and all the other main items apart from 'Der Messingkauf'.

The Messingkauf Dialogues. ('Der Messingkauf' less the poems, practice scenes, etc., translated by John Willett.) Methuen, London, 1965.

'On Experimental Theater.' ('Über experimentelles Theater', from *Schriften zum Theater 3*, translated by Carl Richard Müller.) *The Tulane Drama Review* (New Orleans), Autumn 1961. The text in *Brecht on Theatre* has been cut. This is complete.

'Brecht on Theater 1920.' (From 'Augsburger Theaterkritiken' in *Schriften zum Theater 1*, translated by James L. Rosenberg.) *The Tulane Drama Review*, Autumn 1962.

'Prospectus of the Diderot Society.' ('Prospekt der Diderot-Gesellschaft', unpublished in German.) *The Quarterly Journal of Speech*, XLVII, April 2, 1961, p. 114.

For alternative translations of items included in *Brecht on Theatre*, see the bibliographical note at the end of that volume.

6. FILMS

The *Texte für Filme* added to the collected edition in 1969 consists of two volumes. Vol. 1 contains three early scripts (*Drei im Turm*, *Der Brillantenfresser* and *Das Mysterium der Jamaika-Bar*) followed by a reconstituted script for *Kuhle Wampe* (1932) and a 1955 script for the cancelled film version of *Mother Courage*. Vol. 2

includes some thirty-odd shorter film stories, treatments and ideas of all periods, among them 'Die Beule', Brecht's treatment for the Pabst *Threepenny Opera*.

Fuller material on the two major films is contained in *Versuche 3* ('Dreigroschen-film, Dreigroschenprozess'), 1931, and in *Kuhle Wampe oder Wem gehört die Welt? Filmprotokoll und Materialien*, Reclam, Leipzig 1971. See also the 'Über Film' section of the *Schriften zur Literatur und Kunst* (below).

7. POLITICAL WRITINGS

Apart from the *Me-Ti* aphorisms in the *Prosa* division, and the various political songs and poems in the *Gedichte*, these are supposedly grouped in the 360-page *Schriften zur Politik und Gesellschaft* of the *Schriften*. This overlaps however with the Art and Politics section of the *Schriften zur Literatur und Kunst*, which includes Brecht's two major speeches of the 1930s and his anti-Nazi essay 'Fünf Schwierig-keiten beim Schreiben der Wahrheit'.

In translation:

'Writing the Truth: Five Difficulties.' (Translation by Richard Winston of 'Fünf Schwierigkeiten', etc.) In Dorothy Norman (ed.): *Art and Action*, Twice a Year Press, New York, 1948.

(Brecht's evidence) in House Un-American Activities Committee: *Hearings Regarding Communist Infiltration of the Motion Picture Industry*, 80th Congress, 1st Session, 20–30 October 1947.

(Brecht's statement, disallowed by the Committee.) In Gordon Kahn: *Hollywood on Trial*, New York, 1948.

8. CRITICISM AND MISCELLANEOUS

The *Schriften zur Literatur und Kunst* print Brecht's occasional writings and notes on literature, the visual arts (including the writings on Brueghel and Barlach), film, radio and architecture, but also devote a long section to the Formalist–Realist controversy of the 1930s (embracing the so-called 'Expressionismus–Debatte') and include such essays as 'Weite und Vielfalt der realistischen Schreibweise' and 'Volkstümlichkeit und Realismus'. The notes on poetry are rather more fully given in the 'Edition Suhrkamp' volume *Über Lyrik* (1964), selected by Elisabeth Hauptmann.

Das Wort, a monthly literary review edited by Brecht, Feuchtwanger and Willi Bredel, was published by Meshdunarodnaya Kniga, Moscow, from July 1936 to March 1939.

In translation:

'Über reimlose Lyrik', 'Kulturpolitik und Akademie der Künste', 'Volkstüm-lichkeit und Realismus', and the notes on Brueghel are all included in *Brecht on Theatre*.

'Notes on the Barlach Exhibition.' (Translation by Daniel C. O'Neil of 'Notizen zur Barlach-Ausstellung') in *The Massachusetts Review*, Amherst, I, 3 May 1960.

9. BIOGRAPHICAL

Tagebücher 1920–1922. Autobiographische Aufzeichnungen 1920–1954. (Diaries and autobiographical notes, edited by Herta Ramthun.) Suhrkamp, 1975.

Arbeitsjournal. Suhrkamp, 1973. Vol. 1, 1938–1942. Vol. 2, 1942–1955. (An illustrated journal, centering on Brecht's work and the political background to it, with a separate volume of notes by Werner Hecht. Also issued in 1974 as two supplementary volumes of the collected edition.)

Klaus Völker: *Brecht-Chronik.* Hanser, Munich 1971. Chronology of Brecht's life, partly based on the above. (English translation: *Brecht Chronicle.* Seabury Press, New York 1976.)

In addition, the following provide first-hand accounts of Brecht at different stages of his life:

Hans-Otto Münsterer: *Bert Brecht.* Erinnerungen aus den Jahren 1917–1922. Die Arche, Zurich 1963.

Werner Frisch and K. W. Obermaier: *Brecht in Augsburg.* Aufbau, East Berlin and Weimar 1975. Suhrkamp, Frankfurt 1976.

Arnolt Bronnen: *Tage mit Bertolt Brecht.* Desch, Munich 1960.

Fritz Sternberg: *Der Dichter und die Ratio.* Sachse und Pohl Göttingen 1963.

Hans Bunge: *Fragen Sie mehr über Brecht.* Rogner und Bernhard, Munich 1972. (Transcript of recorded interviews with Hanns Eisler, mostly in relation to Brecht.)

Bernhard Reich: *Im Wettlauf mit der Zeit.* Erinnerungen aus fünf Jahrzehnten deutscher Theatergeschichte. Henschel-Verlag, East Berlin 1970 (contains two sections on Brecht in Berlin and Brecht in Moscow, totalling about 60 pages).

For accounts of Brecht in the U.S. see Lee Baxandall: 'Brecht in America, 1935' in the symposium *Brecht* edited by Erika Munk for Bantam Books, New York 1972 (originally in *TDR* 12, 1, 1967), and James K. Lyon: 'Brecht's American Cicerone' (on Ferdinand Reyher) in the International Brecht Society's annual *Brecht heute. Brecht Today*, no. 2, 1972, Athenäum-Verlag, Frankfurt.

10. BRECHT'S COMPOSERS

Besides Hans Bunge's Eisler interviews listed above, the main works are:

Andres Briner: *Paul Hindemith.* Atlantis, Zurich, and Schott, Mainz, 1971.

Fritz Hennenberg: *Dessau/Brecht/Musikalische Arbeiten.* Henschelverlag, East Berlin 1963.

David Drew (ed.): *Über Kurt Weill.* Suhrkamp, Frankfurt 1975. (Selection of reprinted articles, with chronology and long introductory essay.)

Notowicz and Elsner: *Hanns Eisler Quellennachweise.* VEB Deutscher Verlag für Musik, Leipzig, n.d. (1966). (Full catalogue and bibliography.)

Kurt Weill: *Ausgewählte Schriften.* Suhr Kamp, Frankfurt 1975. (Includes notes on *Mahagonny* and *The Threepenny Opera* and essay 'Über gestischer Musik', of which English translations are in *Collected Plays 2*.)

Index

Unless adapted by Brecht, works by other authors are given under the authors' names. In general, actors, producers, designers, writers of incidental music, translators, are only indexed if they occur in the body of the book. Otherwise they must be sought under the relevant title in the Analysis of the Plays or the lists of Recordings and Films.

Names have not been indexed where they have been cited only for purposes of general comparison or to support the writer's own opinions (e.g., Britten, Gropius, UPA on p. 224).